WITHDRAWN

DATE DUE

TEXT AND VOICE: ESSAYS 1981-1991

Also by Gabriel Josipovici

FICTION
The Inventory (1968)
Words (1971)
Mobius the Stripper: stories and short plays (1974)
The Present (1975)
Four Stories (1977)
Migrations (1977)
The Echo Chamber (1979)
The Air We Breathe (1981)
Conversations in Another Room (1984)
Contre-Jour: a triptych after Pierre Bonnard (1984)
In the Fertile Land (1987)
Steps: selected fiction and drama (1990)
The Big Glass (1991)

THEATRE
Mobius the Stripper (1974)
Vergil Dying (1977)

NON-FICTION
The World and the Book (1971; 1979)
The Lessons of Modernism (1977; 1987)
Writing and the Body (1982)
The Mirror of Criticism: selected reviews (1983)
The Book of God: a response to the Bible (1988; 1990)
(ed.) The Modern English Novel:
the reader, the writer and the book (1975)
(ed.) The Sirens' Song:
Selected Essays of Maurice Blanchot (1980)

Gabriel Josipovici

TEXT AND VOICE

Essays 1981–1991

Carcanet, Manchester
St Martin's Press, New York

First published in the UK in 1992 by
Carcanet Press Limited
208-212 Corn Exchange Buildings
Manchester M4 3BQ

First published in the USA in 1992 by
St. Martin's Press
175 Fifth Avenue
New York, N.Y. 10010

Library of Congress Cataloging-in-Publication Data

Josipovici, Gabriel, 1940-
    Text and voice : essays 1981-1991 / Gabriel Josipovici.
        p.   cm.
    Includes index.
    ISBN 0-312-08381-5
    I. Title.
    PR6060.064T48   1992
    824'.914--dc20   92-8208
                                                                  CIP

A CIP catalogue record for this book
is available from the British Library
ISBN 0 85635 934 3

The publisher acknowledges the financial assistance
of the Arts Council of Great Britain

Set in 10pt Bembo by Bryan Williamson, Darwen
Printed and bound in England by SRP Ltd, Exeter

To Bernard Harrison

Contents

Acknowledgements

I am grateful to the editors and publishers of the journals and books in which these essays first appeared; I have made only minor modifications.

'The Bible in Focus', the seventh annual *Journal for the Study of the Old Testament* Lecture, delivered at the University of Sheffield on 6 March 1990; published in *JSOT* 48 (1990), pp.101-22.

'Eating Your Words: Dante as Modernist' in *On Modern Poetry: Essays Presented to Donald Davie*, eds Vereen Bell and Laurence Lerner (Nashville: Vanderbilt University Press, 1988).

'Echo and Self-Knowledge' in *Moy qui me voy: The Writer and the Self from Montaigne to Leiris: Essays in Honour of John Cruickshank*, eds George Craig and Margaret McGowan (Oxford: Clarendon Press, 1989), pp.93-107.

'The Balzac of M. Barthes and the Balzac of M. de Guermantes' in *Reconstructing Literature*, ed. Laurence Lerner (Oxford: Blackwell, 1983), pp.81-105.

'Text and Voice' in *Comparative Criticism: A Yearbook*, ed. Elinor Shaffer, Vol.2 (1980), pp.3-25.

'Samuel Beckett: The Need to Fail' in *The New Pelican Guide to English Literature*, ed. Boris Ford, Vol.8: *The Present* (Penguin Books, 1983), pp.164-74.

'Maurice Blanchot', introduction to *Maurice Blanchot: The Sirens' Song*, ed. Gabriel Josipovici (Brighton: Harvester, 1982).

'Perec's *La Vie mode d'emploi*' in *The Yearbook of English Studies*, Vol.15, Anglo-French Literary Relations Special Number, ed. C.J. Rawson (Modern Humanities Research Association, 1985), pp.179-200.

Preface

There is a question which continues to puzzle me: when one acts quite differently from the way one has done in the past, is one showing admirable suppleness, an admirable freedom from the shackles of habit, or is one being false to ones innermost nature? And the same goes for writing. Conversely, when one repeats, albeit in a different way, what one has often said or done before, is one being admirably consistent or merely demonstrating that one remains locked in a set of predetermined postures?

Proust was much concerned with this, as he seems to have been by many of the more interesting questions I find myself asking. Marcel, realizing with horror that the pattern of his relationship with Albertine is starting to repeat that of his relations with all the other women he has been in love with, beginning with Gilberte Swann and even his mother, is felled by the discovery: we think we are free, we think life stretches like an ocean before us and we can plunge into its healing waters whenever and wherever we wish, but this is an illusion, and only the stale sense of repetition lies in wait for us. And yet, throughout the novel, repetition also reveals itself as the door to salvation – for what else is the experience of the madeleine, of the shoelaces, of the uneven paving-stones, but that of repetition?

At the most trivial level the issue arises for me when, retyping a section of a novel or story I am engaged on, I suddenly realize, half-way through a sentence, that there is a better way of concluding it than I had previously thought. I triumphantly type in the new ending, without looking at the transcript from which I have been working, only to find, when I have done, that my new wording was already there in the earlier version. In other words, the very thought that has flashed through my mind as I came to the mid-point of the sentence had already occurred to me the last time round, only I had forgotten. Does this mean that what I now have must be right, or, on the contrary, that I cannot escape a particular turn of thought or phrasing?

By the same token, does my discovery that the novel I have just

finished, and which seemed, in the course of writing, to be excitingly
new – does my discovery, upon reading the proofs, say, that it
closely resembles something I had written many years previously,
prove my consistency over the years or my unfortunate limitations?

Not only Proust but many of his Romantic predecessors were
much concerned by these questions of echo, mirroring and repetition. In one of the essays included in this volume, I explore the
theme as it manifests itself in Wordsworth, Poe and Proust himself.
It is, if not an apology for the rest of the book, at least a tacit acknowledgement that the preoccupations that run through it are by and
large the same ones as have run through my earlier critical books,
The World and the Book (1971), *The Lessons of Modernism* (1977) and
The Book of God (1988): the need to listen to the work of art and
not impose ourselves upon it; the need to make ancient works come
alive for us today; the role of the body in the making and reception
of art; the anxiety of Modernism; and the writer's need to trust –
in time, in language – as he works away in the dark, trying to bring
into being something that did not exist before.

The opening essay, on the Bible, traces the violence done to that
book by post-Reformation theology, and suggests that the Bible
and Homer may have more in common than theologians down the
ages have been willing to admit. In the essays on Dante, Sterne ('The
Body in the Library') and Wordsworth ('Reflections on Echo') I
have tried to bring out the modernity of their work while not, I
hope, wrenching that work out of its cultural context. On the other
hand, in the essay on Shakespeare ('Everything and Nothing') I
wanted to underline our distance from Shakespeare and to draw
attention to the advantages of working without anxiety within a
rich web of tradition and an assured sense of genre, even when the
writer subverts both traditions and genres. In that, I suggest, Shakespeare and Mozart are on one side of a great divide, while Milton
and Beethoven are on the other. If the comparison holds then it
shows that the dividing point will come at different historical
junctures in the different arts, which each have their own history as
well as belonging to the larger history of European culture.

Most of the remaining essays deal with writing in French in this
century: with the work of Proust, Beckett, Blanchot, Robbe-Grillet,
Pinget, Barthes, Ricardou, Derrida and Perec. This is partly fortuit-
ous, in that biographical accident has made me more at home in
French than in German or Russian; but not entirely so, since I see
these authors as being very much at the centre of the literary and
cultural revolutions of our century, and believe that without an

understanding of what they are up to we cannot hope to understand ourselves. It also seems to me that what happened in French literary circles in the 1960s and 1970s contains lessons for us all. There a powerfully argued but partial understanding of the implications of Modernism swept like wildfire through the culture before fizzling out – but not before it had been exported to England and especially to American universities. We need to look closely at what was at stake in the theoretical debates of the time, and this I have tried to do in the title essay and in 'The Balzac of M. Barthes and the Balzac of M. de Guermantes'.

There is one exception to this predominantly French focus on the twentieth century, and that is Kafka, with whom I conclude. 'A Bird Was in the Room' is the last of the four Northcliffe Lectures I was invited to give at University College, London, in 1981, collectively entitled 'Writing and the Body'. In it I try to understand just where the power and pathos of Kafka's last writings reside. I am not referring to his last stories, 'The Hunger Artist', the proofs of which he was still correcting as he lay dying, but to those messages written on bits of paper that were his only means of communication at the end, since his illness deprived him of the power of speech. They are neither philosophical nor 'profound', consisting as they do almost entirely of comments on aspects of his hospital room, stray memories and little requests. Yet it seemed to me then and seems to me still that if one could understand just why these fragments are so moving one would understand a great deal not just about Kafka but about art in general and its place in life. I don't think I fully succeeded, but that too is one of the themes of this book: criticism will always fall short – but that does not mean that it should not be able to tell us *why* that is the case, or, recognizing its limitations, still be able to illuminate both art and life.

Lewes
1 December 1991

1 The Bible in Focus

When I was starting to write *The Book of God*, I often found myself trying to bring the Bible into focus in my mind's eye. What sort of book is it?, I would ask myself. How exactly does it appear to me? Is it like any other book I am familiar with? And if not, in what does it differ?

I soon discovered that I could proceed without having to answer such questions, and so I put them aside. By the time I had finished the book I had begun to sense that the notion of focus itself was one about which the Bible had much to teach us. Those lessons, however, remained implicit in the book as I finally wrote it. I would like to return to them now and see if something more explicit can be said on the subject.

The Bible, among other things, is a particularly interesting book to examine because the history of men's attempt to focus on it is so amply documented. Thus that history may be able to show us, as in a mirror, what happens whenever we engage in the activity of focusing on a book.

I

I have no intention of running through a history of biblical interpretation. What I want to do is to look at what happens when people begin to focus on the Bible as a book available to everyone. In other words, I propose to begin with the Reformation.

In 1520 Luther published his *Address to the Nobility of the German Nation*. There he prayed that he might be given the trumpet of Joshua with which to bring down the three 'walls' of the modern Jericho. The second of these 'walls' was the claim that the Popes alone were 'the Lords of Scripture':

> Since they assert that the Holy Ghost has not deserted them, however ignorant and bad they may be, they venture to decree just what they please. But if this be so, what need or use is there

for Holy Scripture? Why not burn it all, and content ourselves
with these unlearned lords at Rome, who have the Holy Ghost
within them . . . ?

These are, of course, rhetorical questions. Luther goes on, with
characteristically aggressive and ironical use of Scripture: 'Balaam's
ass was wiser than the prophet himself. If then God could speak
through an ass against a prophet, why can he not speak through a
godly man against the Pope?'

In other words, if we have to wait to hear from someone else
what we should make of the books we read we might as well not
read at all. But since the book is there to be read, should each of us
not be allowed to make up his own mind about it? Is this not the
sort of thing we tell our students every day? Be independent, we
say, read for yourselves, don't just rely on the critics.

'Scripture', Luther insists, 'is of itself most certain, simple and
open. Scripture is its own interpreter, proving, judging and illuminating everything.' All we need to do therefore is to read it, and
we will understand it 'by that spirit in which [it] was written'.

However, as soon as Luther starts to comment on specific passages
of Scripture, we see that things are not that simple. 'I so hate Esther
and 2 Maccabees', he remarks with touching honesty, 'that I wish
they did not exist. There is too much Judaism in them and not a
little heathenism.' It seems therefore as though Luther has dethroned
the Pope only to find within himself an equally arbitrary ruler
instructing him to read.

'Arbitrary' is perhaps the wrong term. As we know, for Luther
the heart of Scripture lies in the notion that justification from sin
lies in faith, which is, as a modern theologian has put it, 'an existential
personal relationship grounded in God's initiative of grace towards
men'.[1] Thus everything in Scripture is read by Luther in the light
of this belief, and he naturally sees as central those books of the
Bible which seem most clearly to express it: John's Gospel, Paul's
Epistles, 1 Peter; Genesis, Isaiah, Jeremiah and Psalms.

Luther is often a perceptive reader of Scripture; it is illuminating,
however, to see how his convictions also frequently cause him to
misread. Why did Jacob deceive Laban? 'Even though this was deceit
and falsehood', answers Luther, 'nevertheless Jacob did it under
divine authority.' For, 'when God commands his saints and faithful
men to do anything, without any doubt that deed is right and holy'.

We find exactly the same argument in Tyndale:

Jacob robbed Laban his uncle; Moses robbed the Egyptians: And

Abraham is about to slay and burn his own son: And all are holy works, because they were wrought in faith at God's command-ment. To steal, rob and murder are no holy works before worldly people: but unto them that have their trust in God: they are holy when God commandeth them.

The episodes Tyndale mentions have all troubled readers of the Bible, and the explanation he and Luther give must have occurred to many of us. Yet I think that this kind of explanation is inadequate, since at one stroke it does away with all the puzzles in the text, and those puzzles are so ubiquitous as to suggest that they are somehow part of the meaning. I will come back to this.

The great strength of Luther as reader (and of the whole Protestant tradition which stems from him) lies in his ability to project himself imaginatively into what he is reading. And he himself is fully aware of this as a key issue:

I hate myself because when I see Christ laid in the manger or in the lap of his mother and hear the angels sing my heart does not leap into flame. With what good reason should we all despise ourselves that we remain so cold when this word is spoken to us, over which all men should dance and leap and burn for joy. We act as though it were a frigid historical fact that does not smite our hearts, as if someone were merely relating that the sultan has a crown of gold.

Again, we must surely applaud the sentiments, for do we not daily try to make books come alive for our students? Yet again the very strength of Luther's response reveals concomitant weaknesses.

Take Luther on Noah. 'How Luther marvelled at Noah, who had the courage to believe in God's Word and to build an ark when there was no cloud in the sky', writes Roland Bainton, paraphrasing Luther,

How his neighbours must have mocked him for constructing a sea-going vessel far from the coast! It was all the harder for Noah because lived so long. Not only while the ark was under con-struction but for hundreds of years beforehand he must have endured the taunts of unbelievers.

'If I had seen such men in the camp of the ungodly opposing me', Luther concludes, 'I should have thrown down my ministry in sheer desperation. Nobody knows how hard it is for one man to stand out against the consensus of all the other churches and against the judgment of his noblest and choicest friends.'

Luther's own circumstances make it possible for him to empathize with Noah; yet they also make him read the story of Noah in a strangely distorted manner. We could never have told from his comments that there was absolutely nothing in the Bible either about Noah's courage or about the mockery of others. Noah, we are simply told, 'found grace in the eyes of the Lord'. And then, when God has told him how to build the ark: 'Thus did Noah; according to all that God commanded him, so did he' (Gen. 6.8, 22).

It is striking how often we find, in early Protestant exegesis, that the reader's personal concerns lead him to focus on one aspect of a passage at the expense of the whole. Take the story of Joseph sold into slavery in Egypt. Luther focuses on Joseph in prison, falsely accused, and with no one to vindicate his good name. Calvin focuses on the way in which the brothers become the unwitting instruments of God's providence. Castellio, who was himself the victim of persecution, focuses on Reuben's plea for Joseph's life, and sees the whole episode as a denunciation of the iniquity of persecution.[2] No doubt the episode says something about all three views. But one can see the problems that are bound to arise when each interpreter is convinced that his is the one true view.

Take, as one final example, the most intense and imaginatively committed reading of any biblical episode known to me, Kierkegaard's book-length struggle to find the meaning of Genesis 22, which he called *Fear and Trembling*.

Here we find faith being extolled once again, as it had been by Luther and Tyndale, but with a new twist. Like Luther filled with wonder at Noah's courage in believing the word of God when there was not a cloud in the sky, Kierkegaard is filled with wonder at Abraham's faith in setting out to kill the beloved son who carried within him God's promise to increase and multiply his people. For, says Kierkegaard, unlike the simple choice before Agamemnon, either to do his duty as commander of the fleet or as Iphigeneia's father, the choice before Abraham was literally beyond his comprehension. Did Abraham not feel, he wonders, that perhaps he had misheard, or that the command had come not from God but from the Devil? For here was God, who had given him Isaac in his old age and promised him a progeny more numerous than the sands of the sea, now telling him to kill his only son, his loved one. What can Abraham have made of such a command?

I think that if one of our students brought us *Fear and Trembling* as his week's essay on Genesis 22 we would have no option but to give him an A+ and then sit down and try to teach him how to read.

For the first point about the Hebrew Scriptures, which any child immediately grasps, is that they consist of stories in which God speaks to men. Sometimes, as with Saul, God withholds his voice, but he never deceives. It is a basic convention of these narratives that when they say: 'And God said unto Abraham', we are not for an instant to doubt that God did indeed speak to Abraham – and Abraham is not to doubt it either.

The trouble with biblical reading as it is practised in the wake of Luther is that the notion that the Bible speaks directly to us carries with it the implicit corollary that we do not need to pay attention to its conventions or make any effort of the historical imagination. It is striking that Kierkegaard, who could do just that where ancient Greek literature was concerned, as we will see, was quite incapable of doing the same for the Bible. But that was of course because the alternative to the Bible speaking directly to us seemed to be that we must wait for some authority – Pope or Councils or scholars – to pronounce before responding to it at all. And that was clearly unacceptable.

But already in Luther's day he was himself being outflanked by extremists such as Muntzer and Franck, who accused him of being addicted to the dead letter rather than the living spirit. Muntzer called him 'a Bible gobbler', and Franck argued that of course there were contradictions in the Bible, since it is a book of paradoxes, 'a book sealed with seven seals which no man can open unless he has the key of David which is the illumination of the Spirit through the way of the Cross'. Here, in 1539, we are not a thousand miles from Bultmann.[3]

Two and a half centuries later, in 1793, Tom Paine would be equally convinced that he could see for himself what Scripture was saying, though its spirit struck him rather differently from the way it had struck Luther and Franck. Nowhere, he remarks of the New Testament, has he ever found 'so many and such glaring absurdities, contradictions and falsehoods as are in these books'. And, about the Old Testament,

> When we read the obscure stories, the cruel and barbarous executions, the unrelenting vindictiveness with which more than half the Bible is filled, it would be more consistent that we called it the work of a demon than the work of God.[4]

Is it my imagination or can one hear the characteristic tones of F.R. Leavis in such pronouncements?

The desire to bring the Bible into focus, to find the key and break the seals, could and did take other forms than those of the illumination of the spirit or the exercise of common sense. In 1678 Richard Simon told a startled world that Moses was not the author of the Pentateuch, that the chronology of various parts of the Old Testament was confused, and that within the framework of some of its books the order of their contents had been transposed.[5] And so began the melancholy history of the so-called 'Higher Criticism', which still dominates the study of the Bible today, as these remarks from Volume III of the *Cambridge History of the Bible* (1963) attest:

> It is not too much to say that the nineteenth century critics, both 'higher' and 'lower', have provided us with the indispensable foundation for any proper appreciation of the Bible and with the tools with which modern scholarship must work as it seeks by fresh insights to discover facets of the truth enshrined within the sacred canon.[6]

Note the implicit assumptions in every one of these phrases: 'the indispensable foundation', 'any proper appreciation', 'fresh insights', 'facets of the truth enshrined within the sacred canon'. There is really no need to tease them out.

In the nineteenth century, Joseph Parker had already been moved to ask: 'Have we to await a communication from Tübingen or a telegram from Oxford before we can read the Bible?'[7]

The trouble was that potential readers of the Bible seemed to be torn between having to accept the latest word from Tübingen or Oxford with no possibility of judging for themselves; or having to depend on the way the spirit moved them, with no way of controlling it. This strange state of affairs seemed to pertain *only* to the Bible; we would never feel that these were the alternatives where, say, *Hamlet* or *The Prelude* were concerned.

It might be that the Bible was indeed unique in this respect, and that we would simply have to live with the consequences. On the other hand, the stark alternatives of scholarship or spirit might themselves be the result of some profound and historically conditioned misunderstanding.

II

That it was probably the latter became clear from the work, published in the immediate aftermath of the Second World War, of two men, Erich Auerbach and Northrop Frye. I speak of them in the same breath because though *The Great Code*, the book Frye devoted to the Bible, only appeared in 1981, Frye's basic approach was already clearly adumbrated in *Fearful Symmetry* (1947) and *Anatomy of Criticism* (1956); while *Mimesis*, though written during the war, was not published in English till 1953.

Let me deal with Frye first.

Already in Puritan sermons of the seventeenth century 'the corporate drama of the human race, which fell before the wiles of Satan in the person of the First Adam and vanquished the Tempter in the person of the Second Adam, had been set forth with imagery, similitude and illustration as the individual biography of every human being'.[8] What Frye did was to remind us of this and other related lost traditions, and show how their principles were not confined to sermons but pervaded some of the chief works of English literature, notably the epics of Spenser, Milton and Blake.

This was important, but more, it seems to me, as a rehabilitation of lost modes of reading these writers than of reading the Bible itself. Although Frye's approach did help one to see the Bible as a whole, it did so at a cost which I for one have found too great. Of course Frye said quite openly that he was giving us a Christian reading of the Bible, and Jews are likely to feel that this only perpetuates a misreading of the Hebrew Scriptures which began with the New Testament. Yet even with the Christian Scriptures I wonder whether a reading in terms of romance can help, for instance, to distinguish the canonical Gospels from those Gnostic gospels rejected by the early Church.

However, the very boldness of Frye's approach at least raised questions about the relations of part to whole in the Bible which neither the Lutheran/existential nor the scholarly/critical traditions had thought to raise, and for this reason he has left us all in his debt.

Frye's importance lay in the fact that he did not believe we could read the Bible properly without some effort of the historical imagination: he asked us to look at something strange rather than at something familiar. But he perhaps did not take us far enough back. Auerbach, through the simple expedient of laying a passage of Homer alongside a passage of Genesis, asked us to do something which went against the grain of nineteen centuries of Christian exegesis: he asked us to look at the Bible both as a very ancient work and as one which could speak to us today as much – or as little – as Homer.

The comparative method, as far as the Bible is concerned, has its roots in Romanticism, yet there is still a great deal of prejudice against it. This is actually not surprising when one recalls that a

central theme of both Hebrew and Christian Scripture is its uniqueness. Throughout history, if there has ever been any inclination to
focus on the Bible in relation to other books, it has always been in
a spirit of competition: the Hebrew God *against* the gods of the
nations: Jesus *against* the holy men of other cultures; biblical narrative
against the myths and legends of the Canaanites and Greeks. Before
he had even written one word, therefore, Auerbach had already let
a breath of fresh air into the closed chambers of biblical study.
Unfortunately, in the process of comparing Genesis 22 and *Odyssey*,
Book 19 it seems to me that Auerbach contrived to misread both.
It may be instructive to see just how and why he did so.

By focusing on just one episode, and that the binding of Isaac,
Auerbach was of course following in Kierkegaard's steps. Like Kierkegaard he stresses the darkness of the story, and suggests that the
minimum of information we are given forces us to imagine Abraham's anguish and solitude in the face of the enormity of what he
has been asked to do. Auerbach appears to bring out strikingly the
relation of theme to narrative style in the episode, yet a reading more
attuned to the range of Hebrew narratives might rather wish to
stress the companionship of the two protagonists, than their solitude.
It would alert us to Abraham's threefold *hinneni* ('here am I') – to
God, to Isaac and to the angel; it would stress the phrase 'and they
went both of them together', repeated twice in the space of three
verses (6, 8); and it would insist on the happy outcome of the episode
rather than its tragic potential.

To read Genesis 22 in this way is to note, by contrast, how very
Lutheran is the tone of Auerbach's analysis. Auerbach's too is a
'hidden God', and Auerbach's way of filling in detail omitted by
the narrative by attempting to empathize with the protagonists is
one which will by now be familiar to us: 'Bitter to him is the early
morning in which he saddles his ass, calls his serving-men and his
son Isaac, and sets out...'[9]

This view of scriptural narrative naturally colours his contrasting
view of Homer:

> The Scripture stories do not, like Homer's, court our favour,
> they do not flatter us that they may please us and enchant us...
> Far from seeking, like Homer, merely to make us forget our own
> reality for a few hours, it seeks to overcome our reality.[10]

But does Homer really seek to 'court our favour', to 'flatter us',
merely to make us forget our own reality for a few hours? Does this

not sound more like a description of Agatha Christie or Barbara Cartland than of Homer?

It is not just that Auerbach slights Homer in his eagerness to do justice to the Bible – though there is that. It is that his austere view of the Bible will not allow him to see either its narrative or Homer's for what they are. This is a great pity because I believe that Auerbach's initial impulse is the right one, and that a comparison of the Bible and Homer which takes seriously the distance that separates us from both as well as the effect they both can have upon us, is the best way to proceed if we are to have any hope of reading the Bible as it should be read.

It is therefore to this that I would now like to turn.

III

From its beginnings, in Plato, criticism of Homer has been bedevilled by concentration on the gods and their so-called immorality. If, however, we focus on what is central to Homer, namely man, I think we will find that he has more in common with the Bible than is generally supposed.

What distinguishes man from the gods in Homer is the simple fact of death. Death is both final and completely natural: 'The life-giving earth will hold him fast, she that holdeth ever him that is strong' (21. 62-63).[11] The earth is life-giving in that crops grow in it and men can live off it; but when a man's days are done, however great and strong he may have been, the earth will close over him for ever.

The *Iliad* is the tragic evocation of this fact. That is, in the poem, which ends with Hector being returned to his father and his people so that he may be ritually buried and lamented, we see a community coming to terms with the fact of death. But it requires only a slight shift of perspective to see the coming of death as part of a larger cycle:

> Even as are the generations of leaves, such are those also of men. As for the leaves, the wind scattereth some upon the earth, but the forest, as it burgeons, putteth forth others when the season of spring is come; even so of men one generation springeth up and another passeth away (6. 146-48).

Though these words appear in the *Iliad* they describe the perspective of the *Odyssey*. For there it is the sense of natural renewal and continuity that is celebrated. Odysseus chooses to return to the mortal

Penelope rather than acquiring immortality by remaining with the nymph Calypso. And in the story of his return, as Norman Austin has noted,[12] we see a man and a woman rediscovering a communal rhythm after twenty years of following their individual destinies; and they do so in the darkest time of the year, when Odysseus, his bald head shining in the firelight of the hall, comes back to rout the pirates who have been desecrating the wealth of his house. For, as in the *Oresteia*, it is the house, the *oikos*, not the individual, which is the true hero of the poem.

In much of the Bible too death is the ultimate fact: 'I shall go to him but he shall not return to me' (2 Sam. 12. 23), says David when his and Bathsheba's first child dies. And, as Achilles laments Patroclus, so David laments Saul and Jonathan and his beloved son Absalom. At the same time we have, in the Hebrew Scriptures, the celebration of the triumph of the people, Israel, rather than Abraham or Moses or David, while the New Testament reveals a pattern of death and rebirth whereby the torn fabric of life is mended as a deeper rhythm is made manifest.

Of course something which is central to the Bible is missing in Homer. This is often said to be a sense of time, but that does not seem to me quite accurate. If generations pass like leaves, it is nonetheless important to remember and honour them, and what all men strive for is *kleos*, fame, a good name among those not yet born. And, as we will see, the *Iliad*, no less than the Bible, celebrates the fact that men can change, that the wholly unexpected can come to pass.

No. What distinguishes the Bible from Homer is this: from the start the relations between God and Israel have to do with a future yet to be realized, while the central assertion of the New Testament is that in Jesus that future *has been* realized. This idea of future realization is quite absent from Homer. And yet there is of course one ancient epic which is concerned almost exclusively with this theme: Virgil's *Aeneid*.

For Dante it seemed nothing short of providential that Virgil, writing in Rome at the very time when Jesus was active in Palestine, should have produced a work celebrating the history and destiny of the Roman people and reaching its climax with the advent of Augustus as ruler of the civilized world, which seemed exactly to parallel the biblical narrative of the history and destiny of the Hebrew people, with its climax in the advent of Jesus.

Dante was quite right. The *Aeneid* does contain something which does not exist in Homer but which is central to the Bible. Yet when

I read Virgil I feel myself to be much further from the Bible than I do when I read Homer. Why?

We can begin with local effects. Even when Virgil sticks closest to Homer we can see the difference between them at once. Here is Odysseus:

> So she spoke, and I pondered in heart and was fain to clasp the spirit of my dead mother. Thrice I sprang towards her, and my heart bade me clasp her, and thrice she flitted from my arms like a shadow or a dream, and pain grew ever sharper at my heart. And I spoke and addressed her with winged words (*Od.* 11. 204-209).

Virgil was so struck by this image that he used it at least three times in the *Aeneid*. Here is Aeneas meeting the shade of his dead wife in the burning ruins of Troy:

> When thus she had spoken, she left me weeping and fain to tell her much, and drew back into thin air. Thrice there I strove to throw my arms about her neck; thrice the form, vainly clasped, fled from my hands, even as light winds, and most like a winged dream (2. 790-94).

There is an energy in Odysseus – 'thrice I sprang towards her' – which imparts itself to the narrative. There is also an objectivity in his description, even when he is talking about his feelings: 'My heart bade me clasp her', 'pain grew ever sharper at my heart', 'she flitted from my arms like a shade or a dream'. Everything here is as precise as possible, and Odysseus is clearly as fascinated as he is upset by what has occurred. By contrast, everything in Aeneas's telling of the story is designed to heighten the pathos, to make us feel and suffer with him. He begins by telling us that Creusa left him though he wept and still had much to tell her. For Homer 'thrice I sprang towards her...and thrice she flitted from my arms like a shadow or a dream' simply describes the occurrence; for Virgil the repeated 'thrice' sounds like a knell: 'Thrice there I strove to throw my arms about her neck; thrice the form, vainly clasped, fled from my hands'. Even in translation the effect is potent. I think it is that 'vainly' *(frustra)* which does the trick. It gives us a comment, from within Aeneas's own consciousness, of what occurred. There is no equivalent in Homer and one cannot imagine Odysseus ever using the word.

Virgil's whole poem, of course, is personal in a way Homer's is not. From the start it is an 'I' who sings: *arma virumque cano*. The *Iliad*, on the other hand, begins: *mēnin aede thea* – do *thou* sing, O

Goddess. Virgil calls upon the Muse for help, but we feel her to be more decorative than real. And the same is true of all Virgil's gods. He is more interested in the sense of loss Aeneas feels when his goddess mother leaves him than in the larger role of the gods in the affairs of men.

In fact for Virgil man is alone, unrelated to nature or to the larger rhythms of the universe, except through an effort of the will. Aeneas founds Rome, and Rome, the poem foretells, will grow and expand until its full flowering under Augustus. But this is always a matter of bitter effort, and is brought about only by the suppression of what is most human in Aeneas. What makes the poem great, of course, is that Virgil is never certain that the cost is worth it.

By contrast, what the Bible constantly asserts is that by walking in God's way Israel will flourish. But this flourishing will also be a fulfilling of each individual. By remembering what God has done for Israel, by obeying the commandments and by joining in the communal praise, each man will find himself as he lets go his personal fears and desires. Aeneas, by contrast, goes on feeling guilty in relation to Dido for abandoning her, even though that was clearly his duty.

The contrast is enforced by something we take for granted in the Bible, but which is in fact a crucial element: the sense of teeming generations and innumerable episodes – far more than we can ever remember. The *Aeneid*, on the other hand, presents us with selected types and carefully chosen episodes, each of which is carefully crafted to make a point.

Well, it will be said, what can you expect? One is a communal work, a massive series of chronicles and stories joined together, written over a thousand years by many people; the other is one man's attempt to produce a large public work. But that is exactly my point: if Aeneas has difficulty upholding his task, then so has Virgil. We sense the effort it cost him to write his epic poem; no such effort is visible in the Bible – or in Homer.

The contrast between Virgil on the one hand, and Homer and the Bible on the other, can help us to see a little more clearly what the latter two works have in common. It may be that the word 'communal' can be seen to refer not just to their origins but also to how they ask us to respond to them.

To begin with, both Homer and the Bible writers believe in their gods. The system, in both cases, is coherent, matter-of-fact and objective. What this means, among other things, is that human motive and action are accepted as mysterious. *Because* the gods exist, man is not solely responsible for his deeds, though he is not free of responsibility either. In other words, evil deeds have an objective as well as a subjective dimension. It is striking that Kierkegaard, who, we saw, so notably failed to read Genesis 22 as it was meant to be read because he did not feel that he needed to enter imaginatively into a world different from his own where the Bible was concerned, was able to make this imaginative leap in the case of the Greeks. Talking of Sophocles' Antigone (and Aeschylus and Sophocles are at one with Homer on this and many other issues), he tells us that the individual, in the Greeks, rests 'in the substantial categories of state, family and destiny'. He goes on:

> Life-relationships are once and for all assigned to them, like the heaven under which they live. If this is dark and cloudy, it is also unchangeable. This furnishes the keynote of the Greek soul, and this is sorrow, not pain. In Antigone the tragic guilt concentrates itself about one definite point, that she had buried her brother in defiance of the king's prohibition. If this is seen as an isolated fact, a collision between sisterly affection and an arbitrary human prohibition, then *Antigone* would cease to be a Greek tragedy, it would be an entirely modern tragic subject. [13]

Why and how a man acts in Homer and the tragedies depends on his being embedded in a reciprocal network of relationships. What is *philos* is not what a man loves in our – or Virgil's – sense of the term. *Philos* signifies not a subjective emotion but what belongs to a man: his arm, his heart, his son, his retainer. A network of duties and affections ties a man to his relatives and dependants, and this does not necessarily have anything to do with his feelings.

It is thus possible for Oedipus, in *Oedipus at Colonus*, to insist that he is both polluted *and* innocent. That distinction has gone, by and large, in Virgil – and in the New Testament. But it is very much there in the Hebrew Scriptures: Isaac's blessing has gone to the wrong son, yet once given it cannot be retrieved; Jephthah's vow was a foolish one to make, but once made it has to be carried through, no matter what.

Homeric man, Hermann Frankel has said, does not grow confused or depressed, he grows angry with someone or grief-stricken over something, and he always retains the power to express himself. [14] This is true of Greek tragedy as well, and it is an apt description of both Jacob and David. David is grief-stricken once he realizes that God has seen what he has done to Uriah, and at once confesses his sin. He is punished, and never appears to think about the incident again. Here too, as in Antigone, 'life-relationships are once and for all assigned, like the heaven under which men live, and if this is dark and cloudy, it is also unchangeable'. This is what gives the characters in both the Hebrew Scriptures and ancient Greek literature their buoyancy and lightness despite their often appalling afflictions.

The similarities do not end there. Homer, like the biblical authors (including the authors of the Gospels), knows that man is a weak and vulnerable creature, liable at any time to be overtaken by disaster. What is important is not to imagine that one is in control of one's destiny, but to accept that the world is other than one could ever have imagined it:

> Nothing feebler does earth nurture than man, of all things that on earth are breathing and moving. For he thinks that he will never suffer evil in time to come, so long as the gods give him prosperity and his knees are quick; but when again the blessed gods decree him sorrow, this too he bears in sore despite, with steadfast heart; for the spirit of men upon the earth is even such as the day which the father of gods and men brings upon them (*Od.* 18. 130-37).

Such a sentiment, as Martha Nussbaum has argued,[15] is the hallmark of Greek tragedy as well; it is given philosophical backing by Aristotle; and it is the subject of Plato's most tenacious criticism. Man does not *need* to be feeble, vulnerable, argues Plato; if he turns away from the world of the senses he can come to a sure, safe haven.

Reading Nussbaum's *The Fragility of Goodness* one cannot but be struck by the similarity between Plato's advice and that given by many voices within the Christian tradition: withdraw from the world, trust in Christ, and even death will have no power over you. But one must also be struck by the fact that this is, by and large, *not* the attitude of the Bible. The Bible, in fact, is far closer to Homer, the tragedians and Aristotle: no one knows what will happen to him, when disaster will strike; we cannot plan for it, and what happens will always take us by surprise and teach us what and who we are. What is important is to walk in God's way and accept our human vulnerability. 'Who am I?' Moses asks God, 'that I should go unto Pharaoh, and that I should bring forth the children of Israel out of Egypt?' And Jesus in Gethsemane: 'Abba, Father, all things are possible unto thee; take away this cup from me; nevertheless, not what I will, but what thou wilt'.

It is events which teach. Mere introspection cannot reveal to us who or what we are. The death of Patroclus starts a chain of events which in the long run teaches Achilles that he will only find rest if he returns the body of Hector to Priam. Haemon's suicide teaches Creon that the state is not, as he had supposed, everything. What happens in Egypt teaches Joseph that his father and brothers are not simply figures in his dreams. The proximity of his own death teaches Jesus that he too can be afraid. Again and again, in the Bible and in the Greeks, people are brought by events to the realization of their own needs, of their terrible vulnerability. And yet, strangely, that realization is also deeply comforting, for with it comes awareness of a larger pattern, beyond our understanding, but which, at such moments, we are allowed to glimpse – or perhaps it would be better to say: whose rhythms at such moments become manifest.

Of course the Bible differs from Homer in that such a world-view is more difficult to sustain if you believe in a single creator God. For then the question of motive and responsibility becomes even more pressing. Yet it is striking that the Bible is able to avoid answering the question of final responsibility, as though aware instinctively that all answers will be the wrong answers.

Thus when Michal, Saul's daughter and David's wife, rebukes him for dancing in front of the ark, David haughtily replies that where the Lord is concerned he will do what he sees fit. The narrative goes on: 'And to Michal the daughter of Saul there was not to her a child until the day of her death' (2 Sam. 6. 23). Was this *because* she criticized the Lord's anointed? Or for some quite different reason? Or for no reason at all? Clearly the Authorized Version translators thought they were justified in seeing a connection, and so began the sentence with 'therefore': 'Therefore Michal the daughter of Saul had no child unto the day of her death'. But the Hebrew – deliberately, it seems to me – leaves the connection between cause and effect obscure.

Then there is the story of the crowning of Saul, a story so full of contradictions that it is impossible to draw from it the conclusion either that Saul was pusillanimous from the start or that he was rightly modest, either that he had been chosen by God from the start or that his happening to wander into Samuel's orbit at the crucial time made of him the chosen one. It takes a high and conscious art to retain ambiguity over so long a stretch, yet our instinct when we read is of course to dismantle that ambiguity, to 'sort the story out'.

The Lutheran tradition, desiring to respond as fully as possible to the text, inevitably subjectifies it, and thus obscures the crucial principle that event nearly always precedes and is in excess of interpretation. Of course that desire to understand, to control, by making action spring from meaning ('I do this because...', 'God does this because...') is not confined to the sixteenth century and after. It lies behind Plato's critique of Homer and behind developments within the Bible itself. For in the course of the Bible, alongside what we might call its Homeric and tragic component, we find many instances of the Platonic spirit at work. We find it sporadically in the prophets, then quite clearly in apocalyptic, and finally, explicitly, in the New Testament, where Jesus first insists that *he* is the key to history, and this is taken up by both St Paul and the author of the Epistle to the Hebrews to drive the point home that now at last the pattern is fully visible – except of course to those who do not wish to see.

What we have here, it seems to me, is another example of what Nietzsche called the quarrel between the 'fable of the one true world' and the actual multiplicity and variety of the real world. For Plato the one true world cannot be grasped except by clearing the mind of clutter and focusing on the essence. Narrative, to this view, is dangerous and misleading, for it always implies an excess, action which cannot be directly tied to meaning. The author of Daniel or Revelation too offers us a key to the narrative of history, which, once understood, obliterates the messiness of that history; and so too, in his different way, does the author of the Epistle to the Hebrews.

For Nietzsche, for Homer, and for the bulk of the Bible, however, the world is multifarious, always in transformation, and can only be grasped through juxtaposition and discontinuities and in the dimension of time: our partial vision is itself the guarantor of the world, and our attitude to it should be one not of *focus* but of *participation*.

IV

If Achilles is only brought to understanding by what happens to him and what he finds it in himself to do, then only narrative can do justice to his case. But a certain kind of narrative, in which action and speech go hand in hand, and where explanation has no place.

The *Iliad* is a communal poem in more than its origins. At its climax it is a poem about communal lament – about the need and possibility of a communal sharing of grief in order for life to go on: not Achilles alone and Priam alone, but both together and each with his people, allowing the given forms of public mourning to take the burden of grief from their individual shoulders.

It is communal also in a less public sense. For what happens at the end is that public mourning is found not to be enough to lift the burden of grief from Achilles' shoulders. As Book 24 opens he is still tossing and turning, unable to sleep for thinking about Patroclus, whom he will never see alive again. It takes the arrival of Priam, with his preposterous request, for the miracle to occur: Achilles suddenly understands what one of the foe must be feeling – and with that leap of the imagination comes release: he lets Hector's body go:

> But when goodly Achilles had has fill of lamenting, and the long-ing therefor had departed from his heart and limbs, forthwith then he sprang from his seat, and raised the old man by his hand, pitying his hoary head and hoary beard: and he spake and addres-sed him with winged words: 'Ah, unhappy man, full many in good sooth are the evils thou hast endured in thy soul. How hadst thou the heart to come alone to the ships of the Achaeans, to meet the eyes of me that have slain thy sons many and valiant. Of iron verily is thy heart. But come, sit thou upon a seat, and our sorrows will we suffer to lie quiet in our hearts, despite our pain' (*Il.* 24. 513-23).

Achilles could not tell he would suddenly feel pity for the old man, could not tell he would speak these words – and neither could we, as we listen or read. But he does, and we with him.

What Homer's poem does is to lead us to join in, to let go our own individual sorrows and anxieties and partake of a communal rhythm. And that too is the way of the Bible. Not only in the poems of celebration and lament which make up the book of Psalms, and which have always been communal poems for Jews and Christians, but also in the public repetition of the saving history which punc-tuates the narrative from Joshua to Stephen.

The Israelites are commanded to remember, and to cause their children to remember, what God has done for them. And at the end of the Christian mass the injunction is 'Ite missa est' – it is done, go forth. Even in St Paul, where, as in Virgil, we find a new, more private concept of character emerging, the central emphasis is on community in Christ.

We read in Nehemiah:

> Now in the twenty and fourth day of this month the children of Israel were assembled with fasting, and with sackclothes, and earth upon them... And they stood up in their place and read in

the book of the law of the Lord their God one fourth part of the day... Then the Levites... said, Stand up and bless the Lord your God for ever and ever: and blessed be thy glorious name, which is exalted above all blessing and praise. Thou, even thou, art Lord alone; thou hast made heaven, the heaven of heavens, with all their host, the earth, and all things that are therein... Thou art the Lord the God who didst choose Abram, and broughtest him forth out of Ur of the Chaldees, and gavest him the name of Abraham... (Neh. 9. 1-7).

As readers we too speak the saving history. We are not asked to understand, to extract meaning. Understanding is never at issue. We are asked to take part.

In the Talmud tractate on Esther (*Megillah* 18a) we are told that to recite the book of Esther by heart is not enough: it must be read aloud. The Talmud explains this in its usual elliptical fashion by analysing the form of two injunctions which contain the obligation to remember. In one case, after Joshua's war against Amalek in Exodus, Moses is told to 'write this in memory (*zikaron*) in the book' (Exod. 17. 14). In Deuteronomy there is a double injunction: 'Remember what Amalek has done to you... do not forget' (Deut. 25. 17-19).

'Do not forget', suggests the Talmud, concerns memory as conservation in the heart. Thus if it was only a matter of not forgetting, then reciting by heart or reading silently would be enough. But there is also a positive aspect to memory: *zekōr*, remember. The difference between not forgetting and remembering is the difference, the Talmud suggests, between silent reading and the more active form of reading aloud, *zekōr bepê*, memory by the mouth. What such active reading does is what all activities do, but which the (Platonic) notions of focusing and interpreting play down. It takes us where we did not expect to go, makes us discover things about the world and ourselves which we did not know were there.[16]

Achilles, speaking to Priam, discovers what was always there but which, in the silence of his tormented heart, he could not have discovered for himself. The Israelites, reciting with the Levites, learn again who and what they are.

Both Homer and the Bible, then, ask to be read aloud, even if only with the voice of the imagination. They ask not for an act of concentration or focusing but for what we might call relaxed participation.

Surely when we have read best in our lives we have read like that.

We have read not to understand but to participate. No great book can ever come fully into focus. For focus suggests control and great books ask us to let go, to *speak* them, not to *know* them.

One of the unexpected benefits of the secularization of Scripture may then be this: that it will allow the Protestant image of the book to give way to another. We will cease to see books as objects to consult for our salvation or a source of truth or knowledge, and come to see them as beings which ask us to take part in an activity, assent to which will lead to our rediscovery of our place within a larger rhythm.

In other words, that will teach us to read *secular* (as well as *religious*) works as they were always meant to be read, but which certain post-Reformation prejudices and, if I may so put it, professional malformation, have too often prevented us from doing.

2 Eating Your Words: Dante as Modernist

There are two and only two kinds of modern artist: the one who feels that certain things can no longer be done, and the one who has never known such feelings. The trouble with the attitude of the former is that such knowledge erodes confidence and eventually leads to silence; the trouble with the attitude of the latter is that whatever he produces soon comes to seem irrelevant and outdated, no matter how good a craftsman he is. The greatest artists of the century have been those who have accepted that they have eaten of the apple and yet somehow found means of avoiding or evading the stark conclusion to which that ought to lead. This is what unites Eliot and Stevens, Valéry and Yeats, despite all their differences. Recent attempts to treat Stevens as a latter-day Keats or to replace Eliot by Hardy in the pantheon of modern poetry have not been convincing, though one can see why they have occurred: poets and critics have been desperate to find a tradition that would absolve them from having to make the impossible choices of modernism; but as with theological attempts to bypass the insights of Kierkegaard and Nietzsche, they have demonstrated only that there is no escape.

But one could also argue that the recognition of the dilemma can lead to a renewal of art rather than its extinction. Proust was able to write *A la recherche* only when he accepted that he could not write like the Goncourts, and it is surely not by accident that Wallace Stevens placed the same poem at the head of both his *Collected Poems* and his *Selected Poems*, and that the poem 'Earthy Anecdote' deals with precisely the issue we are considering: every time the bucks go clattering over Oklahoma the firecat bristles in the way, forcing them to go either to the right or to the left; yet when eventually the firecat closes his bright eyes and sleeps, leaving the direct way open, the poem comes to an end.

One way modern artists have had of coming to terms with the dilemma is to search for allies in other ages, other traditions. Proust turned to the *Arabian Nights*, Eliot to Dante and Donne, Kafka to the Bible, Brecht to Chinese stories and poems. Just as it is often a relief when a friend confesses to having experienced feelings one might have been tempted to think were peculiar to oneself, so an artist can take heart from realizing that others, in distant times and places, encountered and overcame the problems that seem to him so paralysing. Think of Dante. Did not he too, like the bucks of Wallace Stevens, try first to run straight up the mountain toward his goal and find himself forced back by those medieval firecats, the lion, the leopard, and the wolf? He learned the hard way that in order to go up you must first go down, and that there is no straight road but that he who would reach truth 'about must and about must go'. Where language is concerned he learned that we cannot confer automatic authority on our work by use of an authoritative language, but that the use of the vernacular does not by itself confer authenticity, any more than Latin confers authority. The equivalent of the spiral downward and upward in linguistic terms is the forging of a vernacular that *through use* becomes both authentic and authoritative.

Dante, as Eliot sensed, has much to teach us about the temptations of false and superficial solutions to questions of morals, metaphysics, and aesthetics; so, rather than rehearsing once again the old yet still crucial debates of modernism, I propose to look in some detail at the closing cantos of the *Inferno*. For it is only by submerging ourselves in an artist's world that we can understand the choices with which he presents us and which we can use to illuminate our own lives and work.

As you approach the centre of an inverted cone – which is, after all, what Hell is – you naturally find yourself going faster and faster as the circumference grows smaller and the incline steeper. At the end of the *Inferno*, Dante – and the reader with him – is going to zoom through the centre and, turning as he climbs down the hairy flanks of Satan, King of the Underworld, climb up to find himself in sight of the stars for the first time and at the foot of the mountain of Purgatory. From the point of view of God he has not been going down in his long journey through Hell, but up, so that the journey from the rim of Hell to the tip of Purgatory is one long ascent. It is only in our inverted world, as denizens of Satan's kingdom, that it has seemed as though we were going down.[1]

Dante is careful to make connections between the beginning and the end of the *Inferno* and between the beginning of the *Inferno* and the beginning of the *Purgatorio*. In *Inferno* XXXIII Ugolino dreams of a wolf, which reminds us of the third of the beasts of Canto I, and in talking of the relation of bodies to souls on earth in Canto XXXIII, Dante uses the unusual word *ruina* ('ella ruina in si fatta cisterna'; 'she falls headlong into this cistern', 133) which takes us back to the striking image of the pilgrim Dante falling back at the start: 'Mentre ch'i ruvinava in basso loco' ('while I was ruining down into the depths', I. 61). Both echoes help us to see how foolish it was of the pilgrim to try to run straight up the mountain. At the same time the echoes of *Inferno* I in *Purgatorio* I, so well brought out by Singleton,[2] help to confirm us in our sense that at the start of the second canticle Dante is once again in the position he was in at the start of the first, at the foot of a mountain surrounded by desert and water, but that this time it will be possible for him to climb to the very top.

As always in Dante the theological and the artistic cannot be separated. Artistically, the poet wants to bind his great structure together, and to give us a sense of a huge physical and mental distance to be traversed and of how that distance can be compressed in the imagination. Theologically, Dante wants to remind us that the poem is about himself, about *his* escape from the dark wood of his life, *his* conversion and purgation to the point where he can answer to his own name (at the top of the mountain of Purgatory), and finally be ready to see God as well as to write the poem we are reading (at the end of *Paradiso*). For this to become possible he has to arrive at a new understanding of his relation to the world – to other people, that is, and to language.

In a sense the whole poem is about the relations between speech and love. It is about the right and wrong uses of both, for we can understand the right only when we have grasped its opposite, and the wrong uses of love are inseparable from the wrong uses of language. As the poem accelerates in the lower reaches of the cone of Hell, the cantos cease to be distinct, and we need to read XXXI-XXXIV as a single unit. We are in the lowest of the nine pits, the place where the treacherous are stuck for all eternity. Though even here Dante is concerned to make us grasp nuances, distinctions (between treachery to kindred, to country, to guests, to lords and benefactors), the four kinds merge imperceptibly into each other as earlier distinctions did not.

Yet what this merging should alert us to is that in reality *all* the circles merge into each other, that it is ultimately one state being explored from beginning to end of the *Inferno*. In *Paradiso*, Beatrice tells Dante that all the souls are really gathered together in the great rose, and it is only to accommodate Dante's earthly understanding that they are reflected in the different planetary spheres. This is because theologically Heaven does not recognize the distinctions between better and best. But even in Hell the divisions are only an accommodation; ultimately, there is no difference between Francesca, clinging to the man she loves, and Ugolino, gnawing at the head of the man he hates.

St Augustine had argued that there are basically only two attitudes we can adopt: *amor sui* and *amor dei* (love of self and love of God). Once we put love of ourselves at the centre of our affective life, we are already headed down the cone of Hell toward Satan's gaping mouth – unless we are supple enough in spirit to repent, to re-orient our will, which, in this life, is always a possibility. This is why there is a symmetrical relation between Hell and Purgatory as well as between Hell and Paradise.

Dante makes this clear, as I have suggested, by placing at the beginning and end of the *Inferno* two episodes that could not at first sight be more different, but are in fact profoundly similar. For Dante the pilgrim and perhaps for us the first time we read the poem, they do indeed seem very different, but one of the functions of the journey is, after all, to teach both Dante and ourselves how to read aright. We are able to do this because Dante the poet, who is the product of the journey, gives us the clues to both ways of reading, though it is only when we, too, have got to the end that we can read the beginning as it ought to be read.

In both Canto V and Cantos XXXII-XXXIII we come across two figures, only one of whom speaks. Yet the two are bound together through eternity, Paolo and Francesca by a desperate love, Ugolino and Ruggieri by hatred; the first two embrace and remember how they kissed, the second two eat each other and remember other acts of cannibalism. Both Francesca and Ugolino make long speeches – among the longest in the entire poem – which evoke the horror and pity of the listener and lead to a dramatic response from the pilgrim Dante. Yet the poet Dante takes care to give us, the readers, the chance to experience the speeches quite differently from either the way the speaker wishes them to be taken or the way the pilgrim understands them. And in both cases we who come seven centuries after Dante have the advantage of seeing in the reactions of speakers over the intervening centuries how easy it is to misread, to take, in Dante's terms, the letter for the spirit. That does not mean, however, that we can afford to feel superior, for there is no certainty that we, too, are not misreading in our turn.

'Una medesma lingua pria mi morse' is how Canto XXXI begins;

'One and the same tongue first stung me, so that it tinged both my cheeks, and then it supplied the medicine to me.'[3] It is typical of Dante that in this simple and straightforward account of the effect of Virgil's words on him he should also give us the key to the whole canto, for its theme is language and the division of tongues. Soon Dante and Virgil come upon the giant Nimrod, said to be the chief builder of the Tower of Babel, which led to the fragmentation of peoples and languages. The giant cannot speak any language we or the pilgrim can understand. 'Raphel may amech zabi almi,' he howls, and Virgil says to him: 'Stupid soul, keep to thy horn and vent thyself with that when rage or other passion takes thee' (70-72). Then, turning to Dante, he explains, 'He is his own accuser. This is Nimrod, through whose wicked device the world is not of one whole speech' (76-8). Nimrod, who had wanted to bypass speech and build a tower that would allow him to assault God and wrest his power from him, finds himself robbed of speech. Dante makes the point that to speak at all we have to make an initial sacrifice. The baby cries when it wants food; learning to talk gives it a new mastery of the world, but only at the cost of some repression of immediate desire. To speak means to learn the language of others, and to abide by its laws. Responsibility to speech is thus bound up with the acceptance of the fact that we are not alone in the world with our desires. But if speech can help us to interact with others, such an initial repression results in gain as well as loss. It is another example of the need to go to the right and to the left if one is to move forward. The pattern of the acquisition of speech, moreover, parallels the central lesson of the poem, that love of God rather than love of self is what allows man to fulfil his true potential: 'In his will is our peace' (*Par.* III. 85). And we go on reading the poem seven centuries after it was written precisely because Dante does not simply assert this but demonstrates it in action.

At the end of Canto XXXI we come to the frozen lake of Cocytus, which will be the setting for the next two cantos. Here the sinners are frozen into the ice, locked together in a parody of communal life and demonstrably incapable of the movement that alone can lead to salvation: Dante's physical movement through Hell and up the mountain of Purgatory, and the spiritual movement of those who repented in this life and are now in Purgatory.

When Dante enters this area of supreme cold, he calls on the Muses for help:

It is not without fear I bring myself to speak, for to describe the

bottom of all the universe is no enterprise to undertake in sport
or for a tongue that cries *mamma* and *babbo*. But may those ladies
aid my verse who aided Amphion to wall in Thebes, so that the
telling may not be diverse from the fact. (XXXII. 5-12)

The 'tongue that cries *mamma* and *babbo*' is the baby's, but it is also
the vernacular, which Dante chose for his poem, refusing the authority of Latin. These opening remarks of Canto XXXII thus make
the point that with the help of the Muses, trusting himself to the
guardians of tradition, his child's language can develop and extend
so as to take in even what is farthest below speech, as later he will
have to deal with what is farthest above it. As we would expect of
Dante, he does in the end indeed return to the image of the child:
'Now will my speech fall more short, even in respect to that which
I remember,' he says of his final vision, 'than that of an infant who
still bathes his tongue at the breast' (*Par.* XXXIII. 106-8).

So Dante walks over the icy lake and sees the first group of sinners,
those who, like Cain, have been treacherous to kindred; and then
he comes to those who, like Antenor, the Trojan who betrayed Troy
to the Greeks, have betrayed a country or a cause. We are at line
124 and need to start reading closely: 'io vidi due ghiacciati in una
buca' ('I saw two frozen in one hole', 125). Two in one, but what
kind of union do they form? At the end of the whole poem Dante
will contemplate the mystery of the Trinity, and in Canto XXXIV
of the *Inferno* he will see a parody of it in Satan's three heads. But
here already we are set to explore the nature of unity and community.

The theme of the episode that follows is now adumbrated in typical Dantean style, not by assertion but by an apparently precise
description of what the pilgrim sees: 'And as bread is devoured for
hunger, so the upper one set his teeth upon the other where the
brain joins the nape' (127-9). Put very simply, the theme is this:
what is the food that man most needs? What is the bread that will
truly satisfy his hunger? We are fortunate to have a translation of
the whole Ugolini episode by one of our finest poets, Seamus
Heaney, and it is no insult to him to say that his translation just
doesn't work. It is an early piece (it can be found in *Field Work*,
1979), and I suspect that today he would probably agree that he was
just trying too hard:[4]

> I walked the ice
> And saw two soldered in a frozen hole
> On top of other, one's skull capping the other's,
> Gnawing at him where the neck and head

> Are grafted to the sweet fruit of the brain,
> Like a famine victim at a loaf of bread.
> So the berserk Tydeus gnashed and fed
> Upon the severed head of Menalippus
> As if it were some spattered carnal melon.

This is Heaney at his most Lowellian, and the passage is certainly powerful. But the power is that of the grotesque. Dante, for example, has no 'spattered carnal melon', and 'Like a famine victim at a loaf of bread' loses the wonderful way in which Dante, like Aeschylus, gives us images of wholesomeness even in the depths of Hell. For the line says nothing about famine victims, only about the way bread relieves hunger; in doing so, of course, it points us to the bread of the sacrament, but only by way of that most ordinary and natural activity, the eating of good bread to satisfy us after honest toil.

And yet, of course, Dante is too great an artist simply to set good against bad, correct against incorrect behaviour, the natural against its perversion. He makes the journey down precisely in order to understand the reasons for the perversion of the good, the nature of evil. The episode of Ugolino is the greatest exploration in literature (along perhaps with Kafka's late story, 'The Fasting Showman') of the implications of the fact that the mouth is used both to masticate food and to utter speech and that it cannot do both at the same time. What Dante is going to suggest, and demonstrate, is that ultimately, if it comes to a question of choice, speech is a better food than food. But there is a long way to go before we can understand this.

To describe Ugolino gnawing at his enemy's neck and head, Dante chooses an image from the siege of Thebes: 'non altrimenti Tidëo si rose / le tempie a Menalippo per disdegno' (131-2). Heaney misses that 'for rage' by simply talking about 'the berserk Tydeus'. In his version it could have been hunger that drove Tydeus mad, but Dante is careful to tell us that he fed on the other not out of hunger but out of rage – 'per disdegno'. The image makes us realize that we are not dealing with three separate themes in these cantos, the themes of childhood, language, and love (and their perversion), but one theme that unites them all. For we are here in a world of utter regression, where adults have gone back to babyhood, wanting, wanting, wanting, and back even further, to bestiality – the ultimate regression that lies in wait as a possibility for each one of us.

Having described the scene, the poet follows a familiar strategy by having the pilgrim enquire of the damned about their condition:

'O you who by so bestial sign show hatred against him whom you devour, tell me the wherefore' (133-5). John Freccero, in a fine essay to which I am greatly indebted,[5] has made the point that signs exist only within society and that a bestial sign is a contradiction in terms, the sign of the giving up of signs. Dante is here dealing with what lies beyond words, and as usual he is punctilious in his poetic response. On the one hand, we must not assimilate bestiality to our system of signs and thereby falsify its import; but on the other, without designating it by our signs we would remain in its power. Dante's solution here is not unlike Chaucer's in the General Prologue: the pilgrim wanders through Hell in an oddly innocent way. He talks as though everything around him were perfectly normal and as though there was no problem in conveying what he is experiencing: 'Tell me the wherefore', he says to the sinner in the ice, 'on this condition, that if you with reason complain of him, I ... may yet requite you in the world above, if that with which I speak does not dry up' (135-9). Heaney, subscribing to a romantic aesthetic, which says that art must be what it tells, has no room for irony or the deferral of meaning: his task is to squeeze as much horror as he can out of the scene. But since in the end he has only words, he always falls back in failure. Dante, on the other hand, is prepared to be patient. The calmness of the narration and the narrator's lack of horror are the truly terrifying aspects of the episode.

Without a break we move into the next canto. Again the horror of the scene is conveyed by the pilgrim's down-to-earth narration. But as the scene unfolds, we start to go back in our own minds to an earlier scene and to hold the two in balance.

> Tu vuo' ch'io rinovelli
> disperato dolor che'l cor mi preme
> già pur pensando, pria ch'io ne favelli.
>
> (XXXIII. 4/6)

(You will have me renew desperate grief, which even to think of wrings my heart before I speak of it.)

Thus the figure in the ice. And we recall Francesca:

> Nessun maggior dolore
> che ricordarsi del tempo felice
> nella miseria.
>
> (V. 121-23)

(There is no greater sorrow than to recall, in wretchedness, the happy time.)

The tone is the same, though the two passages naturally differ about the earlier time. Ugolino's remark is actually closer to what lies behind both passages, Aeneas's first words of the story of his adventures before he reached Carthage: 'Infandum, regina, iubes renovare dolorem' ('A sorrow too deep to speak do you order me, O queen, to tell once more,' *Aeneid* II. 3-6). But where Aeneas calls the sorrow 'infandum', beyond speech (from which our word *infant* comes), Ugolino, like Francesca, is actually only too glad to speak, though doing so is painful.

But they are glad for different reasons. Francesca wishes to tell the world about her great love; Ugolino, on the other hand, speaks so that 'my words are to be seed that may bear fruit of infamy to the traitor I gnaw' (6-8). In other words, his story will merely act out in verbal form his revenge on the one he is condemned to bite forever in hatred. It is worth noting, too, the inversion here of the idea of seed and fruit: for Dante there can be growth from the baby's babbling, from *mamma* and *babbo* to the entire *Commedia*; for Ugolino the act of speech is only another form of cannibalism and vengeance.

Yet the tale he tells seems to be full of pathos and has often been taken as such. The Monk in *The Canterbury Tales* retells it as an example of tragedy, and tragedy for him is in essence pathetic. In so doing he fills it out and makes it even more of a tear-jerker than it is in Dante. But he is in effect only 'reading' the story as Ugolino himself would have us read it, not as Dante wants us to. For Ugolino is silent on two crucial issues, one I think through deliberate choice, and the other through a kind of psychological compulsion. I will come to the second aspect in a moment. As for the first, it is important to note that throughout his speech Ugolino says nothing at all about *his own guilt*. Yet, as the footnotes tell us, and as we can guess from the fact that he is where he is, Ugolino is himself a traitor; he betrayed his city, Pisa, to its enemies, before being betrayed in turn by his erstwhile ally, Archbishop Ruggieri.

Francesca had said to the pilgrim: 'If thou hast so great desire to know our love's first root, I shall tell as one that weeps in telling' (V. 124-6). Ugolino says: 'If my words are to be seed that may bear fruit of infamy to the traitor I gnaw, thou shalt see me speak and weep together' (9). Yet the really striking fact is that Ugolino does not weep. (We will see later why weeping is a physical impossibility in this part of Hell.) And though he speaks, and at length, it is clear that his motive is not to recount what has happened in the past but to take present revenge on his enemy.

To that end he begins by explaining to Dante who he and his

victim are: I am Count Ugolino, he says, and this is Archbishop Ruggieri. 'Now I will tell you why I am such a neighbour ['tal vicino'] to him. How, by effect of his ill devising, I, trusting in him, was taken and thereafter put to death...' (15-18). Both 'neighbour' and 'trust' are being misused here, for Ruggieri and Ugolino form a parody of neighbourliness, and their mutual trust was in the service of betrayal of their city. Ugolino leaves it to Dante, as a Florentine, to draw his own conclusions about the neighbourliness and trustworthiness of Pisans, and this the poet duly does at the end of Ugolino's speech (79-90). In this outburst against Pisans, Dante makes two points that help us retrospectively read Ugolino's own story correctly, and it is therefore worthwhile jumping forward to it for a moment. First he compares Pisa to Thebes, and then he castigates the city for putting his [i.e. Ugolino's] children 'to such torture'. Dante has already referred to Thebes twice, and as Freccero reminds us, the city was a byword in antiquity and the Middle Ages not just for treachery and brutality, but for the mutual destruction of its ruling family. Oedipus killed his father, and then his two sons killed each other as they fought for possession of the city. Thebes is thus an apt symbol for the City of Man, which St Augustine contrasted with the City of God. It is the place where each man is for himself, and where a neighbour is only a person who occupies space you might have yourself, and eats food you might yourself wish to eat, and who is likely to betray you if you do not betray him first.

But what, then, of the City of God? In paraphrasing Dante's remarks about what the city did to Ugolino's children, I did not do justice to Dante's precise words: 'non dovei tu i figliuoi porre a tal croce' ('You should not have put his children to such a cross', 87). The words cannot help but alert us to a quite different father–son relationship from that in Oedipus's family, one in which a cross figures not as an instrument of torture but as an instrument of redemption. Just as the image of the bread evoked echoes of a world far from the immediate one before the pilgrim Dante's eyes, so here his own words remind us of another world, unknown to the denizens of Hell, but known to us. In the City of God fathers and children will trust each other, and each will work for the good of the community. By the time Dante wrote the *Commedia* his hopes of the realization of such a city on earth had all but vanished, but that did not stop him understanding that it was nevertheless the only alternative to Thebes. In this poem the psychological, the metaphysical, the aesthetic, and the political can never be separated.

Let us return now to Ugolino's account of his experiences. He powerfully conjures up the tower in which he and his four little children were shut up, and then tells of his terrifying dream of a wolf being ripped to pieces by pursuing hounds. He goes on: 'When I awoke before the dawn I heard my children, who were with me, crying in their sleep and asking for bread. You are cruel indeed if you do not grieve already, to think what my heart was foreboding; and if you weep not, at what do you ever weep?' (37-42). Though he had said that he would 'speak and weep together', now he tries to draw tears of sympathy from his listener. To this end, he describes how he heard the tower door being nailed up ('e io senti'chiavar l'uscio di sotto / a l'orribile torre', (46-7), those lines Eliot used so well as an image of solipsism in *The Waste Land*. (In fact Eliot must have sensed how much of this canto was about the ultimate solipsism that is the regression into bestiality, and must have felt its power more acutely than we can, since he had just recovered from a breakdown.) Ugolino goes on to say how he looked into his children's faces, 'without a word': 'Io non piangëa, sì dentro impetrai' ('I did not weep, I so turned to stone within', 49). Everything comes together in this simple line, the theme of tears again, the impossibility of tears then, and how, instead of the bread for which the children had asked (39), Ugolino can only give them stone – the stone he has now become.

The image of the self as stone, unfeeling and indifferent, is one that had long haunted Dante. He had written some wonderful sestinas about a *donna pietra*, a stony woman or *belle dame sans merci*, who tormented him by her indifference, and he knew well what it was like to reach the point where we can no longer feel. Here, instead of the traditional criticism by the sensitive lover of the indifferent beloved, we have an exploration of the reasons why people turn into stone. We today, sated as we are with reports and images of people crammed and locked into cattle trucks or forced to watch their children beaten to death before their eyes, can perhaps better understand what he was on about than most nineteenth-century critics. Indeed, an admission that their hearts had been turned to stone by their experiences would often be more honest than attempts to convey the nature of the Nazi atrocities by those who have experienced these at first hand or delved into the archives.

What follows in Canto XXXIII is the heart of the episode. It touches us to the quick but should not for that reason cloud our understanding nor make us forget that the events are being mediated through Ugolino's own words. One son looks up and asks his father

what is the matter. Ugolino does not answer. Instead he bites his
own hand in grief. At which his children, misreading his action,
say: 'Father, it will be far less pain for us if thou eat of us' (61-2).
Still he does not answer. Four days go by, and another child throws
himself at his feet, cries out, 'My father, why do you not help me?'
(69), and dies.

As Freccero points out, there can be no doubt that here we are
being presented with other signs, which, if properly understood,
will counter the 'bestial signs' we have encountered so far. Instead
of the stone that is Ugolino, his children offer him bread, not literal
bread, of course, but the bread of Heaven, which is the sacrifice of
oneself for another. For Ugolino there is merely the pathos of their
gesture, a sense that they have misread his anguished gnawing at
his own arm as a sign of hunger. For us there is the sense, in that
gesture of selflessness, of Christ's offer of his body as the true bread
of the Heavenly City. For did not Christ say, after feeding the five
thousand: 'I am the living bread which came down from heaven: if
any man eat of this bread, he shall live for ever: and the bread that
I will give is my flesh, which I will give for the life of the world'
(John 6:51)?

Behind Jesus' sacrifice lay another episode of father and son, the
story of Abraham and Isaac. Here the son trusts the father as the
father trusts God, and as God speaks to Abraham, so father and son
can converse together. Ugolino speaks at length to Dante about
what happened, but in response to his children's gesture he can only
remain silent, even their words cannot turn that stony heart into
flesh again. But even when he speaks to Dante, it is not out of
understanding or remorse but only to bring tears to the pilgrim's
eyes and so manipulate him that his later retelling of the story will
be a kind of revenge by Ugolino on Ruggieri.

It is interesting in the light of this to compare the Monk's version
of the Ugolino story with the English mystery cycles' versions of
the Abraham and Isaac story. The Monk's Tale is sentimental
because, for him, tragedy equals pathos; the cycle plays are moving
yet dignified because they are part of a larger story that is, in the
end, a comedy. (It may be that Chaucer, too, meant us to think of
the Monk's tragedies taking place within the larger comedy of the
Tales as a whole.) But there is more. In the difference of tone between
the two lies much of the difference between the Middle Ages and
the Renaissance with its aftermath, Romanticism. Once this is understood it is possible to see that both Ugolino and those critics who
see mere horror or pathos in the Dantean episode are looking at it

from what we might call a post-Renaissance point of view. That is, they ask us to see it from a point of view in which individuals are merely themselves and nothing more; Dante the poet, on the other hand, and the authors of the mystery cycles see individual lives as part of a continuum, as embedded in a world that is ultimately meaningful, even if we mere mortals cannot hope to grasp the meaning.

But why should I, as a non-Christian, assent so readily to Dante's poem and to Dante the poet's point of view, and feel it to be much closer to reality than that of Ugolino or Dante's romantic critics? I think it is because Dante never preaches but is content to give a psychological account of the difference between the two cities. He asks us to see in the children's act of spontaneous selflessness not a mere sign of some higher truth, but an example of possible human response to horror, just as Aharon Appelfeld, in his wonderful novel *The Age of Wonders*, presents us not only with Jews who hurriedly married gentiles and covered over their tracks in the wake of the Nazi invasion of Eastern Europe, but also with some who proudly asserted their Jewishness and went to their deaths in dignified fashion. Both Dante and Appelfeld ask us to imagine a world where genuine community is possible because what drives people is generosity toward each other; and both insist on the fact that the alternative to speaking to each other is eating each other.

This perhaps helps resolve what has long been seen as the chief crux of the passage before us. 'There he died', says Ugolino, ignoring his son's last words, and he goes on to recount how – always in silence – the other children also soon succumb. 'Therefore,' he concludes, 'I gave myself, now blind, to groping over each and for two days called on them [now he speaks!] after they were dead. Then fasting had more power than grief' ('poscia, più che'l dolor, poté'l digiuno', 75). The question is whether the last line implies that Ugolino eventually died of hunger, which, rather than grief, has the power to kill, or whether then hunger overcame even grief, and he ate them. Ugolino stops abruptly at this point, and Freccero rightly refers us back to Francesca's 'quel giorno più non vi leggemmo avante' ('that day we read in it no further', V. 138). Both sentences, he points out, are examples of the rhetorical figure of *reticentia*, a form of ellipsis designed to make us imagine more than language can convey. In both cases we are to imagine what follows, but in Francesca's case it is the act of love while in that of Ugolino it is an act of cannibalism. His present self may refuse to face this, yet his actions tell all, as Freud found when he said of one of his patients: 'Her painful legs began to "join in the conversation" during our analyses.'[6] For when Ugolino had finished speaking, writes Dante, 'with eyes askance he took hold of the wretched skull again with his teeth, which were strong on the bone like a dog's' (76-8). This is the final bestial sign. As in their lifetime Ugolino failed to respond to his children's appeal, would not or could not speak to them when they spoke to him, so after their death he reverts to that other, more primitive use of the mouth and tries to stave off his own death by feeding on them. Stone that he has become, he finally accepts literally their offer of food, even though they made it out of a misunderstanding of the signs he offered them, and so in eternity he is condemned to bite forever the head of his fellow-traitor.

That is the last we see of Ugolino, but what follows has retrospective force. Dante moves on along the ice and sees more figures locked in there. Only now do Ugolino's many references to tears acquire their full meaning, for this is the ultimate horror of Hell, that the most natural movement of sympathy in humans, the welling up of tears, is blocked as the ice freezes the water in their eyes. 'Lift from my face the hard veils,' cries out one of the sinners, 'that I may give vent for a little to the misery that swells my heart, before the tears freeze up again' (112-14). The Italian says, 'il duol che'l cor m'impregna' ('the misery with which my heart is pregnant'), and we recall that Ugolino, too, was 'pregnant' with grief but could not give birth to it. This failure to breed anything except death completes the series of oppositions round which these concluding cantos have been built: children-babble-speech-humanity-tears / beasts-stony hearts-false words-silence-impossibility of tears.

Dante begs the sinner to speak to him, saying that he will help him if he does so. When the soul has complied with his request, it repeats its prayer: 'But now reach out thy hand here: open my eyes.' 'And I did not open them for him,' Dante tells us, 'and it was a courtesy to be a churl to him' (148-50). Modern scholars, in reaction against their romantic predecessors, have been quick to point out that Dante is quite right to act as he did and that there are good theological justifications for his actions. But I am not sure that we can read the poem quite so comfortably. In Canto V Dante had swooned at the end of Francesca's piteous tale; in XX he had wept at the sight of the false prophets so twisted in their bodies that their tears fell from their eyes down to their buttocks. There Virgil instructed him in one of the laws of Hell, rebuking him for his easy sympathy: 'Qui vive la pietà quand'è ben morta' (28). Singleton translates this as 'Here pity lives when it is altogether dead', but the punning line is perhaps better rendered as 'Here piety lives when pity is quite dead.' In Beckett's story, 'Dante and the Lobster', the hero, quaintly called Belacqua, asks his Italian teacher the meaning of the line. She nimbly avoids the question, but it is one the story faces. Belacqua is, in fact, testing the teacher and challenging us to indict Dante for his callousness. It is in keeping with this that he should feel sympathy for the murderer he reads about in the paper and who is due to be hanged the following day, and for the lobster he has brought his aunt and which she is about to drop alive into her boiling pot. The aunt, like Virgil, is quick to condemn him: 'You make a fuss and upset me and then lash into it for your dinner.' Implicitly she rejects his pity as too easy and only a form of self-indulgence. Of course it is a shock to our post-romantic sensibilities to think of empathy as ultimately selfish and unproductive, but there is much truth in what both the aunt and Virgil are saying. Pity, the sufferings of the gentle heart in sympathy for others, is, finally, a destructive sentiment, what brings Francesca to her present plight, and there is no place for it in Purgatory. (Graham Greene's finest book, *The Heart of the Matter*, is an extended exploration of precisely this self-destructive quality of pity.)

But is that the whole truth? The story suggests that Belacqua's response to the imminent death of the lobster is a better one than the aunt's. Just because we can never fully imagine the sufferings of another does not mean that we should not try. What the story suggests is that at least the awareness of our inability is itself a kind of life, whereas the stony heart of the aunt is not. And so I wonder whether those modern critics, armed with St Augustine and St Thomas, who criticize Dante the pilgrim for swooning over Francesca and praise him for his action in Canto XXXIII are entirely right. It may be that the pilgrim Dante's only way of getting through Hell is to make his heart stony, and that that is the lesson he learns between Cantos V and XXXIII. But the heart of the poet is not hardened. To write about the stony heart, you have to start with the language of *mamma* and *babbo*. Of course you cannot stop there. You have to be able to distinguish lies from truth, the lies we tell ourselves as well as the lies others tell us. But that is not done by hardening the heart or adopting a position of superiority. It is done by experiencing imaginatively what it means to refuse to enter the world of signs, the world of human speech. For, as Wallace Stevens understood, even 'the absence of imagination had / Itself to be imagined.' Dante the pilgrim will have to learn that while speaking like a child makes us vulnerable, it is also our only hope. Virgil, like all the virtuous pagans, may live a dignified and serene existence, but it is an existence without hope. Dante suggests, I think, that only by accepting how close we are to babyhood, to bestiality, can we find the springs of generosity that, with the right discipline, can lead to the founding of the City of God and the writing not just of the *Inferno*, but of the *Purgatorio* and the *Paradiso* as well.

That is a lesson every poet since Dante has had to learn for himself. We may argue about the validity or otherwise of this or that tradition, this or that poetic strategy, and no doubt both tradition and strategy are important to the poet. But prior to the choice of either comes the choice of what to do with the mouth, with the relation between food and utterance. To ignore that relation is to condemn oneself to a poetry without substance; to conflate the two is to condemn oneself to a poetry of mere indulgence. Somewhere between these two extremes every major modern poet has operated. The question we have to ask ourselves is a simple one, but upon its answer depends the trajectory of the poet's career: what kind of food do I most need?

3 Reflections on Echo

From the start the fates of Echo and Narcissus seem to be inseparable. If they are not exactly mirror-images of each other then at least, in Ovid's retelling of the story, their fortunes are tantalizingly intertwined.

Narcissus' mother, a naiad of the river called Liriope, asks Tiresias if the boy will ever live to a ripe old age, and the seer answers: 'Yes, if he never knows himself.' The meaning of the mysterious prophecy is made clear in what follows. The nymph Echo, who cannot speak except to repeat the last words said to her, falls in love with Narcissus, but he spurns her and she wastes away until she is only a voice. Meanwhile, Narcissus falls in love with his own image, seen in the water:

> Poor boy,
> He wants himself; the loved becomes the lover,
> The seeker sought, the kindler burns. How often
> He tries to kiss the image in the water,
> Dips in his arms to embrace the boy he sees there,
> And finds the boy, himself, elusive always,
> Not knowing what he sees, but burning for it,
> The same delusion mocking his eyes and teasing.
> Why try to catch an always fleeing image,
> Poor credulous youngster? What you seek is nowhere,
> And if you turn away, you will take with you
> The boy you love.[1]

But it is not only the boy's beauty that seduces Narcissus. It is the promise of something more, the hint that what he is seeing can give him what no one else can, understands him better than anyone else in the whole world:

> You promise,
> I think, some hope with a look of more than friendship.
> You reach your arms when I do, and your smile

48

Follows my smiling; and I have seen your tears
When I was tearful; you nod and beckon when I do;
Your lips, it seems, answer when I am talking
Though what you say I cannot hear.

But there is of course a price to pay for such perfect reciprocity, as
Narcissus himself suddenly understands:

What I want is with me,
My riches make me poor. If I could only
Escape from my own body! If I could only –
How curious a prayer from any lover –
Be parted from my love! And now my sorrow
Is taking all my strength away; I know
I have not long to live, I shall die early,
And death is not so terrible, since it takes
My troubles from me; I am sorry only
The boy I love must die; we die together.

To love myself and find myself another – that is the impossible
desire. Since that cannot be it is better to die. That at least will release
me from an intolerable existence. The one sadness is that it will also
mean the death of the one I love. But then another way of looking
at it is that at least we will both die together.

So Narcissus kills himself, and Echo, now only a voice, mourns
him in the only way she can:

you could hear her
Answer 'Alas!' in pity, when Narcissus
Cried out 'Alas!' You could hear her own hands beating
Her breast when he beat his. 'Farewell, dear boy,
Beloved in vain!' were his last words, and Echo
Cried the same words to him.

As the water reflects his image so Echo reflects his words. As he is
forever separated from himself, so she is forever separated from
him. It is as though once that narcissistic duplication had taken place
it is designed to go on splitting into two unsatisfied halves for ever
and ever. Or perhaps one could say that once an echo is heard it is
designed to go on repeating the same words for ever and ever.

Yet Ovid, for all that he touched, in this brief story, the very
heart of Romanticism and its discontents, was a man of the first and
not of the nineteenth century. So his story ends not with death but
with a flower and a bit of traditional lore:

> But when they sought his body, they found nothing,
> Only a flower with a yellow centre
> Surrounded with white petals.

THE WORLD'S ECHO

Wordsworth wrote 'The Boy of Winander' in 1798, and then, as he did with so much of his early poetry, he incorporated it virtually unchanged in *The Prelude* (ll. 364-97). There it becomes an example of those special childhood experiences which can never be recovered in later life, but which the poet, through his art, brings back for us intact.

The poem opens abruptly:[2]

> There was a Boy; ye knew him well, ye cliffs
> And islands of Winander!

There *was* a boy. Presumably he no longer exists. The poem, though, does not go on to tell us his story, but glides instead into the iterative mode:

>   – many a time,
> At evening, when the earliest stars began
> To move along the edges of the hills,
> Rising or setting, would he stand alone,
> Beneath the trees, or by the glimmering lake;
> And there, with fingers interwoven, both hands
> Pressed closely palm to palm and to his mouth
> Uplifted, he, as through an instrument,
> Blew mimic hootings to the silent owls,
> That they might answer him...

The almost aggressive narrative opening has miraculously changed into a cradling rhythm which seems able to dispense with a main verb for far longer than we would have thought possible, while not noticeably distorting the natural rhythms of the spoken language: 'many a time, at evening, when the earliest stars began to move... rising or setting, would he stand...'. This is Wordsworth's special magic, the totally new element he brought into English (and into European) literature.

But even here the sentence is not done. The Boy stands 'Beneath the trees, or by the glimmering lake' (the adjective, we sense, is more than merely formulaic; soon we will see just how it earns its keep); and now, typically, Wordsworth extends the period with a breathtakingly simple 'and', allowing us to keep our balance yet propelling us forward. The second half of the sentence tells us what the boy does. In contrast to Robinson Crusoe on his island, this activity on the part of the boy is not directed outwards, towards the improvement of his position in the wilderness, but rather towards the merging of himself in his surroundings by means of echo and imitation: interweaving his fingers, he blows *mimic* hootings to the silent owls, to get them to respond. 'Uplifted', in line 9, seems to float free of reference. Analysing it after the event we see that it must refer to the hands. But is this a purely physical description? Is there not a sense of the boy himself being uplifted by what is going on?

The mouth and fingers – indeed, the whole boy – become an instrument for those imitations of the owls' hootings, which seem to succeed in calling forth an answer; for, the poem goes on to say,

> they would shout
> Across the watery vale, and shout again
> Responsive to his call . . .

How much less sense we would have of the owls as *responsive* to the boy's call, were that sentence not folded in on itself already, with its 'they would shout . . . and shout again . . .'. Even then the cry is not allowed to vanish but is once again extended by the poet through the naïve but effective use of the dash:

> . . . Responsive to his call – with quivering peals,
> And long halloos, and screams, and echoes loud
> Redoubled and redoubled . . .

This brings us to the heart of the little poem, as echo gives way to silence:

> And, when there came a pause
> Of silence such as baffled his best skill:
> Then, sometimes, in that silence, while he hung
> Listening, a gentle shock of mild surprise
> Has carried far into his heart the voice
> Of mountain-torrents . . .

Wordsworth here deploys one of his favourite devices, the tension between a breath pause at the end of a verse line and the enjambement required by the sense. The voice, like the boy, '*hangs* . . . Listening', just as earlier there is a 'pause . . . Of silence', and the silence is somehow confirmed by the word's almost immediate repetition.

As he hangs, then, listening, 'a gentle shock' carries not just 'into his heart' but '*far* into his heart' the voice of mountain torrents. As so often in early Wordsworth the inner, affective self is somehow expanded, and given contours, by the very breath of the verse, so that we too, as readers, come to feel that the silence after the echoes goes deep inside us, travelling through our bodies rather as the torrents themselves travel through the Lakeland landscape, and carrying with it a rich and complex geology which now speaks within us and through us, but in its own voice and not in either the poet's or ours.

Still the great period has not ended, for now, in the stately climax, the aural echo, which played such a crucial role, as we have seen, in both the poetry and the fiction, is expanded to include a triple *visual* echo (Narcissus is never very far away from Echo):

> or the visible scene
> Would enter unawares into his mind
> With all its solemn imagery, its rocks,
> Its woods, and that uncertain heaven received
> Into the bosom of the steady lake.

'Uncertain' is brilliant here, another non-formulaic adjective, which sends us back to the 'glimmering lake', and sets up the uncertainty in our own minds that is the sign of those last lines: the echo or reflection is in the Boy's mind *and* in the lake *and* in the mind of the reader. Yet if the lake is glimmering it is also steady, and these two adjectives could also be seen as accurate descriptions of the poem. Each would seem to rule out the other, but Wordsworth's distinctive genius consists precisely in making each an index of the other.

Echo and reflection function here not to divide, as in Ovid, but to unite. Through his mimic hootings the boy is bound fast to the owls, the hills, the woods, the mountain torrents and the lake, as the seemingly ponderous iterations of the poem bind us to the boy. We are reminded of the climax of so many early Wordsworth poems, notably the most compressed of the Lucy poems, 'A Slumber did my Spirit Seal', where both girl and poem end 'rolled round in earth's diurnal course / With rocks and stones and trees!' The overt meaning is that Lucy is dead. But death has taken on a new meaning as a result of the poem, neither Christian resurrection nor Romantic annihilation but a mysterious combination of the two.

The boy of Winander too is, of course, now dead. We grasped that with the opening phrase, and the poem, in a concluding section, returns to it:

> This boy was taken from his mates, and died
> In childhood, ere he was full twelve years old.

But the poet does not tell us this as would a novelist, from some position outside and above the orbit of his creature. Wordsworth, in his final section, depicts him wandering through the very landscape the Boy had inhabited and the churchyard where he is buried. 'And through the churchyard when my way has led', he tells us, conveying by this the sense of passivity, of responsiveness, which is so typical of the boy as well. There, on summer evenings,

> A long half-hour together I have stood
> Mute-looking at the grave in which he lies!

The poet is excluded, apart, yet meditating on the past, as we find him in *Tintern Abbey*. Wordsworth wrote an essay on epitaphs which is, in a sense, the last document in European culture to assert the continuity of past and present, the ability of the simple epitaph to sum up a life satisfactorily. Since his day writers have tended to contemplate epitaphs ironically, suggesting that the pious words inscribed on tombstones can tell us nothing about the person buried beneath.[3]

But if the essay is the last of its kind, a poem such as 'The Boy of Winander' is surely the first of another kind. For the poem, unlike those inscribed on tombstones, does not rest content with traditional pieties, but seeks to bring the Boy back to life. The poet may stand mute before the grave, but the result of that silence, we sense, is the poem we have before us, and which allows us to enter the very being of the Boy. That being is summed up in his hooting to the owls, which calls forth an answer from them, and then in that silence which allows the geology of the place to enter into him *unawares*, until he becomes the world in which he stands. He is like Lucy, yet alive. On the other hand, he dies before he can reach adolescence and it is left to the poet, through a radically new use of language, to make him live for us – and, of course, for himself.

It is as though Wordsworth, accepting that a poem will only ever be an echo of reality, turns the tables by revealing how reality itself is, in its essential being, echo, but echo as the assertion of a generous reciprocity.

THE MIND'S ECHO

Edgar Allan Poe wrote a number of essays and meditations on land-scape. Though these are ostensibly written to celebrate the wonders of man's ability to imitate nature in the creation of elaborate gardens and the like, their effect is chilling. For instead of the communion with landscape leading the mind out of itself and so healing its self-divisions and anxieties, that communion only leads man back to himself. Though Poe talks of *Kabbala* and the discerning of the secret languages of God in nature, the effect is only to throw us back on ourselves: we had thought it was other and find it the same. At the same time these essays and meditations also seem to reveal the final bankruptcy of the American dream: instead of infinite spaces to colonize and chart, infinite adventures to recount, there is, in the end, only the sense that we have been here before.

This is also the subject of the tales. 'The Fall of the House of Usher' is particularly interesting in this context, because it is in some ways so close to Wordsworth's 'Boy of Winander', yet almost its polar opposite in the feeling it conveys. As with Wordsworth's poem, the setting is evening and the central image is that of a reflec-tion in a lake. But where one brought renewal and a feeling of life, this brings only a sense of dreariness and death:

> During the whole of a dull, dark, and soundless day in the autumn of the year, when the clouds hung oppressively low in the heavens, I had been passing alone, on horseback, through a sin-gularly dreary tract of country, and at length found myself, as the shades of the evening drew on, within view of the melancholy House of Usher.

Without understanding why, the traveller's soul is filled 'with a sense of insufferable gloom'. It seems to him that his feelings can only be compared to the 'bitter lapse into every-day life – the hideous dropping off of the veil' of the opium addict. Here, he suggests, we have reached reality itself, a reality unredeemed by any 'goading of the imagination'. Trying to grasp the reason for this,

> I reined my horse to the precipitous brink of a black and lurid tarn that lay in unruffled lustre by the dwelling, and gazed down – but with a shudder even more thrilling than before – upon the remodelled and inverted images of the grey sedge, and the ghastly tree-stems, and the vacant and eye-like window.

It is as though the reduplication of the house has robbed it of its life. Those windows like eyes through which no spirit shines have already been referred to in the opening lines, and they are later to be made explicit in the poem sung by Roderick Usher and entitled 'The Haunted House':

> In the greenest of our valleys,
> By good angels tenanted,
> Once a fair and stately palace –
> Radiant palace – reared its head.
> In the monarch Thought's dominion –
> It stood there!
> Never seraph spread a pinion
> Over fabric half so fair.

But alas, 'evil things, in robes of sorrow, / Assailed the monarch's high estate',

> And travellers now within that valley
> Through the red-litten windows, see
> Vast forms that move fantastically
> To a discordant melody;
> While, like a rapid ghastly river,
> Through the pale door,
> A hideous throng rush out forever,
> And laugh – but smile no more.

The mountain torrents, which in the pause between the hootings of the owls had seemed to enter the very being of the Boy of Winander, here become merely a dead image for the madman's loss of his grip on language.

What has led to the deterioration? It is hinted that there is something about the house and its grounds which has affected Roderick Usher's mind – 'above all', the narrator says, 'the long undisturbed endurance of this arrangement, and . . . its reduplication in the still waters of the tarn.' But there is a further, secret mirroring at work in this haunted house: the suggested incest between Roderick and his sister, who has recently died and been buried.

The denouement is both horrific and expected. The dead sister turns out to have been put living in the tomb, and she now, at the climax of the story, appears at the door of the room in which Roderick and the narrator have been talking:

> There was blood upon her white robes, and the evidence of some bitter struggle upon every portion of her emaciated frame. For a moment she remained trembling and reeling to and fro upon

the threshold, then, with a low moaning cry, fell heavily inwards upon the person of her brother, and in her violent and now final death-agonies, bore him to the floor a corpse, and a victim to the terrors he had anticipated.

The narrator flees in horror. A wild storm is beating about the house and grounds. A terrifying light flares in his path, and as he turns to look back he sees that the long zig-zag crack, which had been barely discernible in the façade of the house, has now widened and is letting through the gleam of a blood-red moon:

> While I gazed this fissure rapidly widened – there came a fierce breath of the whirlwind – the entire orb of the satellite burst at once upon my sight – my brain reeled as I saw the mighty walls rushing asunder – there was a long tumultuous shouting sound like the voice of a thousand waters – and the deep and dank tarn at my feet closed sullenly and silently over the fragments of 'The House of Usher'.

The whole narrative, like so many post-Romantic fictions, exists between the moment in the opening lines, when the narrator senses that something is dreadfully wrong, and the eruption of that wrong into the light of day.[4] There is relief, as well as horror, in Roderick Usher's finally succumbing 'to the horrors he had anticipated' – and it is worth contrasting that anticipation in our minds with Wordsworth's 'gentle shock of mild surprise' which forms the climax to *his* narrative. In Poe it is as though the story cannot exist without a sense of a fatal flaw, a primal guilt, and cannot go on once that flaw has emerged into the light of day. That emergence is quite literal here, as the only apparently dead sister rises from her grave in order to die properly by bringing down her *alter ego*, her brother, and the entire scenery that contained the two of them.

At one level this is a psychological tale, with its themes of incest, madness and repression. But its springs lie elsewhere. Like Beckett, Poe makes use of what lies to hand, the banalities filling the popular reader's mind. In his case it is the trappings of Gothic. Like Wordsworth and Beckett, he is concerned with the point at which the literary and the psychological mesh. It is as though such writing cannot go on pretending to be innocent. To do so, to write a story of adventure in the style of Fenimore Cooper, say, would be forcing the living world into the tomb of letters. Once this is recognized the story itself finds its theme: the revenge of life upon letters. Reduplication, echo, is the sign of writing, yet it is also that which writing itself must annihilate, destroying doubleness, leaving the lake empty of reflection.

This is brought out equally clearly in 'William Wilson', Poe's richest tale of doubles. This time there is no narrator distinct from the action. The story opens: 'Let me call myself, for the present, William Wilson. The fair page now lying before me need not be sullied with my real appellation.' Who the narrator is, and what his relation is to his name is what is in question. As usual, Poe turns the clichés of Gothic to his own rather different ends. The fair page should not be sullied with his real name because that name is too dreadful to write down; but also because to put the 'real name' down would so sully any page that that would be the end of all writing. In other words, to go on writing at all, a false name has to be substituted for a real one.

But a false name is, precisely, one that can be precisely imitated. With that opening sentence, therefore, we are at once in a world that refuses the falsehood of an unthinking transposition of life into literature, *and* a world condemned to infinite reduplication. That, however, is left in abeyance as Poe moves easily within the parameters of his chosen genre, describing 'my' ancestry, childhood and schooling. It is the school and its over-symmetrical appearance which he pauses on longest:

> But the house! – how quaint an old building was this! – to me how veritably a palace of enchantment! There was really no end to its windings – to its incomprehensible subdivisions. It was difficult, at any given time, to say with certainty upon which of its two stories one happened to be...

And as the house reduplicates the maze-like grounds, so the school-room reduplicates the house, for

> Interspersed about the room, crossing and recrossing in endless irregularity, were innumerable benches and desks, black, ancient, and time-worn, piled desperately with much-bethumbed books, and so beseamed with initial letters, names at full length, grotesque figures, and other multiplied efforts of the knife, as to have entirely lost what little of original form might have been their portion in days long departed.

It is here, in this palimpsest of a building, that he meets the boy who is to play such a central role in his life. No relation, but bearing the same name as himself, born on the same day, like him in appearance, this *alter ego* seems to take pleasure in imitating him, though no one else, surprisingly, seems to notice either this or any other of the coincidences. Most horrible of all to Wilson is the fact that his rival, as he calls him, 'had a weakness of the faucial or guttural organs, which precluded him from raising his voice at any time *above* a very low whisper' (author's stress).

The horror engendered by this 'twofold repetition', as he calls it, gives the narrator no rest. One night he creeps up to his rival's bed:

> I looked; – and a numbness, an iciness of feeling instantly pervaded my frame. My breast heaved, my knees tottered, my whole spirit became possessed with an objectless yet intolerable horror ... Was it, in truth, within the bounds of human possibility, that *what I saw now* was the result, merely, of the habitual practice of [his] sarcastic imitation? Awe-stricken, and with a creeping shudder, I extinguished the lamp, passed silently from the chamber, and left, at once, the halls of that old academy, never to enter them again.

But of course he flees in vain. The other goes on haunting him, and here too, as in 'The Fall of the House of Usher', the end is both horrible and never in doubt. The narrator, driven to distraction, kills his double, then feels that he is looking into a mirror as he sees himself totter towards himself, 'all pale and dabbled in blood'. But it is not himself – or is it?

> It was Wilson; but he spoke no longer in a whisper, and I could have fancied that I myself was speaking while he said: 'You have conquered, and I yield. Yet, henceforward art thou also dead – dead to the world, to Heaven and to Hope! In me didst thou exist – and, in my death, see by this image which is thine own, how utterly thou hast murdered thyself.

As in Ovid, the hero and his mirror-image converge, but only in the moment of death. Knowing himself, he has to die; or perhaps it is that death brings a kind of self-knowledge. But death, one could also say, is the only way of stilling forever the horror of the echo.

IN SEARCH OF THE LOST ECHO

It is characteristic of Proust that the climax of his novel of repetition and return should begin with a return that is not a return. At the start of *Le Temps retrouvé*[5] Marcel recounts how he went to stay with Gilberte, now Mme de Saint-Loup, at her country house in Tansonville. The scene had already been prepared for as early as

the fourth page of the novel, when Marcel is recalling all the rooms
he has ever slept in:

> j'étais dans ma chambre chez Mme de Saint-Loup, à la campagne;
> mon Dieu! il est au moins dix heures, on doit avoir fini de dîner!
> J'aurai trop prolongé la sieste que je fais tous les soirs, en rentrant
> de ma promenade avec Mme de Saint-Loup, avant d'endosser
> mon habit. Car bien des années ont passé depuis Combray, où
> dans nos retours les plus tardifs c'étaient les reflets rouges du
> couchant que je voyais sur le vitrage de ma fenêtre. C'est un autre
> genre de vie qu'on mène à Tansonville, chez Mme de Saint-Loup,
> un autre genre de plaisir que je trouve à ne sortir qu'à la nuit, à
> suivre au clair de lune des chemins où je jouais au soleil... (i. 6-7)

In the course of their walks Gilberte takes him back over all his
childish haunts, for Tansonville is within walking distance of Combray. Aren't you excited? she asks him. But, sadly, the answer is
no: 'J'étais désolé de voir combien peu je revivais mes années d'autrefois. Je trouvais la Vivonne mince et laide au bord du chemin de
halage' (iii. 692). Even the amazing discovery that the two ways,
that of Swann and that of Guermantes, which had seemed to him
to belong to quite different universes, can in fact easily be encompas-
sed in a single stroll, fails to move him. 'Elle m'étonna beaucoup',
says Marcel, when she reveals this fact to him, as when she shows
him the source of the Vivonne, which he had imagined as something
rather like the entry into Hades, but which turns out to be 'une
espèce de lavoir carré où montaient des bulles'. But 'ce qui me frappa
le plus, ce fut combien peu, pendant ce séjour, je revécus mes années
d'autrefois, désirai peu revoir Combray, trouvai mince et laide la
Vivonne' (693).

And yet the narration of this reaction has a curious effect on the
reader, who has, after all, lived through Marcel's childhood in Combray with him. Paradoxically, it makes him feel the mystery of the
past, and the joining of the two ways only serves to remind him
how they were once fully alive for Marcel and totally distinct; totally
distinct *because* fully alive. Unlike Wordsworth, the visit to a once
sacred spot does not set feeling and memory in motion; unlike Poe,
this meeting with his past self is anything but fatal. And it *is* a meeting
with his past, for Gilberte tells him about her side of the encounter
in the forest path, her view of him then. But Marcel simply cannot
relate past to present. He is no longer in danger, the past cannot
hurt him – but only because he is, in a sense, no longer alive. He is
in the state recommended by Tiresias: he does not know himself.

If we search our minds for a parallel experience to this one we quickly discover it: it is Swann looking back at his love-affair with Odette and wondering how he could have spent the best years of his life on a woman 'qui n'était même pas mon genre' (i. 382). Tansonville, however, is only a stage, perhaps a necessary stage, in Marcel's progress. For had he remained in this mood he would not have written 'Combray', and we would not have known about the Vivonne in another mode. The fact that we do, that we have already experienced it differently, and can therefore register disappointment at this return which seems to be no return, is a proof (available to our senses but not yet to our consciousness) that matters will not end here.

On his last night in Tansonville Gilberte lends Marcel a copy of the Goncourt *Journals* to read in bed. The next few pages consist of a transcription of a dinner party, described by the Goncourts, at which the guests are those old friends of Marcel's, and thus of ours, the Verdurins, Cottard, Brichot, *et al.* As everyone knows, it is reading about that dinner party that makes Marcel at once thankful that he has in fact never pursued his career as a writer – for who would want to do so if that is the end result? – and sad that he never had the gifts required for such a career. But the way the pastiche ends has perhaps not been remarked upon enough. It is difficult to quote from the pastiche, for Proust's point is the evenness of the Goncourts' tone, the way everything is seen in the same light, but we can cut into the passage as it nears its end:

> Et la suggestive dissertation passe, sur un signe gracieux de la maîtresse de maison, de la salle à manger au fumoir vénitien dans lequel Cottard nous dit avoir assisté à de véritables dédoublements de la personnalité, nous citant ce cas d'un de ses malades, qu'il s'offre aimablement à m'amener chez moi et à qui il suffirait qu'il touche les tempes pour l'éveiller à une seconde vie, vie pendant laquelle il ne se rappellerait rien de la première, si bien que, très honnête homme dans celle-là, il y aurait été plusieurs fois arrêté pour des vols commis dans l'autre où il serait tout simplement un abominable gredin. Sur quoi Mme Verdurin remarque finement que la médecine pourrait fournir des sujets plus vrais à un théâtre où la cocasserie de l'imbroglio reposerait sur des méprises pathologiques, ce qui, de fil en aiguille, amène Mme Cottard à narrer qu'une donnée toute semblable a été mise en œuvre par un conteur qui est le favori des soirées de ses enfants, l'Ecossais Stevenson, un nom qui met dans la bouche de Swann cette affir-

mation péremptoire: 'Mais c'est tout à fait un grand écrivain,
Stevenson, je vous assure...' Et, comme, sur mon émerveille-
ment des plafonds à caissons écussonnées, provenant de l'ancien
palazzo Barberini, de la salle où nous fumons, je laisse percer mon
regret du noircissement progressif d'une certaine vasque par la
cendre de nos 'londres', Swann, ayant raconté que des taches
pareilles attestent sur les livres ayant appartenu à Napoléon Ier...

(iii. 716-17)

The anecdote about Napoleon goes on for a further twelve lines,
when Marcel, who has to get up early the next morning, closes the
book. But we have seen enough of the Goncourt style, with its even
movement over objects, people, anecdotes and books, to make us
sense that it is indeed a kind of death-in-life. Everything is equally
important here and nothing has any meaning. We watch a group of
reasonably cultivated people taking dinner in town and we are left
to wonder what point their lives can have. Time does not exist here,
nor do joy or sorrow seem to touch either the writer or the people
he so carefully describes.

That, as all readers of Proust know, forms the turning-point for
Marcel. Proust deliberately blurs the passing of time in the next few
years, as Marcel goes back and forth from his sanatorium to Paris,
and the war destroys the French countryside and the fabric of Parisian social life. But soon he will experience that series of shocks to
his system which will alert him to the fact that the Goncourts have
got it wrong, and will be led to recognize that art is indeed the
central element in his life, but an art which accepts both Echo and
Narcissus.

We watch Marcel coming alive in those last pages of the novel,
until he reaches the point where, understanding fully what his task
is, he is ready to write the book we have been reading. But paradox
holds to the end, for that task, which gives new meaning to his life,
and which, from one perspective, can be seen as his attempt to join
himself once more to his dead mother, condemns him, like Roderick
Usher's sister, to be buried alive for the remainder of his days; not,
it is true, in the exotic House of Usher, but in the cork-lined room
at 102 Boulevard Haussmann.

4 Maurice Blanchot

'Born in 1907, he has devoted his life to writing and literature.' In an age avid for publicity, where even art is often seen as only a stepping-stone to fame and wealth, the austerity of this, the only biographical information Maurice Blanchot will make available about himself is most striking. Blanchot's reputation has slowly spread in French intellectual circles since the early 1940s, when he first began to publish fiction and criticism, but, unlike his younger contemporaries, Barthes and Foucault, he has remained almost unknown to the general public in France and wholly unknown abroad outside a tiny circle of specialist academics. Nor is this surprising. There are no large theories that can be associated with his name, no *isms* or causes with which he can be identified. To the English reader, whose 1066-and-all-that view of French culture consists of a straight line from Baudelaire and the Symbolists through Proust to Existentialism, the *Nouveau Roman*, Structuralism and Deconstruction, with Gide, Mauriac and Maurois hovering uneasily on the edges, the names frequently to be met in Blanchot's work are likely to be puzzling and alien: Lautréamont, Paulhan, Bataille, Char. And when we also discover that his critical books consist for the most part of the mere collection of what were once ephemeral essays and reviews, we are entitled to ask why these should be resurrected and translated. With so much to read, why should we bother with this?

The answer is that Blanchot is, with Walter Benjamin, the finest literary critic of the century, and that not to read him is to deprive ourselves of the knowledge of a body of work of startling originality and perspicuity. Having said that, though, it is difficult to know how to set about substantiating it short simply of thrusting his selected essays at the reader and letting the book make its point. For, unlike Benjamin, there are no intriguing biographical details to arouse our interest or sympathy, nor is there any espousing of such popular causes as Marxism or Mysticism. Unlike Barthes or Derrida, there is no theory of literature with which we can associate Blanchot, and which can be sketched in, in a few deft strokes. On the other hand he hardly seems interested in literary history, and all his essays seem to circle like moths round the questions: Why write? Why literature? – questions which the Anglo-Saxon mind immediately associates with continental abstraction and even perhaps with that dread word, Hegelianism.

The key to Blanchot is, I suspect, that he is a novelist as well as a critic. He is a critic *because* he is a novelist, and for him criticism is simply the continuation of the imaginative exploration which is fiction by other means. His criticism should thus be seen as belonging more with that of Proust, Eliot or Jarrell than with that of Leavis, Frye or Barthes. And, like the very greatest writer–critics, he has the ability to ask questions so unexpected that the very posing of them forces us to reconsider not just the work or writer in question but the nature of writing itself. Why is James in his journals so interested in plot? Why does Proust set aside his almost finished novel, *Jean Santeuil*, though he was willing to publish the much slighter *Les Plaisirs et les jours*? Why does Rimbaud need so much sleep? Why does Virginia Woolf keep a diary? Who speaks in Beckett's works? Where does the light come from that infuses a story like Robbe-Grillet's *Le Voyeur*? These are not questions that will trouble those who take literature for granted, who accept works of art as simply given, and feel that the task of criticism is to elucidate or pass judgement on this given. Nor will it trouble those who are interested purely in aesthetics and wish to answer such questions as: what is the function of art?

It might seem, too, that asking the kinds of questions he does, Blanchot must be prepared to answer them with some kind of psychoanalytic theory, but this is very far from being the case. A psychoanalytic theory, like any other, suggests that the answers to such questions will be boringly uniform. But the striking thing about Blanchot is that each essay is unique. The reason for this is simple: he writes about works of literature to which he is prepared to listen. Each one is different, and they are only worthy of attention because they are excitingly unique. The task of the critic is to bring out that uniqueness.

It follows from this that to give an idea of the flavour of Blanchot's criticism it is no use talking in general terms. What we need to do is to follow him through one of his explorations.

The example I have chosen is not among Blanchot's greatest or most pondered essays; it may well have been sparked off by the arrival of a book for review. But for that very reason it shows his characteristic method and approach more clearly. It is an essay on Beckett's trilogy,[1] and here is how it begins.

Who speaks in Samuel Beckett's books? Who is the tireless 'I' who seems always to say the same thing? What are the author's (and the reader's) expectations – for there must be an author? Or is he trapped in a circuit where he circles blindly, swept along by the flow of stumbling words? Words that are not meaningless but focusless; that neither start nor stop and are eager, nevertheless, demanding; and will never stop; nor could we bear them to stop because then we would be faced with the horrifying discovery that when they are not speaking they continue to speak; when they stop they go on; are never silent, for in them silence ceaselessly speaks.

The first thing to notice is how fast this paragraph moves. We have travelled a very long distance by the time we get to the end of it. The second thing is that Blanchot always starts with our experience of reading; he helps us to articulate that experience by keeping us from turning too quickly to an answer, an explanation, a solution. Notice how carefully he fills out for us what happens when we read Beckett, how concerned he is to find the appropriate words for all that is going on in us: 'Words that are not meaningless but focusless; that neither start nor stop and are eager, nevertheless, demanding'. And then his profound insight into our own expectations: we could not bear for the words to stop. And why? Because then we should find that they do in fact go on, even when they have stopped. So, paradoxically, author and reader seem to be locked in the same enterprise, to try and stop the words that flow out with so little focus; but also, secretly, to keep them going; for, so long as they are going, the illusion exists that they could be stopped.

Having plunged us so rapidly so deep into the experience of reading Beckett, Blanchot stops short and stands back:

What first strikes us is that here someone is not writing for the worthy purpose of producing a good book. Nor does he write in response to that noble urge we like to call inspiration; or to say the significant things he has to say; or because this is his job; or because he hopes by writing to penetrate into the unknown.

The paradox of Blanchot's writing, as I have already suggested, is that each essay, no matter how slight or incidental, comes back to his central preoccupations; and yet that there is no one more scrupulous than he in the attention he pays to the nuances of individual authors and works. Here, for example, he helps us to move deeper into Beckett by carefully removing, and in the process holding up for our inspection, the ghosts of aims which are not Beckett's. First of all, Beckett is not out to produce a well made, marketable work. A writer like Artaud or Joubert is more interesting to Blanchot than Balzac or Hugo. For he has begun to ask himself: 'What does it mean to finish a book?' 'What does it mean to *write* a book?' Balzac, on the other hand, was content merely to keep writing. And what Blanchot suggests, here following Mallarmé, Kafka and Mann, is that there is no external justification for the production of an 'accomplished' novel, play or opera except to satisfy a bourgeois public which needs its quota of entertainment and even of 'art'.

But if there is no genuine external reason for writing a book, as there was for telling a story in an oral culture perhaps, are there not internal ones? What about 'the noble urge we... call inspiration'? Some of Blanchot's greatest essays have been devoted to Kafka (a fascinating volume could be put together out of these) and Blanchot's interest in Kafka stems from the fact that for Kafka the simple opposition between art and society, inspiration and the demands of a Philistine world, which underlies so much Romantic writing, no longer holds. Kafka, to judge by his letters and diary entries, certainly began by believing in this Romantic opposition, but life itself was to give the lie to these assumptions. The decisive years are 1915-17, with the outbreak of the war, the development of his liaison with Félice Bauer, his failure (in his eyes) to produce work with which he could be satisfied, and his discovery of his fatal illness. Though when he was not writing Kafka felt that the only salvation for him was to write, once he was writing he felt that what he was doing was meaningless, without relation to the world or the truth, worse even than meaningless, the perpetuation of a downright lie. His writing is the description of the failure of writing; were his writing to succeed, he would have failed; failing, he perhaps succeeded.

Nor is Kafka's an isolated case, though it is perhaps the purest because Kafka himself was so honest and clear sighted. The same denial of the easy Romantic alternatives (which are still to a large extent the terms in which the general public thinks of the relations between art and life) is to be found in the case of Baudelaire. Blanchot agrees with the famous remark of Sartre's that Baudelaire got the life he deserved: sordid, petty, filled with lies and evasions. But, he says, if we accept this view, we must also accept the opposite, that Baudelaire's life was an unqualified success, for he succeeded in doing what he had set out to do, which was to be a great poet. Nor was the production of *Les fleurs du mal* the result of a stroke of luck. If we speak of Baudelaire's life as being a success we must add:

> And not a fortuitous success, but an intentional one; not some-
> thing superimposed on failure, but something which finds it jus-
> tification in failure, glorifies it, turns impotence into incredible
> fertility and extracts from a basic deception the most radiant
> truth.[2]

Blanchot rightly sees that Baudelaire's life does not exhibit a clash
between the attitude of the Pharisees who surrounded him and his
own unshaken sense of poetic vocation. Its pathos comes from the
fact that Baudelaire too sides with the Pharisees and condemns himself. But this too is, in one sense, only one of the subterfuges of
poetry. For if his failure is the failure of poetry, it is only through
that failure that poetry discovers what it truly is – and thus triumphs:
'Everything happens as though... its realisation depends on its failure'; though even this can be reversed, depending on one's point
of view, and one could say that 'it is not even capable of achieving
the total failure that alone would establish its reality'.

We can now return to Beckett with a clearer idea of what it is that
Blanchot is suggesting Beckett is *not* doing: he is not writing to
produce yet one more novel that will sell; he is not writing under
the intolerable pressure of inspiration, of some inner image or idea
that is struggling to come out. But what then is he doing? As is his
way, Blanchot proceeds by asking a new question: 'Is it then, so as
to get it over with?' This is startling, but it is clearly echoed in
Beckett's own writings, and Blanchot further defines it: 'Because
he is trying to escape from the urge that carries him along by making
himself believe he is still in control and that since he speaks he could
just as well stop speaking?' Blanchot has, of course, already partially
answered this; he is merely making explicit what had been hinted
at earlier. So now, once again, he stands back and changes direction:
'He is struggling, that is obvious'. So obvious, indeed, that the
reader of Beckett might well hesitate before acknowledging even
to himself that this was of central significance. This is because he
would feel that it was he, the reader, who was struggling, and our
culture has made it plain that this is a shameful thing, that it is better
to arrive at some real clarity before even venturing to comment.
Blanchot is sensitive enough and brave enough to bring this central
feature of Beckett's work to the surface and insist that we recognize
it not as an obstacle we have to overcome before we can see properly
but as the thing itself which we have come to see.

Once again he proceeds to qualify and elaborate upon his insight:

> Sometimes he struggles secretly as though moved by a secret he

is hiding from us and even from himself. There is a certain amount of guile in his struggle as well as that other more subtle guile which consists in showing his hand. His first ploy is to put masks and figures between himself and speech.

In this way Blanchot is able to move from general remarks about Beckett's prose fiction to the exploration of the three volumes of the trilogy: *Molloy*, where what is expressed still to some extent conforms to what we think of as a story; *Malone Dies*, where the space explored has none of the resources available in the first novel, being reduced to just one room; and, finally, *The Unnamable*, where the stories do not even try to stand on their own, but 'circle mechanically around the vacant centre occupied by the nameless "I"'.

Who, then, is speaking in *The Unnamable*? The author?

> But to whom can such a term refer since anyhow he who writes is no longer Beckett but the urge that sweeps him out of himself, turns him into a nameless being, the Unnamable, a being without being who can neither live nor die, stop nor start, who is in the vacant site where speaks the redundancy of idle words under the ill-fitting cloak of a porous, agonising I?

This is the question Blanchot has always asked: what is the relation between the self one is and the self which writes? The question itself is both source and substance of most of the important literature from the Romantics to the present, and whenever we think we have finally dealt with it, it always re-surfaces. Blanchot does not try to tackle it head on, but comes at it via Kafka, or Baudelaire or Beckett, or through some ancient myth or story. And we too might be wise to approach it hesitantly and by way of negatives.

Recently, in reaction to the rather naïve biographical approaches sanctioned by the dominant culture of the nineteenth century, the notion has acquired respectability that there is no relation between an author and his work. The work is a 'text', with its own laws and rules, and it is these which must be grasped, rather than any facts about an author's life. An important half-truth has here been blown up into the whole truth and as a consequence a new fallacy has been perpetuated, quite as misleading as the biographical fallacy it has sought to dislodge.[3] For, as we have seen in the case of Kafka and Baudelaire, there would have been no problem, there would not even have been the writing we have, had it been simply a matter of 'working on the text'. The art of Kafka and Baudelaire – and of every major writer of the last 150 years – is precisely an exploration of the limits of art and of the complex interaction of art and life. Any criticism which ignores this, and tries to treat art purely as art, is simply bad criticism.

Mallarmé is often seen as the writer who first dared to think the unthinkable, the total lack of relation between an author and his text. For Blanchot, however, it is not so much Mallarmé as Valéry's version of Mallarmé which is to blame.

> Valéry never ceased to glorify Mallarmé and to study his poetical stance. He was faithful to him to the last, like Plato to Socrates. But, like Plato, he both illuminated and obscured the image of his master by his own success, the vast range of his enquiries, and a way of seeing, admiring and understanding peculiar to these enquiries.[4]

The comparison is apt; and it grows in significance when we recall that the journal which first began to preach the separation of author and text in France (long after this essay of Blanchot's was written), took its name, *Tel Quel*, from one of Valéry's collections of meditations and aphorisms.

In an interesting early essay on Gide, Blanchot came back to the attack. He makes it clear that, though Gide often seems to espouse very traditional and conventional views on art, seemed to hold as strongly as Gautier, say, to the primacy of the well made work, he, Blanchot, nevertheless found him a more interesting figure than Valéry:

> Often more daring, but always less sceptical than Valéry, Gide is infinitely less so where the truth of art and rhetoric are concerned. Valéry sees the means and effects of art as no more than arbitrary, pure convention; and it is only because he denies the true value of form that he assents to and respects its demands: he achieves perfection as a writer only because, for him, perfection contains no truth. But Gide is not so impious. Art, for him, signifies something; to write a work is not a simple exercise; to write well is also to give a greater chance to the truth, to the effort to remain true without ceasing to be daring.[5]

Gide is less radical, but for that reason more profound, 'less easy to satisfy', in Blanchot's fine phrase. Valéry's radicalism is shallow just because he does not seem to be fully aware of all the implications of what he is suggesting. Blanchot has never been a polemical critic. He has written about what he loves and believes in. But he must have been saddened to see in recent years the virtual triumph of

Valéry's shallow radicalism over his own more profound efforts to catch the precise relation between the living author and the written work.

This, after all, is itself the central theme of Beckett's own writing, and it is to this that Blanchot has gently been directing us since the start of his essay. But once again, having raised the question about the nature of the Unnamable, he stands back to remind us of what is at stake in writing of this kind:

> Aesthetic considerations are out of place here. Perhaps what we have before us is not a book because it is more than a book. It is a direct confrontation with the process from which all books derive – with the original point at which the work is inevitably lost, that always destroys the work, recreates endless idleness in the work, but with which too, if anything is to come of it, an ever more primal relationship has to be established.

Two stories, which Blanchot himself sees as central to his own explorations, illuminate this passage. They are the story of Ulysses and the Sirens, and the story of Orpheus and Eurydice. They are, for Blanchot, complementary but distinct. One of them, he says in a prefatory note to that volume, forms the secret centre of *L'Éspace littéraire*, the other is placed at the start of *Le livre à venir*. In Blanchot's hands the Greek stories are not turned into allegories so much as returned to their mythic dimensions.

Ulysses, it will be remembered, wished to listen to the Sirens' song, so he made the sailors fill their ears with wax and asked them to tie him to the mast. Thus the ship was able to sail close to the Sirens but did not destroy itself, while Ulysses heard their voices but did not drown. In this he differs from a fictional character like Ahab, who also heard the Sirens, but was lured by them, in the form of the white whale, to his death; and from a real person like Virginia Woolf. Ulysses was cunning and resourceful, but did he in fact triumph over the Sirens? Did he, from the safety of his ship, really hear the true song? Or is that reserved for those who go to the Sirens openly? One could also say, from another perspective, that Ulysses was not in fact saved, since after hearing them he was condemned to repeat their song for ever in the words of the *Odyssey*. And the case of Orpheus is similarly ambiguous. He went down into Hades to bring Eurydice back to the light, but turned while she was still in the dark and so lost her. Yet it was just because he lost her that he sang; and perhaps he didn't lose her after all, perhaps what he wanted was precisely this, to see Eurydice, but to see her in her darkness; had he waited till they reached daylight it would have been another Eurydice he would have seen.

Both Ulysses and Orpheus are caught in a double-bind, a situation in which whatever they do they are bound to lose; but also one in which whatever they do they are bound to win. It is in the light of these two myths that we can fully understand Blanchot's closing remarks on Beckett. Art, he says, is not for those who see it as an ivory tower, a barrier behind which they can retreat into themselves:

> Art requires that he who practises it . . . should become other, not another, not transformed from the human being he was into an artist with artistic duties, satisfactions and interests, but into nobody, the empty, animated space where art's summons is heard.

This has nothing to do with the conquest of new territories by the imagination, as a naïve humanism is wont to assert; for what is discovered bears no resemblance to our world or to any we might imagine or invent:

> What *The Unnamable* depicts is this malaise of one who has dropped out of reality and drifts forever in the gap between existence and nothingness, incapable of dying and incapable of being born, haunted by the phantom he creates, in which he does not believe, and which refuses to communicate with him.

But this is not the whole truth. *The Unnamable* is 'about' more than its overt subject-matter:

> The whole answer should rather be found in the process by which the work of art seeking its realisation constantly reverts to the point where it is confronted with failure. The point where language ceases to speak but is, where nothing begins, nothing is said, but where language is always reborn and always starts afresh.

To read Blanchot is not to acquire more knowledge or even more understanding, but to find one's way of reading changing, so that by the time one has finished it is difficult to talk to someone who has not undergone the same experience. But then that is what happens with any major author, and no amount of introductory matter will bridge the gap between the person who has and the one who has not read Dickens, Eliot or Rilke.

Like all the greatest critics, Blanchot is the master of the telling contrast. Thus, discussing Kafka's breaking off of his engagement with Félice, he points out that a parallel has often been seen – was seen at the time by Kafka himself – between Kafka's actions and those of Kierkegaard. But, says Blanchot,

> The two cases are really very dissimilar. Kierkegaard can give up Régine, he can give up a normal life. Such a sacrifice does not hinder his access to religious experience – indeed, it rather facilitates it. But if Kafka renounces the satisfactions of a normal existence he simultaneously renounces the satisfaction of doing right, becomes an outlaw, deprives himself, and to a certain extent law and order, of the stability and basis required to exist.[6]

Again, trying to define more precisely Rilke's attitude to absence and death, he contrasts his relation to these things with that of Mallarmé:

> Mallarmé... can turn absence into something positive, death into an action and voluntary death, which gives complete control over nothingness, into the essence of poetic achievement. But Rilke, while turning likewise towards death, as to the origin of poetic experience, seeks a deeper contact with it, sees voluntary death as the sign of a violence and despotism which can never be the basis on which poetic truth is founded, sees it as a sin against death itself, a disregard for death's intrinsic unobtrusiveness and for the patience proper to its invisible force.[7]

Sometimes, as in his essay on Marguerite Duras, Blanchot has to step very far back in order to bring the work under consideration into proper focus.[8] As usual, he immediately isolates the key element in a writer's work. In Duras' case it is dialogue. But what *is* dialogue? An English or American critic who asked this kind of question would probably seek to answer it by turning to Buber or Heidegger. Blanchot is actually more pragmatic. He turns to the use of dialogue by three other writers, who all differ significantly in this respect from each other and from Duras: Malraux, James, and Kafka.

In his two great novels, *La condition humaine* and *L'Espoir*, Blanchot argues, 'Malraux restored art and life to a very old tradition, that of the debate'. The representative of the debate is of course Socrates, who was convinced that through argument agreement could always be reached. By contrast, 'If we listen to the two unsophisticated voices in [Duras'] *Le Square* we notice that they do not seek agreement, like the voices of those who discuss and go from proof to proof until coherence is automatically achieved'. These two, the travelling salesman and the servant girl, don't even seek mutual understanding:

Perhaps all they want is to talk, to make use of the one faculty they are still lucky enough to possess and which they cannot be sure of having for long. It is this last feeble and threatened resource which gives an element of gravity to the simple exchange. From their first words we sense that, for these two people, and more especially for one of them, the space and air required to make talking possible are all but exhausted.

But this, far from making dialogue impossible, enables us in fact to see 'the moment at which people are capable of dialogue'.

They talk to each other and they do not agree. They do not altogether understand each other. They do not share that common space where understanding takes place, and their whole relationship is based only on their intense and simple feelings that they are both *equally* outside the common system of relationships.

Nevertheless, even this is a great deal:

It creates an immediate proximity and a kind of total agreement-less agreement where their attentiveness to the words of the other and the carefulness and scrupulous truthfulness with which they express themselves are so great, precisely because what is said can only be said once yet cannot be said, could not benefit from the superficial understanding current in the ordinary world, the world where we so rarely experience the fortuitousness and pain of true dialogue.

Duras' tact and sensitivity are here matched by the critic's own. He manages to put into words just what we feel when we read her strange books, and once again he does so by opening them up, so to speak, and revealing that beneath or through the simple exchanges the very largest questions are at issue. These are questions we don't usually ask precisely because they touch on the limits of language and thought, the very tools we are using. For what Socrates is upholding is a view of the world as finally susceptible to understanding, a unitary world. And it is out of the unquestioned belief in this unity that our philosophy and indeed our whole Western culture, has sprung, and which modern art since Mallarmé, and modern thought since Nietzsche have begun to question. But to talk is already to some extent to acknowledge meaningfulness, unity. Hence Nietzsche's problems with the rhetorical strategy he should use in his philosophy, and Mallarmé's equivalent problems with poetry. In the Duras essay Blanchot hints at the problem when, contrasting her work to that of Malraux and Socrates, he talks about the two characters not sharing 'that common space where understanding takes place'. Only literature can create an alternative space where the notion of a common space can itself be called into question. This, says Blanchot, is precisely what Mallarmé was trying to do in *Un Coup de dés*, a work which 'opens up a new dimension for literature in a combined effort of dispersal and concentration'. Mallarmé had said that the mind was 'volatile dispersal', and Blanchot argues:

> A book that gives access to the mind will thus give access to an immensely destructive force. . . . It is a process of dispersal which must not be repressed but, on the contrary, preserved and garnered as such into the space it projects and to which this process responds. . . . Such a book, always in motion, always on the verge of dispersal, will also always unite from all directions through this dispersal and according to its necessary division.[9]

He comes back to the problem in his essay on Mann's *Dr Faustus*.[10] He notes Mann's expressed lack of sympathy with post-Wagnerian music, and goes on, 'It is as a cultured man that he shies at *Ars Nova*, just as it is as cultured men and not, I am convinced, as political theoreticians, that certain socialist leaders bitterly condemn non-figurative art.' What these people condemn and, 'not without reason', dread, is that element in artistic experience 'which alienates it from any form of culture. There is an acultural aspect to literature and art which is hard to accept wholeheartedly'. New music helps us to grasp what an abyss separates art and culture.

> It is rigid, hard, austere . . . and makes no concessions to the 'human touch' which society is always so ready to use as a mask behind which it conceals its inhumanity. Culture, on the other hand, is based on the notion of humanism, the notion that man is naturally reflected in his works and never distinct from himself, that progress is continuous, an uninterruptable continuity which ensures the flow of past into present, since culture and accumulation go hand in hand. Thus culture requires results from art because only results can be stored in the vast storehouses of culture. So an art which has no answers but only questions, which even questions the existence of art, cannot fail to be seen as disturbing, hostile and coldly violent.

Ars Nova, the mediaeval term for new music, which Blanchot appropriates for the music of Adrian Leverkühn and, by extension, for modern art in general, is, he suggests, 'the ordeal of thought trying to free itself from the tyranny of unity'. It would be easy to find parallels to Webern in painting and literature, but Blanchot is never one to indulge in vague generalizations. Instead, he says,

> I shall resort to a metaphor: the fact that the universe is curved is more or less undisputed, and it has often been assumed that the curve must be a positive one, whence the image of a complete, boundless sphere. But is there any logical reason to exclude the hypothesis of a universe (a consequently misguided term) that could not be represented figuratively because it would correspond to no optical requirement nor to any concept about the universe?

What, in fact, would happen 'were we to accept the notion that the curvature of the universe and even that of our world bears a negative sign?'

In this essay Blanchot is clearly raising questions which could easily take on political dimensions (e.g. 'culture and accumulation go hand in hand'), and his critique of culture does of course have much in common with that of the early Barthes. But Blanchot has always maintained that to sing of the Revolution is to betray the Revolution, that if you want to change the world you write *Capital* and not *War and Peace*. Nor is there any difficulty in understanding why anyone should write *Capital*. But *War and Peace*? That is the much more troubling question to which he has always addressed himself.

No less than Barthes though, he has taken a stand against academic humanism. However, remembering Proust's great essay on Flaubert's style, written in outraged response to an article by Albert Thibaudet claiming that Flaubert had no style, we should perhaps see in Blanchot not so much the theoretician standing up for his view of 'literature' as the writer eager to defend what he sees as the truths of writing and refusing to allow these to be distorted by those who only profess and do not practise. Thus the Mallarmé essay from which I quoted, a spirited defence of *Un Coup de dés* and an exploration of the concept of a 'literary space', was sparked off by Jacques Scherer's misguided attempt to prove that the scattered notes left by Mallarmé at his death can be meaningfully reconstituted as that Book which so haunted the imagination of the poet and on which he had for years claimed to be working. Blanchot argues against this that the 'Livre' is always 'à venir', 'to come', is never realizable, and that to imagine we can simply piece it together and publish it is to misunderstand the whole nature of the enterprise. Rather, he says, *Un Coup de dés* is as near as Mallarmé (and we) can ever get to any ideal Book, though it may be only its blueprint or even negative.

Similarly, reviewing the posthumous publication of Proust's early unfinished novel, *Jean Santeuil*, Blanchot takes the opportunity to show up the errors of Albert Feuillerat's argument that *A la Recherche* in its initial state was wholly inspired by 'the fleeting magic of involuntary memories', and for this reason was a far better book than the one we now have, swollen as it is and coarsened by the inclusion of so much 'inferior' material.[11] What Blanchot shows is that *Jean Santeuil*, which does try to give us only the 'pure moments', is in fact largely taken up with extremely conventional descriptions of people, places and actions. Proust, it is clear, is still writing here as he thinks novels have to be written – in other words, as Flaubert and James were writing. This is because no novel can be made up entirely of 'pure moments', and to imagine that it can means that there is a contradiction at the heart of the creative impulse, a cloud over the author's central aims. It was only when Proust put *Jean Santeuil* aside and faced up to the full implications of what he wanted to do that his masterpiece began to emerge. It did so because Proust discovered, in the course of working, that though the flashes of joy he experienced were indeed related to certain privileged moments, they were related not to some ungraspable essence but to the sudden unexpected conjunction of two elements quite ordinary in themselves, unique only in combination. Indeed, *A la Recherche*, is, in the end, a long paean of praise for the forgotten, the ordinary, the trivial, the banal – not at all, as Feuillerat's etiolated Symbolism would have us believe, for the delicate, the exquisite, the refined. Far from Proust spoiling his novel by the introduction of 'impure' elements, it is those very elements which make for the book's greatness.

Blanchot ends his essay on *Jean Santeuil* with a moral as solid and in a way as humanistic as even Leavis might have wished for, but one which, to my mind, has a quality of reverberation no English critic has ever approached:

> When we read *Jean Santeuil* or any of the numerous intervening versions where he tried out the theories he wished to express, we can see how much he owes to that corrupting time which was an accessory to his work both with and against himself. Haste was the great threat to the accomplishment of his work. The longer it dragged on the closer it came to itself. In the book's

progress we can detect the deferment which holds Proust back as though, foreseeing his death at its completion, he were trying, in order to avoid it, to swim against his own tide.

Thus at first:

> Proust's natural indolence is an impediment to easy success; then indolence gives way to patience and patience to tireless labour, to the feverish impatience struggling against the clock as he comes to realise that his years and then his days are numbered.

Ironically, it was the war, time in its most destructive guise, which helped to free Proust from the pressures of immediate publication and allowed his novel to grow in its own good time:

> Had *Jean Santeuil* been completed and published, Proust was lost, his masterpiece forever unachieved and time irretrievably mislaid. Thus there is something almost uncanny in the resurrection of this manuscript which reveals how the greatest writers are threatened and how much energy, indolence, inertia, care and carelessness they require to accomplish their tasks.

Our temptation is always to reduce art – the activity and the objects – to something else. As we have seen from his remarks about Beckett, Mallarmé, Duras and Proust, Blanchot is always trying to dispel these errors and to draw us back to the central mystery of the nature of writing and reading, of the uniqueness of this author, this book. One final contrast will perhaps help to clarify the nature of Blanchot's own enterprise.

Heidegger, like Blanchot, is concerned to escape from the false issues of academic humanism; like Blanchot he recognizes that with the Romantics something decisive happened to literature, that in a sense it came into its own. Heidegger has a predilection for the notions of habitation, construction, shelter, presence. We find in his later essays a wealth of richly suggestive remarks: 'Upon the earth and in it, historical man grounds his dwelling in the world... The work lets the earth be an earth'; 'the ground is the soil in which to strike root and to stand'; 'the poetic is the basic capacity for human dwelling'; 'What is it to dwell?'; 'When Hölderlin speaks of dwelling, he has before his eyes the basic character of human existence'; 'Men alone, as mortals, by dwelling attain to the world as world.'[12] His favourite subjects of meditation are the farmhouse, the table, the bread, the jug, Van Gogh's peasant boots, the rooted poetry of Hölderlin, Rilke and Trakl. All this gives a peasant-like, very German and Protestant cast to his thought. For Blanchot, on the other hand, the key terms are dispersal, wandering, erring, exile. The Word for him is not that which shelters or brings you back to yourself, but that which drives you into exile. It is not the bread and wine of the Eucharist or the opening of St John's Gospel which lie behind much of his thought, but the Old Testament desert. And as he says in his essay on Borges:

> What if the geographical wilderness were to become the Biblical wilderness which can no longer be crossed in eleven days but in the space of two generations, of the whole of human history or perhaps longer? To the regulated, regular man a room, a wilderness and the world are precise, well defined spaces. To the nomadic labyrinthine man condemned to wander on a journey which is inevitably a little longer than his life, the same space will be truly infinite even when he knows – and the more so when he knows – that it is not.[13]

Where Heidegger's thought and language consciously reach out to the Greek and especially the pre-Socratic, those of Blanchot are Jewish. But we must be careful here. Blanchot himself is not Jewish, and, as Françoise Collin rightly points out in her excellent book on him, when we say this kind of thing we are not talking about historical Judaism but about a kind of Jewish myth: 'The veritable Jewish space-time is not history but wandering [*errance*]. And wandering is not then the way but error, "the error, the fact of being on the way without ever being able to stop." '[14]

The Jewish philosopher Emmanuel Levinas has been a lifelong friend of Blanchot's, but I suspect it was the experience of reading Kafka which coloured Blanchot's mind in this way. Or rather that experience gave him the strength to explore his own predilections. For it is striking how full Blanchot's novels are of rooms whose doors won't shut, of corridors through which people wander restlessly, of the dead who will not die, and the living who cannot live. It is these novels, just as much as Kafka's, which he could be describing in his remarks on exile and the Biblical desert. Nevertheless it is perhaps significant that he should have used those images and not others, for here again he and Benjamin join hands. They are our two greatest spokesmen for the distinctively modern in modern art because they both recognize that it is an art of exile and that there is no fatherland to which to return. This looks like a gloomy position but in fact it is oddly positive. Heidegger and Mann, believing, like the Romantics, in an ideal 'home' to which we may one day be able to return, can only despair when the homecoming does not occur and blame us for our 'inauthenticity'. But, as Blanchot says: 'If, among all words, there is one inauthentic word, that word is certainly the word "authentic".'[15] What he and Benjamin would argue is that exile, lack of fullness, lack of rootedness, is man's essential condition, and that what modern art does is to help him to understand that condition and rejoice in it.

Like Benjamin, Blanchot re-establishes for us the strangeness of literature, the infinite distance from us of something we tend too easily to take for granted. Blanchot helps us to see in each writer the lineaments of Orpheus and Odysseus, but he is always conscious of the way every embodiment is unique. Reading him, we are made to work to grasp an experience which is always startlingly new: the encounter with Kafka, or Rilke, or Virginia Woolf. But we are also relieved to find that our doubts and confusions as readers are not things to be brushed aside by superior knowledge or intelligence; they are part of what reading these authors is about.

For Blanchot not only reminds us that it is an extraordinary thing for people to be writing books – an activity which can never, *pace* Plato, be assimilated, however indirectly, to the making of beds or tables – but also that it is an extraordinary thing to be reading them. The Burghers of Calais stand on the Embankment at Westminster whether anyone sees them or not. But can the same be said of *War and Peace* or Eliot's poems? The precise answer may be left to the philosophers; we need only to recognize the mystery. And in so doing recognize that reading itself, though a most serious activity, need not for that reason be other than light and careless. Indeed, it is only careless, unburdened reading that will yield the desired results. Blanchot's essays miraculously restore that lightness which characterized our most profound – because most innocent – reading experiences.

5 Samuel Beckett: The Need to Fail

'I am only interested in failure,' Beckett told his friend Thomas McGreevey when he saw him again after the war. And this was not a boast but a simple statement of fact. In 1946 he was forty and his life seemed to have been a total failure. Born with remarkable gifts, as a sportsman, an intellectual, a poet, he seemed, by the end of the war, to have squandered them all. He had rejected a promising academic career which was his for the asking; he had cut himself off from his family in Dublin; and all he had to show for it were an eccentric volume of stories and a novel, a few poems and translations which had appeared in French literary journals in the pre-war years, and an extensive circle of acquaintance in the bohemian and avant-garde world of Paris. The novel, *Murphy*, had been rejected by forty-two publishers before it was finally accepted in 1938, and when the pattern started to repeat itself with *Watt*, the novel he had worked on throughout the war, with publishers justifying themselves by saying that at this point in time what they were looking for was something more positive and heroic, Beckett could say with feeling to McGreevey: 'I am not interested in heroism and success. I am only interested in failure.'[1]

Yet less than ten years later he had achieved success and recognition to a degree he cannot ever have dreamt of. *Waiting for Godot* (1954) and the publication of the Trilogy made Beckett, overnight, the most talked-of writer of his time, and his life, despite himself, had become the fulfilment of a Romantic fairy-tale: the struggling, solitary artist, refusing ever to compromise, suddenly hailed as the voice of a generation. Of course nothing in his work had fundamentally changed; only the public's recognition of it. And the extraordinary thing is that Beckett has been able to take success in his stride just as he took failure, and simply go on being himself. Now, at seventy-five, he seems younger than any other writer, and each new work is still a venture into the unknown, the taking of risks which nearly all writers would balk at. In fact, though Beckett could never stand the posturing of Yeats, it is of the old Yeats and the old Wallace Stevens, artists whose late work constitutes their greatest achievement, that he now most forcibly reminds us.

Yet, if Beckett became famous in the 1950s, he has never been exactly popular. His plays have never been performed in the West End, his prose has been more talked about than read. Compared to a Hemingway, a Graham Greene, a Saul Bellow, his is clearly a minority following. In this he reminds us more of the great masters of modernism – Eliot, Webern, Mondrian – than of his contemporaries. The sociology of art cannot deal with such artists because there is no clear or simple correlation between their significance and their popularity. For some they have changed the history of art; for others they are nothing but charlatans. And, especially in the case of Eliot and Beckett, their work seems both to invite and to resist criticism. It invites it because it seems to suggest a mystery to be uncovered; and it resists it less because that mystery proves difficult to uncover than because criticism, no matter how sensitive and intelligent, never seems able to bridge the gap between the immediate impact of the least of their works and any subsequent explanation.

What is the nature of this gap? Why does it exist? Such questions clearly cannot be answered in the abstract. Let us look briefly then at the best of Beckett's early stories (published when he was twenty-six), 'Dante and the Lobster'.

'It was morning and Belaqua was stuck in the first of the canti in the moon. He was so bogged that he could move neither backward nor forward.' Belaqua is not Dante's slothful character but a Dublin intellectual and layabout. No explanation is given for his name, which engenders in the reader a curious unease: the details of his life and actions are too specific for this to be allegory or even Joycean replaying of myth, but the name is too odd, too literary, for us to feel entirely at ease within the fiction. As we will see, both the style and the content of the story will reinforce such feelings in the reader.

Belaqua's situation as he struggles with the opening canti of the *Paradiso* parallels Dante's own as he seeks enlightenment from Beatrice:

> Blissful Beatrice was there, Dante also, and she explained the spots on the moon to him. She shewed him in the first place where he was at fault, then she put up her own explanation. She had it from God, therefore he could rely on its being accurate in every particular.

It is difficult to decide if 'he' in this last sentence is Dante or Belaqua, but it doesn't matter. They are both mortal, incapable of full understanding, driven by needs other than those of pure intellect or pure love.

Indeed, as midday strikes Belaqua triumphantly closes his book and prepares for lunch. In the afternoon he has to collect a lobster which he is bringing to his aunt for supper, and then have his Italian lesson. But first, lunch:

> Lunch, to come off at all, was a very nice affair. If his lunch was to be enjoyable, and it could be very enjoyable indeed, he must be left in absolute tranquillity to prepare it. But if he were disturbed now, if some brisk tattler were to come bouncing in now with a big idea or a petition, he might just as well not eat at all, for the food would turn to bitterness on his palate, or, worse again, taste of nothing... The first thing to do was to lock the door. Now nobody could come at him. He deployed an old Herald and smoothed it out on the table. The rather handsome face of McCabe the assassin stared up at him... Now the long barrel-loaf came out of its biscuit-tin and had its end evened off on the face of McCabe. Two inexorable drives with the bread saw and a pair of neat rounds of raw bread, the main elements of his meal, lay before him, awaiting his pleasure. The stump of the loaf went back into prison, the crumbs, as though there were no such thing as a sparrow in the wide world, were swept in a fever away, and the slices snatched up and carried to the grill.

We may at first be tempted to see the prose as merely mannered and self-conscious, and conclude that Beckett is simply trying to be funny. He succeeds, too, quite as well as Wodehouse and Waugh. But instinctively we feel that there is more to it than that. In a peculiar way, though it is only the cutting of two slices of bread that is being described, we feel that something much more serious is going on than in the two English writers. Serious, of course, does not mean solemn; on the contrary, seriousness here is obviously connected with laughter. But how? Provisionally we may say that it has something to do with the fact that here there is no way of establishing that comfortable distance between reader and story, author and character, which is one of the delights of Wodehouse and early Waugh. On the contrary, our laughter is tinged with panic because there is something excessive about the manner of both hero and writer, and we cannot easily perceive the reason for this excess. But, as with all the best fiction, these feelings remain latent and we read on.

McCabe the assassin, like Dante and the lobster, is mutely present throughout the story. In the pub where Belaqua finally settles down to eat his toasted sandwich, so lovingly prepared, and now filled

with a mouth-burning mixture of salt, pepper, mustard and Gorgon-
zola, he learns that

> the Malahide murderer's petition for mercy, signed by half the
> land, having been rejected, the man must swing at dawn in
> Mountjoy and nothing could save him. Ellis the hangman was
> even now on his way. Belaqua, tearing at the sandwich and swil-
> ling the precious stout, pondered on McCabe in his cell.

He is clearly still pondering when, having collected the lobster,
in the course of his Italian lesson he asks the teacher to translate
Dante's punning line: 'Qui vive la pietà quand' è ben morta.' ' "Do
you think," she murmured, "it is absolutely necessary to translate
it?" ' Her reticence may seem puzzling at first. For after all a translation is certainly possible. Virgil is here rebuking Dante for feeling
sympathy for the damned, and he says: 'Here *piety* lives when *pity*
is quite dead.' But what the teacher senses and what it will take the
rest of the story for Belaqua to grasp, is that what is at issue here is
not translation *into English*, but *into reality*. For how can our liberal
secular culture make any sense of Dante's distinction?

Belaqua finally arrives at his aunt's house and hands her his parcel.
She undoes it and lays the lobster out on the kitchen table:

> 'They assured me it was fresh,' said Belaqua.
> Suddenly he saw the creature move, this neuter creature.
> Definitely it changed its position. His hand flew to his mouth.
> 'Christ!' he said, 'it's alive.'

Unperturbed, the aunt bustles off to the pantry and returns with an
apron on and her sleeves rolled up. 'Well,' she said, 'it is to be hoped
so, indeed.'

> 'All this time,' muttered Belaqua. Then, suddenly aware of her
> hideous equipment: 'What are you going to do?' he cried.
> 'Boil the beast,' she said, 'what else?'
> 'But it's not dead,' protested Belaqua.

Gently she explains to him that lobsters are always boiled alive.
'They must be.'

> She caught up the lobster and laid it on its back. It trembled.
> 'They feel nothing,' she said.
> In the depths of the sea it had crept into the cruel pot. For
> hours, in the midst of its enemies, it had breathed secretly. It had
> survived the Frenchwoman's cat and his witless clutch. Now it

was going alive into scalding water. It had to. Take into the air my quiet breath.

Belaqua looked at the old parchment of her face, grey in the dim kitchen.

'You make a fuss,' she said angrily, 'and upset me and then lash into it for your dinner.'

She lifted the lobster clear of the table. It had about thirty seconds to live.

Well, thought Belaqua, it's a quick death, God help us all.

It is not.

Everything comes together here: the problem of God's mercy to the damned, raised by Dante's punning line; the question of the fate of McCabe the murderer; the reason for Belaqua's aggressive way with objects and the writer's aggressive way with language. None of these has been overtly dealt with so far, they have merely troubled the stream of the narrative. In the face of the aunt's calm, 'They feel nothing', we are forced to face them.

The aunt's attitude suggests a refusal to open oneself to another's sufferings, and we naturally side with Belaqua's horror and disgust. Though in the end he too tries to anaesthetize himself with a cliché, 'It's a quick death, God help us', the last three words, uttered not by him, we feel, but by some absolute impersonal authority, show that in the face of what he has witnessed clichés will have little effect: 'It is not.'

Yet do Belaqua's horror and pity for both the lobster and McCabe do anything for them? Is Dante not perhaps right? To feel pity is meaningless. It only makes the pitier feel better. It could even be argued that Belaqua's pity is worse than his aunt's realism, for he wishes to salve his conscience, yet is not above tucking into the lobster. And now we can begin to understand something about why the story is written as it is. For is Belaqua's attitude very different from that of the writer? By imaginatively conveying the lobster's agony the writer puts himself on the side of honesty, sympathy, truth. But is this sympathy not bought far too cheaply? Does he in fact really understand the agony of McCabe or the lobster? Is there not even a monstrous presumption in imagining that he does?

Belaqua can ponder the fate of McCabe and the lobster but he will always be denied a full understanding of them because he, unlike them, can escape. And this is the case of Beckett as well. He is thus caught in an impossible situation. He wants to make us sense what McCabe and the lobster are suffering, *and* to make us recognize that,

however much we project ourselves imaginatively into their situations, we will never have any conception of the horror of those last
thirty seconds.

But there is a further twist. For McCabe and the lobster the time
of imagining, of prevarication, of 'being stuck', is over. Now they
are locked in their horrible reality. And for this they are to be envied
as well as pitied. Imprisoned, hopeless, they await their end. Yet
we, who think ourselves free, are also imprisoned. Our end too will
come. But, because there are no bars we cannot imagine it, and live
as though we were immortal. Now the reason for Belaqua's violence
('the crumbs... were swept in a fever away') and his masochism ('It
was like eating glass. His mouth burned and ached with the exploit!')
is clear: instinctively he tries to make himself feel the vulnerability
of his own body, to prepare himself for his own impending death.

And again, behind Belaqua is his maker. 'The stump of the loaf
went back into prison, the crumbs, as though there were no such
thing as a sparrow in the wide world, were swept in a fever away.'
Just because it is so easy to make a sparrow fly in fiction, fiction
cannot convey the miracle of a sparrow's flight, of its freedom.
Conversely, the reason why there is such an insistence on enclosure
in Beckett, on the lack or loss of limbs, such a denial of generosity,
such apparent cynicism, is that movement of the body or the spirit
is felt by him to be bought too easily in words. Words can do anything; by the same token, they can do nothing. And so, since fiction
is helpless in the face of reality, only the fiction of helplessness will
be real. Here it is only the loaf that is maimed and pushed back into
its box; later, it will be the protagonist himself.

The pleasures of the imagination are not *innocent* pleasures. This
is the driving force behind all Beckett's work, from first to last. The
very act of writing and of reading distorts reality, the central reality
that we are imprisoned in our bodies and will soon be no more.
Beckett thus tries to use the imagination against the imagination.
But each time we say 'I see', each time we are moved to feel for the
suffering of McCabe or the lobster, Beckett has failed. Each time
he has to add an 'It is not', but then that too becomes part of what
we 'understand' and he has to start again. The more he succeeds
then, the more he fails. But failure, of course, is not in its turn
transmuted into success. It remains itself.

For the next fifteen years Beckett struggles to escape this contradiction. He struggles against himself, his gifts. The brilliance and
bitterness of *Murphy*, *Watt*, and *Molloy* stem from this sense of un-
resolvable struggle. Beckett, from now on, denies himself the

authority of God or Beatrice, the false authority of those last three words, and tries to get the truth to reveal itself by undermining all its false impersonations from within. Looking back from our vantage-point, we can see him moving slowly forward, shedding one skin after another in his effort to say that which is true. The Trilogy becomes the great testing-ground for these matters, its very length an essential part of the process. First there was Molloy, still just about able to move; then Malone, dying in his closed room; finally the Unnamable, able to identify himself only in negative terms: not Molloy, not Malone, not Worm, only that which refuses to be named because each name, each history, will fix him, freeze him, deny him that which is most precious to him, his potential for movement, change. At the same time, it is unbearable to live in a perpetual state of metamorphosis. The organism longs for stability, rest at last.

It is important to realize how much the act of writing is implicated in the search. Joyce had moved forward from *Dubliners*, with its calm narrative tone, to the *Portrait*, with its stream-of-consciousness technique, before finding himself in the impersonality of *Ulysses*. But *Ulysses* is still a very nineteenth-century work in its confidence that the act of making an object out of words is a good in itself. Beckett lacks that confidence, or refuses to be taken in, depending how you look at it. The memory of the living lobster, the realization that in the act of imaginative sympathy the greatest betrayal occurs – this cannot be put aside.

It is because art is so powerful that it is so suspect. Beckett senses reality forming under his hand as he writes, but what kind of reality is it? Is he himself not more of a prisoner even than McCabe or the lobster? For he sits at his desk in his room and half believes his imaginative projections.

Belaqua drew near to the house of his aunt. Let us call it Winter, that dusk may fall now and a moon rise. At the corner of the street a horse was down and a man sat on his head... A lamplighter flew by on his bike, tilting with his pole at the standards, jousting a little yellow light into the evening.

Most writers would be more than satisfied with such gifts. But for Beckett the gifts themselves are a sign of damnation. 'One has to be very strong to deny onself the luxury of such speculations,' Wittgenstein remarked to a friend who showed him a book of metaphysics. And Wittgenstein's constant attempts at flight from philosophy have much in common with Beckett's own attempts at escape from his art. For no horse was down, no lamplighter at his rounds, there was no aunt or even Belaqua, for that matter, only Samuel Beckett, whoever he might be, needing to write. But why? Where does such a need come from? How can it be satisfied?

He still has an uneasy conscience at the ease with which it is possible to conjure a world out of paper when he comes to the end of *Molloy* (1955). The second part of that book had opened in good classical first person style: 'It is midnight. The rain is beating on the windows. I am calm. All is sleeping.' It ends: 'Then I went back into the house and wrote, It is midnight. The rain is beating on the windows. It was not midnight. It was not raining.'

We have grown so used to this kind of thing that we dismiss it with glib remarks about Chinese boxes and novels about writing novels. As with all art, everything depends upon our sense of the artist's responsibility. In Beckett it is not a joke or a clever way to end, but a mute cry of despair: Why am I writing this? Why going through with this fraud?

The Trilogy grew out of the attempt to face this. As with Proust and the First World War, the isolation forced upon him by the Second World War pushed Beckett through the barrier and to the point where he was no longer in conflict with himself. In 1946 there was a moment of positively Proustian revelation, described by Deirdre Bair in her biography of Beckett. One night, by the sea in Dublin, as Beckett was visiting his mother, he was overcome by the sense that 'the dark he had struggled to keep under' was the real substance and source of his work. 'I can now accept this dark side as the commanding side of my personality,' he said later. 'In accepting it, I will make it work for me.' The Trilogy is the product of that acceptance.

For Beckett did not stop at the end of *Molloy* and look round for *another* novel to write. There seemed to be no way forward, yet he found he could go on moving. And he could do so, precisely, by reducing the fictional protagonist's own possibility of movement. And so he went from Molloy and Moran circling round each other in the forest to Malone dying alone in his room, and from Malone to that which can only be named in negative terms: not Molloy, not Malone, not Worm. The unnamable is the source of both light and dark, speech and silence, and it cannot be grasped as an essence, only seen in its operations.

In the earlier work, as we have seen, the sense of bitterness and anger stemmed from frustration at being locked in an impossibly contradictory enterprise: there seemed to be no way in which 'It is not' could detach itself from the fiction and acquire the unquestioned status of Beatrice's lessons to Dante in the *Commedia*. But now, with *Malone Dies* (1956) and *The Unnamable* (1958), we start to feel that Beckett's acceptance of impossibility frees him, releases new energies: he will not name and then point in derision at the name; instead he will show the operations of the unnamable.

Between these two novels came *Waiting for Godot*, and the theatre was of course an important factor in this transformation. For the theatre is the real locus of illusion. In one sense it is a place of far more dangerous illusion, since these figures are only apparently as free as we are; in reality they are doomed to repeat the same words over and over, every evening. What Beckett does is to use this greater appearance of reality in the theatre to force us into a recognition of the complex interplay of memory, imagination and desire in our own lives. The central question remains, as always: what does it mean to be alive? But in the theatre this question acquires a new sharpness and immediacy.

Not I, written in 1972, is the culmination of the Trilogy. Here a mouth, unattached to any body, talks to us or to itself from a darkened stage. We see the mouth, we hear it speak, but we also see that there is no body. We are thus forced to accept both its reality and its separation from the body. And so Beckett makes it impossible for us to avoid awareness of the fact that we too are never wholly where we are, that we can never speak what we know or know fully what we speak, can never attain a fullness of speech that takes account of our bodies.

Between mouth and audience stands a shadowy figure. What is it doing there? It reminds us that none of Beckett's stage monologues is ever quite that. Krapp has his tape, Winnie her Willie. We are never unified, never one even when most alone. Moreover, our voice is not attached to our body as our hands and feet are, while neither voice nor body is fully alive without the other. The theatre is the place where the inevitable distance between them can be demonstrated.

The mouth cannot say what it is, but it is present to us. And the more it cannot say the more aggressive it seems to become. The mouth is the body reduced to a minimum; it is a hole, but a hole only exists by virtue of what surrounds it. The mouth is the place of connection between sound and meaning, and it is the presence of the shadowy figure which saves it from falling back into either the one or the other. The unpleasant though powerful effect of the television version, which dispensed with the figure and filled the whole screen with the mouth, was due to the fact that it left one with too immediate an identification of that organ with the vagina. The connection is there, of course, just as the tape is *Krapp*'s, but the space between Krapp and crap, between mouth and vagina is precisely the space where art can – just – exist.

The figure has its instructions:

> Movement: this consists in simple sideways raising of arms from sides and their falling back, in a gesture of helpless compassion. It lessens with each recurrence till scarcely perceptible at third. There is just enough pause to contain it as MOUTH recovers from vehement refusal to relinquish third person.

Why will the mouth not relinquish third person? As so often in Beckett, there are two contradictory answers. (Art can contain such contradictions, but criticism has to fight its own tendency to dissolve them.) The mouth will not accept responsibility for what it says, denying that it is attached to any body. But it also knows that to speak in the first person is to perpetuate a falsehood, since that which is the source of utterance is never a single 'I'. This is what constitutes the drama. Somewhere something which is not the mouth keeps wanting it to use the first person, to acknowledge that speech comes from a person, with the responsibilities we all share; but another part of the self knows that to say 'I' is to lock out major portions of the self. The only acknowledgement of the force that seeks to say 'I' is a violent denial, and this is followed by the figure's gesture: '. . . and she found herself in the –. . . What?. . . who?. . . no!. . . she!. . . (*Pause and movement*).' Once this is grasped we can see that the compassionate figure is deeply ambiguous: father confessor but also judge; friend but also betrayer.

Beckett, since *Godot*, seems to have moved from stage to page and back as a way of unblocking, of keeping the forward momentum going in spite of everything. *Not I* was a kind of culmination, but since it was written he has published two long prose pieces which are more relaxed, lyrical and all-embracing than anything he has done, *Company* (1979) and *Mal vu mal dit* (1981).

In *Company* we once again have a narrator unable to say 'I'. 'A voice comes to one in the dark. Imagine.' The voice speaks, tells stories, but 'only a small part of what is said can be verified'. All that can be asserted is that someone is lying on his back in the dark, and that to this someone comes a voice, telling him stories:

> Use of the second person marks the voice. That of the third that cankerous other. Could he speak to and of whom the voice

speaks there would be a first. But he cannot. He shall not. You cannot. You shall not.

Of course it would be wonderful if he / you could. 'What an addition to company that would be. A voice in the first person singular. Murmuring now and then, Yes, I remember.'

The entire tradition of novel and autobiography depends on just this sleight-of-hand. A voice murmurs: 'Yes, I remember,' but even the most truthful of autobiographers omits to ask himself: 'Even if the stories the voice tells me are familiar to me, how am I to know they are stories about myself?' It may be that repetition has made him imagine that they belong to him. And what is 'a story about myself' anyway? We say: 'This is how it was', or 'This is what I did' – but in what sense is this 'I' oneself? Is it not a construct made up of social, psychological and literary clichés?

This does not mean, as some recent theorists have maintained, that there is no self, only that it is less an entity than a source of potential. For Beckett all that can be said is that a voice comes to one in the dark, and that to listen to this voice is to acquire a sense of company. All that can be said with certainty is: 'Devised deviser devising it all for company. In the same figure dark as his figments.' And so a kind of provisional truth is arrived at:

> Huddled thus you find yourself imagining you are not alone while knowing full well that nothing has occurred to make this possible. The process continues none the less lapped as it were in meaninglessness. You do not murmur in so many words, I know this doomed to fail and yet persist. No. For the first personal and a fortiori plural pronoun had never any place in your vocabulary.

Though *Company* is clearly there in embryo in the early stories, it was of course impossible to imagine it till Beckett had written it. And the tone has changed. Now there are no sudden jerks and shifts of register; the ambiguities concerning self, voice and imagination are explored, gently played with rather than aggressively butted against.

Like any writer, Beckett has made use of autobiography. It is important to grasp this, because critics have tended to talk about his work too much in terms of aesthetics and metaphysics, and not to see the wonder that lies in the transformation of the local and personal. Deirdre Bair tells us that Beckett's mother used to walk about the house at night, unable to sleep. Another writer might have told the story of an old lady wandering about the house at night, unable to sleep. Or he might have used that to 'say something' about parents and children, or about generations and guilt – as Joyce did in *The Dead*, for example or Yeats in *Purgatory*. This is not Beckett's way.

Footfalls was written in 1976. Beckett was seventy. It is a tiny play; it cannot last more than twenty minutes. As always, Beckett uses the stage with utter precision. This is not because he is a 'good craftsman' (the excuse for a multitude of sins) but because all depends on what cannot be said but can be shown, the gap between the image before us, the flesh and blood person we see on the stage in front of us (and the person he or she represents) and the totality of life, of the actor's life and the character's life. Like our own life, it is always more than what we see of bodies existing in space, more than we can ever formulate. But more in what way? By destroying the 'commonsensical' reality of the figure on the stage – she is the actress so and so, playing the role of so and so – Beckett actually lays bare something very important about ourselves and our lives.

In his stage directions he explains exactly how the character is to look and walk:

> MAY (M), dishevelled grey hair, worn grey wrap hiding feet, trailing.
> WOMAN'S VOICE (V) from dark upstage.
> Strip: downstage, parallel with front, length nine steps, width one metre, a little off centre audience right.

$$L \; \frac{r \; l \; r \; l \; r \; l \; r \; l \; r}{l \; r \; l \; r \; l \; r \; l \; r \; l} \; R$$

> Pacing: starting with right foot (r) from right (R) to left (L), with left foot (l) from L to R.
> Turn: rightabout at L, leftabout at R.
> Lighting: dim, strongest at floor level, less on body, least on head.
> Voices: both low and slow throughout.

So M paces and V speaks. But at once the simple division of activity is complicated, for M also speaks. In fact she starts: 'Mother.' V answers: 'Yes, May.' M asks if she was asleep and the mother answers that she was. So far all is clear and straightforward. Now a new complication is introduced. The mother continues: 'I heard you in my deep sleep. (*Pause*) There is no sleep so deep that I would not hear you there.'

What are we to make of this? Is this a ghost story? Or is the mother's voice perhaps only in May's head? The romantic quality and rhythm of the last sentence is typical of Beckett: we roll it round our tongues with pleasure, but its very beauty renders it suspect; a seed of doubt is sown: no one would actually speak like this, though that is the kind of phrase someone alone might make up, the rhythm itself generating the words.

Is May imagining V then? She begins to pace again, and V goes on, counting her daughter's steps: 'One two three four five six seven wheel one two three four five six seven wheel.' The conversation between them picks up again, realistic at first, with May asking: 'Would you like me to inject you again?' It quickly moves once more into that grey area where we are no longer sure of our bearings: 'What am I now?' M asks. V responds by asking in her turn: 'And I? And I?' May tells her she is ninety, while she, May, is in her forties. 'I had you late,' says the mother. 'Forgive me again. Forgive me again.' May resumes her pacing and the mother calls out to her: 'May... Will you never have done? (*Pause*) Will you never have done revolving it all?' May stops, asks: 'It?' The mother: 'It all. In your poor mind. It all.' May resumes her pacing then all is in darkness again and the steps cease.

What have we seen? First there was the clear separation of mother and daughter. Then we wondered if the daughter was imagining the mother's voice. And finally we are led to wonder if the daughter's movements, her pacing and wheeling, are not a projection of thoughts or memories revolving in a mind – May's? The author's? Ours?

The second movement. Lights fade up on May, still. V speaks:

> I walk here now. (*Pause*) Rather I come and stand. (*Pause*) At nightfall. (*Pause*) She fancies she is alone. (*Pause*) See how still she stands, how stark, with her face to the wall.

A new element is thus introduced: is the figure we see perhaps the mother, or the mother's image of herself? The voice asks: 'Where is she?' And answers that she is in the old house, where it first began. She has not been out since girlhood. 'But let us watch her move in silence.' May starts to pace again. V goes on: 'Watch how feat she wheels...' May turns, walks, stops. The mother now starts to tell a story. It is the story of how the child would walk on the deep carpet until one day she said to her mother that she needed to hear her footsteps, her footfalls. 'May: I mean, Mother, that I must hear the feet, however faint they fall.' She goes on pacing, and V goes on speaking. 'Does she still sleep, it may be asked?' Yes, even as she walks she snatches a little sleep. And she tries to 'tell how it was. Tries to tell how it all was. It all. It all.' Then there is darkness again and the steps cease.

We now have five possibilities: that V and M exist, as mother and daughter, and speak and move as we see and hear them; that V is May's projection of a remembered or wished-for mother; that May is V's projection of a remembered or wished-for daughter; that May is V's projection of herself in childhood; that both are the projection of the author's remembered or wished-for or merely imagined mother and childhood.

In the final scene it is May who has the single long speech. But it is not a soliloquy, for she talks about herself in the third person, as the mother did. Moreover, she finds it difficult to get into any rhythm, either in pacing or talking:

> Sequel. (*Pause. Begins pacing...halts...*) Sequel. A little later, when she was quite forgotten, she began to – (*Pause*) A little later, when as though she had never been, it had never been, she began to walk... (*Resumes pacing...halts*). The semblance. Faint, though by no means invisible, in a certain light. (*Pause*) Given the right light. (*Pause*) Grey rather than white, a pale shade of grey.

She resumes her pacing, halts again. At last she is getting into her stride, but what is she now saying? She too is telling a story:

> Old Mrs Winter, whom the reader will remember, old Mrs Winter, one late Autumn Sunday evening, on sitting down to supper with her daughter after worship, after a few half-hearted mouthfuls laid down her knife and fork and bowed her head. What is it, Mother, said the daughter, a most strange girl, though scarcely a girl any more. What is it, Mother, are you not feeling yourself? (*Pause*) Mrs W did not at once reply. But finally, raising her head and fixing Amy – the daughter's given name, as the reader will remember...

It is as though we cannot speak about ourselves except through stories. As May is to Amy so Beckett is to May; as May is to herself so Beckett is to himself – but so also are we to ourselves. It is nonsense therefore to say: Is this true? Did it really happen? Who is she really? Because we are a multiplicity of voices, memories, imaginings. Instead of shutting the lid on this and forcing only one voice, one memory, to block out all the others, Beckett allows them all free play, and in so doing comes close to certain truths about ourselves as beings existing in time and space.

The story proceeds:

> ...fixing Amy full in the eye she murmured, Amy did you observe anything...strange at Evensong? Amy: No, Mother, I did not. Mrs W: Perhaps it was just my fancy?...You yourself observed nothing...strange? Amy? Amy? No, Mother, I myself did not, to put it mildly. Mrs W: What do you mean, Amy, to put it mildly? Amy: I mean, Mother, that to say I observed nothing...strange is indeed to put it mildly. For I observed nothing, of any kind, strange or otherwise. I saw nothing, heard nothing, of any kind. I was not there. Mrs W: Not there? Amy: Not there. Mrs W: But I heard you respond. (*Pause*) I heard you say Amen. (*Pause*) How could you possibly have responded if you were not there? (*Pause*) How could you possibly have said Amen if, as you claim, you were not there? (*Pause*) The love of God and the fellowship of the Holy Ghost, be with us all, now and for evermore. Amen. (*Pause*) I heard you distinctly.

Now May resumes her pacing, and finally stops. She goes on with her story: 'Amy.' She pauses. 'Amy.' She pauses. 'Yes, Mother.' She pauses again. 'Will you never have done?...Never have done ...revolving it all? It all. In your poor mind. It all. It all.' The light fades, then fades up a little. But there is no one there.

So, just as May and V are transmuted in May's story into Amy and her mother, but the effort to keep the story going cannot be kept up indefinitely and we return to May and V, so Beckett can only speak by creating May and V, and, after a certain time, that effort is too much; they vanish and all vanishes, and we are back to the silence and the next effort to speak and once more try to lay the old ghosts.

Yet something has happened. As Stevens puts it: 'After the leaves have fallen, we return / To a plain sense of things. It is as if / We had come to an end of the imagination.' But to get there we have actually been through something much more violent and painful than we ever experienced sitting through *Who's Afraid of Virginia Woolf* or *Look Back in Anger*. For it is our own ghosts which have been raised, and given an airing, and so exorcised, though only temporarily, by the power of art.

There is repetition as compulsion and repetition as release. It is not always easy to separate the two. *Footfalls* is as difficult to talk about as any of Beckett's works, because it only exists when it is over, so to speak, and before it starts again. What it does is to make us sense that what lives in us and makes us live is less a history or a set of memories than a certain rhythm, which, in the end, may be simply the rhythm of our own breathing. Curiously, we can only apprehend that rhythm through another. Beckett's work leaves us with a powerful feeling of another's rhythm. To pay it the attention it deserves is to grow conscious of our own. But the paradox is always there: we become conscious of who and what we are only in the moment that we recognize that that is what, once again, we have failed to be.

Barthes was the most intelligent critic of his generation. He was not perhaps the most perceptive (that honour surely goes to Butor), or the most profound (*that* honour must go to Blanchot), but he was the most wide-ranging, the most elegant stylist, and each of his books is a pleasure to read because Barthes, the student of rhetoric, was himself a master of critical rhetoric. Yet, I want to argue, there is a large area of darkness at the centre of his work. He who illuminated so many of our conscious and half-conscious habits failed to answer satisfactorily a question he came back to again and again: What happens when we read a novel?

I don't myself have an answer to this question, and in fact doubt very much whether it can ever be completely elucidated. But I believe Barthes' mistakes and partial answers help point us in the right direction, and that an understanding of what he was up to in the course of his enormously various critical career can illuminate this mysterious topic.

I

Barthes had a wonderful nose for the phoney and the meretricious; he was adept at helping bad taste, by an almost imperceptible turn of phrase, to reveal itself. Reviewing Mankiewicz's famous film of *Julius Caesar*, he goes straight for two apparently innocuous traits: the hair-styles of the protagonists and the abundant sweat they seem to produce:

> comme la frange romaine ou la natte nocturne, la sueur est, elle aussi, un signe. De quoi? De la moralité. Tout le monde sue parce que tout le monde débat quelque chose en lui-même; nous sommes censés être ici dans le lieu d'une vertu qui se travaille horriblement, c'est-à-dire dans le milieu même de la tragédie, et c'est la sueur qui a charge d'en rendre compte.[1]

But Barthes was never content, like Tynan or Clive James, to point and pass on. More solemn or perhaps more intelligent than they, better read at any rate in Nietzsche and Brecht, he wanted to chase such insights home, to try and uncover the roots of bad taste in our society.

Like Nietzsche and Brecht, he realized that those roots lay in our society's positing of cultural and historical factors as purely natural, rooted in the eternal verities of human nature and human society. Barthes' classical studies made him realize that Mankiewicz's notion of tragedy was not that of either the Romans or of Shakespeare, just as Barrault's notion, exemplified by his production of the *Oresteia* was a travesty of Aeschylus. Wherever Barthes turns his attention, to the cult of the child poet Minou Drouet, to travel guides, to newspaper reports, to the use of plastic, he finds bad taste going hand in hand with self-righteousness, with an ineradicable belief that matters are like this and can be no other way. And everywhere he sees the characteristic of popular literature, middle-brow literature, as reinforcing such attitudes: 'Marguerite Gautier, "touchante" par sa tuberculose et ses belles phrases,' he ends his little piece on *La Dame aux camélias*, 'empoisse tout son public, lui communique son aveuglement.'[2] What was needed was a little Brechtian irony in the writing, a sense on the part of the writer of how foolish as well as how pathetic she is: 'Sotte dérisoirement, elle eût ouvert les yeux petits-bourgeois. Phraseuse et noble, en un mot "sérieuse", elle ne fait qui les endormir.'

Barthes thus takes it upon himself to lay bare what we might somewhat barbarously call the Norpoissisms and the Verdurinisms of our time. Like Proust and Brecht he recognized that such attitudes go hand in hand with the perpetuation of certain forms of art: the classical novel in its debased form, or boulevard theatre. But this is actually too weak a way of putting it. Is it not the traditional novel, the traditional play, well-made both of them, which are the culprits? Is there really a radical difference between the novelistic equivalent of the Mankiewicz film and a Balzac novel, between a Dumas melodrama and the plays of Euripides? Barthes, developing these ideas in *Le degré zéro de l'écriture*, joins Kierkegaard and Nietzsche in something which is more than a critique of bad taste and becomes a critique of the world in which we have lived, in the West, from at least the time of the French Revolution.

In *Mythologies* Barthes was a loner: watching, sarcastically, as the follies of society unrolled before him. In *Le degré zéro* he found allies in that very history of literature he was examining. For what is characteristic of modernism, in all the arts, as well as in philosophy, is precisely this critical response to the surrounding culture. Monet, Schoenberg and Flaubert, to take but three representative examples, define themselves in relation to the art of their contemporaries, and they themselves feel that they move forward to the degree that they *see through* the assumptions upon which these are operating. It is the same with the philosophers: Kierkegaard does not simply criticize Hegel's ideas, nor Nietzsche Kant's. To say what they want to say they have to discover a new way of writing philosophy, for what they recognize is that form is never neutral.

That form is never neutral is what Barthes tries to demonstrate in *Le degré zéro de l'écriture*. He shows how the past tense of the traditional novel and its use of the third person work on us in such a way that we feel both safely insulated from the narrative and yet convinced of its truth. Thus, like Kierkegaard on Hegel and Nietzsche on Ranke, he states: 'La finalité commune du Roman et de l'Histoire narrée, c'est d'aliéner les faits: le passé simple est l'acte même de possession de la societé sur son passé et son possible.'[3]

These are difficult matters to grasp because the very tools we use to grasp them, our intelligence, our consciousness, are themselves already complicit with the material. The only way to understand is to recognize alternatives. That is why Kierkegaard, for instance, in *Fear and Trembling*, decides to tell so many versions of the Abraham and Isaac story. For what Kierkegaard wants to make us see is that to tell the story at all is to rob Abraham of his freedom: the essence of Genesis 22 for Kierkegaard, why it can be set up against the entire Hegelian system of history, is precisely that it presents us with something which cannot be turned *into* story.

For the same reason it is easier for us to grasp the points Barthes is making about narrative in *Degré zéro* if we can see what alternatives there are. In the 1950s and 1960s Barthes wrote many fine essays on some of his contemporaries, particularly Queneau, Robbe-Grillet and Butor. The essay on Butor's novel, *Mobile*, is perhaps the most useful from our point of view. There he makes the point that 'le discontinu est le statut fondamental de toute communication; il n'y a jamais signes que discrets'. A tree or a baby merely grows, as Stevens would say, but a poem or a book is made up of sentences which are made up of words which are made up of letters, as a painting is made up of individual brush-strokes and even *Tristan* is made up of individual notes. We cannot choose our letters, but we have to choose our words and sentences, and that choice will be determined by the aim we set ourselves, which is of course itself determined in large part historically and culturally, and by our own resources, which are themselves also to a large degree determined. The central problem for the maker is thus 'De savoir comment mobiliser ce discontinu fatal, comment lui donner un souffle, un temps, une histoire'. What Barthes dislikes about the traditional novel is that it pretends to be all of a piece, to exist apart from such individual choices. What he likes about *Mobile* is that it makes no attempt to hide the way it is put together, nor does it present one with a false 'souffle', 'temps' or 'histoire', since its mode of progression depends not on the simulation of reality but on following the most arbitrary yet strict rules, in particular the progression of the alphabet.

The essay on *Mobile* is brilliant, and rich in *aperçus*, none of which I have space to detail here. It should be read by anyone interested in understanding how narrative works. But a nagging doubt remains. Is development in narrative only a convention, as Barthes suggests, on a par with the Alexandrine and the quatrain? Why then has story-telling *always* tended to be sequential? Is there something in man's very make-up, in his constitution as a human being, which makes him need to invent and listen to sequential narratives? If that is the case is it not perfectly natural that a work which moves forward according to an alphabetical sequence should be felt by the reader as an affront? To say that *Mobile* is no more and no less arbitrarily constructed than *Le Père Goriot* is in one sense true: both are made up of words put together by a human being who can choose at each stage to go in one direction rather than another. But at the same time we feel that such a way of putting it is not quite right. We can assent to the individual steps of Barthes' argument but not (quite) to his final conclusion. With narrative fiction we seem to be in deeper waters than we ever were with news reports or with the sweat on the foreheads of the Romans in *Julius Caesar*.

Barthes seems to have felt some of these doubts himself. The problem of narrative continuity clearly wouldn't go away as easily as he had imagined in *Degré zéro* and the Butor essay. The only way was to go back over the material and look at it more closely. After flirting briefly with attempts to develop a scientific theory of narrative on a par with generative grammar, Barthes, thirteen years later, returned to the source of the trouble, Balzac. The result was one of his longest and densest books, *S/Z*.

The characteristic of the realist novel, of which Balzac's novella, *Sarrasine*, is a good example, is the smoothness of its surface. It offers no purchase for criticism, since it seems to be all of a piece. As a result critics of novels have tended to speak in the terms the novels themselves have presented them with – at its crudest, asking questions about the 'lives' of the characters. But of course novels are not babies, they do not grow, they are made. Barthes, in *S/Z*, is therefore determined to go against the grain of the novel, to break it up, to open it out for inspection, to return it to its elements, so to speak.

These elements, he argues, consist of strings of five 'codes'. Much has been made of these codes in subsequent discussion of *S/Z* and in imitations of it. But though Barthes himself insists that there are five and only five, and though his always impressive critical rhetoric invested them with an almost classic status as soon as they appeared, I think we should not be taken in by this. Certainly his distinction between on the one hand the two codes which can only move forward, the 'proaretic' and the 'hermeneutic' (the codes of 'background reality' and of 'plot'), and on the other the 'semic', the 'cultural' and the 'symbolic', is a valuable one. It even allows Barthes to present us with a convincing analysis of the first chapters of *Sarrasine* in the form of a musical notation, with the hermeneutic code functioning like classical melody, the proaretic like classical harmony, and the other three giving orchestral 'colour', thus making more tangible the often repeated assertion that there is a profound equivalence between nineteenth-century music and the nineteenth-century novel. But as the book progresses the symbolic code seems to dominate more and more. This is the atemporal code of inner-outer light–dark oppositions, the code of the central term of castration itself. It takes over partly because Barthes himself never seems to have responded to narrative continuity; he has always, like Frye, tended to see works of art as spread out before him in space rather than unfolding in time. But also, I suspect, because his approach in *S/Z* has allowed him to face up to aspects of himself which had previously been kept rigorously out of the picture. I will return to this. For the moment I want to suggest that *S/Z* is interesting less for its theoretical armature than for its local insights, that is, for the very same reason as his analyses of the mythologies of contemporary France were interesting: his unsurpassed ability to spot the elements of bad taste and his ability to relate these to large but unrecognized needs on the part of writer and audience.

Let me give two examples. Examining the lines: 'Elle sourit tristement, et dit en murmurant: – Fatale beauté! Elle leva les yeux au ciel', Barthes comments:

Dérivée d'un code pictural multiple, la Zambinella connaît ici sa dernière incarnation, ou expose sa dernière origine: *La Madone aux Yeux Levés*. C'est un stéreotype puissant, élément majeur du Code Pathétique (Raphaël, le Greco, Junie et Esther chez Racine, etc.). L'Image est sadique... elle désigne la victime pure, pieuse, sublime, passive... dont les yeux levés au ciel disent assez: regardez ce que je ne regarde pas, faites ce que vous voulez de mon corps, je m'en désintéresse, intéressez-vous-y.[4]

The very last line of the novella is related to this image. Now it is the woman to whom the narrator has told the story of Sarrasine and Zambinella who is the subject: 'Et la marquise resta pensive'. Barthes comments:

> Pensive, la marquise peut penser à beaucoup de choses qui ont eu lieu, mais dont nous ne saurons jamais rien: l'ouverture infinie de la pensivité (c'est précisément là sa fonction structurale) retire cette ultime lexie de tout classement.[5]

But, since every element *in* the story is at the same time part of the message *of* the story, Barthes is able to show that for Balzac as well as for the marquise this is in fact the perfect ending:

> Comme la marquise, le texte classique est pensif: plein de sens (on l'a vu), il semble toujours garder en réserve un dernier sens, qu'il n'exprime pas, mais dont il tient la place libre et signifiant ...la pensivité (des visages, des textes) est le signifiant de l'inexprimable, non de l'inexprimé. Car si le texte classique n'a rien de plus à dire que ce qu'il dit, du moins tient-il a 'laisser entendre' qu'il ne dit pas tout; cette *allusion* est codée par la pensivité, qui n'est signe que d'elle-même: comme si, ayant rempli le texte mais craignant par obsession qu'il ne soit pas *incontestablement* rempli, le discours tenait à le supplementer d'un *et cetera* de la plénitude. De même que la pensivité d'un visage signale que cette tête est grosse de langage retenue, de même le texte (classique) inscrit dans son système de signes la signature de la plénitude: comme le visage, le texte devient *expressif*... doué d'une interiorité dont la profondeur supposée supplée la parcimonie de son pluriel.[6]

Barthes has clearly not changed radically from the scourge of French middle-brow culture he appeared in *Mythologies*. And he is still concerned, as in *Degré zéro*, with the attempt to demythologize the novel, to show that its 'naturalness' is a pseudo-nature, that characters are only bundles of ticks with names stuck on them like labels. He still confesses that the attempt of the work of art to appear 'natural' makes him 'sick', that it gives him 'nausea', that it makes him feel that he is stifling. But there is a crucial difference. In *Mythologies* he had reluctantly come to the conclusion that the critic's stance must always be one of 'sarcasm'. Now he no longer disguises the very real pleasure he takes in the work of unmasking. In fact, his own pleasure in the task now becomes a very important plank in his theoretical argument.

There are, he says, two kinds of reading of a work like *Sarrasine*. There is the ordinary, naive reading, which is pure consumption, and there is *his* kind of reading, which is in effect a re-reading, and which does not simply follow where the text leads but finds active pleasure in going against the text, breaking it up, unmasking it:

> La relecture, opération contraire aux habitudes commerciales et idéologiques de notre société qui recommande de 'jeter' l'histoire une fois qu'elle à été consommeé (dévorée), pour que l'on puisse alors passer à une autre histoire, acheter un autre livre, et qui n'est tolérée que chez certaines catégories marginales de lecteurs (les enfants, les vieillards et les professeurs), la relecture est ici proposée d'emblé, car elle seule sauve le texte de la répétition (ceux qui negligent de relire s'obligent à lire partout la même histoire), le multiplie dans son divers et son pluriel... elle n'est plus consommation, mais jeu.[7]

One of the difficulties Barthes had had with the Marxian and Brechtian mode of demythologizing was that it left no place for pleasure. This is as much as to say, for the individual, since it is through pleasure that I sense myself as myself and no one else. We see Barthes, in *S/Z* and the books that follow, trying to find a way of assimilating pleasure into his notion of the critic's task, without thereby giving up his critical cutting edge. The two kinds of reader he here presents us with is the first step in that direction. Later, in interviews, in *Le Plaisir du texte*, and in his last three, much more personal, books, we are going to see him develop it to such an extent that the early, 'sarcastic' Roland Barthes almost disappears.

There is no doubt that Barthes' instinct is once again correct. A critical attitude of sarcasm may be useful, but a fully developed theory of reading must take the reader's pleasure into account. But I have grave doubts about the steps he takes to introduce it. I believe it leads to a misunderstanding of how we read novels, of the nature of fiction itself, and even of the thrust of Barthes' own earlier insights. Let me try to explain my misgivings.

II

There are, says Barthes, two kinds of readers: naive readers, who are 'mere consumers', and sophisticated readers. The first are like the audience at a strip-tease joint, the second like lovers. We all like to think we belong to the second category rather than the first, but I am not so sure that we can divide our attitudes either to sex or to reading that easily. Is our experience of reading well, of experiencing continuous and quite altruistic pleasure not often gained when reading a book for the first time? And though it's true that children ask for stories to be re-read to them again and again my own memory of childhood reading is that, once one had found an author to one's taste, one devoured his books and threw them aside as soon as they were read. And, if our own childish reading experiences are touchstones for us of what reading well means, can we really put 'les enfants, les vieillards et les professeurs' into the same category?

Instead of arguing the question theoretically let us put beside Barthes another great reader of Balzac – not, it is true, a real person, but the creation of Marcel Proust. I am sure, though, that the author of *Roland Barthes par Roland Barthes* would not feel that the comparison was for that reason invalid.

I am thinking of the Duc de Guermantes. 'Dans la petite bibliothèque du second,' Proust tells us in *Contre Sainte-Beuve*, 'où, le dimanche, M. de Guermantes court se réfugier au premier coup de timbre des visiteurs de sa femme, et où on lui apporte son sirop et ses biscuits a l'heure du gouter, il a tout Balzac, dans une reliure en veau doré avec une étiquette de cuir vert, de chez M. Béchet ou Werdet.' The Duke knows every Balzac novel practically by heart, every character in *La Comédie humaine* is an old acquaintance. We could call him an Honorite. And so, it seems, is his brother, for when the latter comes to visit him they often turn to Balzac, 'car c'était une lecture de leur temps ils avaient lu ces livres-là dans la bibliothèque de leur père, celle précisément qui était maintenant chez le comte qui en avait herité'. And Proust points out that their taste for Balzac was coloured by 'des lectures d'alors, avant que Balzac ne fût devenu grand écrivain, et soumis comme tel aux variations du goût littéraire'.

Proust is already drawing a distinction between the solidity of a response based on childhood reading and family tradition and the vagaries of adult 'literary' taste. But more is to come. Not only is M. de Guermantes fonder of little-known Balzac than of the more famous works, but his instinctive taxonomy stands 'sophisticated' literary response on its head. For Proust goes on to tell us that the Duke would often cite works by Balzac's now totally forgotten contemporaries, like Roger de Beauvoir and Céleste de Chabrillon with no apparent awareness that these were not by Balzac himself, and for the simple reason that in his library they were all bound in the same style:

> Quand on les ouvrait et que le même papier mince couvert de grands caractères vous présentait le nom de l'héroïne, absolument comme si ce fût elle-même qui se fut presentée à vous sous cette apparence portative et confortable, accompagnée d'une légère odeur de colle, de poussière et de vieillesse qui était comme l'emanation de son charme, il était bien difficile d'etablir entre ces livres une division prétendue littéraire qui reposait artificiellement sur des idées étrangères à la fois au sujet du roman et a l'apparence des volumes![8]

Clearly M. de Guermantes does not fit into either of Barthes' categories. He is neither a 'mere consumer' nor is he a 'sophisticated' critic. His relation to Balzac, we could say, is magical. And what is more, the narrator, though he hardly presents him to us as a paragon of good sense or intelligence, sides with him on this point. And that is why an essay on the critical method of Sainte-Beuve has to tell us about the *sirop* and biscuits consumed by the Duke, about a ray of light on a balcony, about the narrator's mother, and much else that the literary critic might find irrelevant. For the distinction we unthinkingly make between books and life is being ceaselessly eroded by this book, and not in order to say that they are the same thing but to make us think again about both.

In case we should think the narrator is merely having a bit of fun at the expense of the 'division prétendue littéraire', he goes on:

> Et je demande quelquefois si encore aujourd'hui ma manière de lire ne resemble pas plus à celle de M. de Guermantes qu'à celle des critiques contemporains. Un ouvrage est encore pour moi un tout vivant, avec qui je fais connaissance dès la première ligne, que j'écoute avec déférence, à qui je donne raison tant que je suis avec lui, sans choisir et sans discuter.[9]

The only progress he feels he might have made on this score since childhood, and the only point of disagreement with the Duke, 'c'est que ce mond inchangeable, ce bloc dont on ne peut rien distraire, cette réalité donneé, j'en ai un peu étendu les bornes, ce n'est plus pour moi un seul livre, c'est l'œuvre d'un auteur'.

Does this mean that he is now able to relate the books of Balzac to Balzac the man? Not at all. The whole of *Contre Sainte-Beuve* is expressly designed to counter this view. Sainte-Beuve, after all, was the leading exponent of biographical criticism in late nineteenth-century France, and, especially in the essays on the noted critic's relation to Stendhal and Baudelaire, Proust shows the utter crassness of a critical method which would relate the work directly to the man. But Proust, unlike Barthes and Foucault and Derrida, does not, for that reason, decide that the unit of criticism must be the 'text'. Indeed, though he does not know the term, it is as much against such a view as against Sainte-Beuve's that his book is directed.

To understand what Proust's view is and its close links with that of the unthinking Duc de Guermantes we need to look at the rest of *Contre Sainte-Beuve*, that unfinished masterpiece which was in effect to be a trial run for *A la recherche du temps perdu*, though Proust did not know it at the time. The chapter which precedes the one we have been considering is Proust's own 'Balzac'. Despite his assertion that for him writers are all of a piece, that he cannot go along with academic critics who praise one aspect of a book and condemn another, Proust is the least dogmatic of critics, the most flexible, never allowing a theory, even a theory about instinct, to override his instincts. Just as he begins his great late essay on Flaubert, an impassioned defence of that novelist against the imputation that he has no style, by pointing out that Flaubert is by no means his favourite author, that he is coming to his defence simply because he cannot let so monstrous an accusation go unchallenged, so he begins the essay on Balzac with a fine inventory of Balzac's weaknesses. He is in no doubt about Balzac's vulgarity, both in his own life and in his writing; he notes that for Balzac both art and love seem to be merely the means to social advancement, and that he makes no effort to hide the fact. Yet Proust cannot deny the power of the man, his confidence in himself, and the way this manifests itself in his writing. In a footnote in which he moves, as only he could, in the course of one sentence, from literary criticism to medicine to cannibalism, without the least hint of strain, he asks:

La vérité, du point de vue de Flaubert, Mallarmé, etc. nous a-t-elle un peu rassasiés et commencerions-nous à avoir faim de l'infinement petite part de la verité qu'il peut y avoir dans l'erreur opposeé (comme quelqu'un qui après un long et utile régime d'albumine aurait besoin de sel, comme ces sauvages qui se sentent 'mauvaise bouche' et se jettent, selon M. Paul Adam, sur d'autres sauvages afin de manger le sel qu'ils ont dans la peau)?[10]

Proust is struggling here to understand the power of popular literature. He recognizes instinctively that there is no absolute division between naive and sophisticated pleasures where literature is concerned, and his remarks are close to those of Graham Greene in 'The Lost Childhood':

> Of course I should be interested to hear that a new novel by Mr E.M. Forster was going to appear this spring, but I could never compare that mild expectation of civilized pleasure with the missed heartbeat, the appalled glee I felt when I found on a library shelf a novel by Rider Haggard, Percy Westerman, Captain Brereton or Stanley Weyman which I had not read before.

Both Greene and Proust assert the immediate and violent effect popular literature can have on us, both insist on a continuity between our deepest reading experiences and our reading in childhood of certain books, no matter how trashy. It would be wrong, however, to take their remarks as a stick with which to beat certain writers or movements in art, or to play down the very real criticism which Proust has previously levelled at Balzac. What is important is to see that in writing about Nerval, Baudelaire and Balzac in *Contre Sainte-Beuve* Proust was instinctively weighing up his own potential against the greatest French writers of the nineteenth century; when the time came he would write a book that would have elements of all three and could have been written by none of them.

But what really interested Proust in Balzac was not his ability to make characters come alive, not his self-confidence, but something else. It was the fact that a lot of separate novels had been transformed by the simple addition of a title. The central theme of *Contre Sainte-Beuve* is the radical distinction between the writer as social being and the writer in his work. To discover that what you had thought of as a number of discrete poems or stories really formed a unity was confirmation for Proust of his fundamental insight. That Hugo, calling his poems *La Légende des siècles*, and Balzac, calling his stories *La Comédie humaine*, should have sensed this already, could only give him confidence in the truth of his insight. For these titles were not imposed on the material, they emerged from it.

Yet there is, of course, a crucial difference between Proust and the earlier writers, and it does not lie in the fact that he, unlike them, had from the start seen a unifying thread in his life and art. It is rather that the unifying thread, once found, turned out to be nothing other than the insight that such a thread exists.

How does Proust's Balzac differ from Barthes'? Barthes would make a distinction between the novels and stories and their author, and so would Proust. But for Barthes the distinction is between author and text; for Proust it is the distinction between Balzac the man and Balzac the writer. And the latter is not the sum of his books, simply. 'He' is what comes through in the interstices between each book, 'he' is the 'secret signature' which is not to be located in any one work but which is to be found in those elements which are common to at least two. These are not tangible, but they are apprehensible, emerging for the attentive reader as he listens to the Balzacian music: 'Dès que je lisais un auteur, je distinguais bien vite sous les paroles l'air de la chanson, qui en chaque auteur est différent de ce qu'il est chez les autres.'

At this point Proust adds the last stone to the edifice he has slowly been building in *Contre Sainte-Beuve*: it is, he says, the sensing of this 'air' which gives him an experience that can only be described as joyous, and this joy does nothing less than bring him back to life:

> Mais si dans le second tableau ou le second livre il aperçoit quelque chose qui n'est pas dans le second et le premier, mais qui en quelque sorte est entre les deux, dans une sorte de tableau idéal, qu'il voit en matière spirituelle se modeler hors du tableau, il a reçu sa nourriture et recommence à exister et à être heureux. Car pour lui exister et être heureux n'est qu'une seule chose.[11]

Even here, at the very end, Proust is groping to explain his experience. Of the experience itself he is in no doubt. Yet one could be forgiven for thinking that he was referring here to some kind of Platonic ideal, the essence of all an author's books. His earlier remarks, however, make it clear that this is not at all what he has in mind, and I think it is important to understand why.

'Il n'y a pas de beauté, mais de femmes belles.' The abstract desire for beauty is *fade*, since it imagines it according to what we already know, whereas a new person brings us precisely that which we couldn't imagine: 'Ce n'est pas la beauté, quelque chose de commun à d'autres, c'est une personne, quelque chose de particulier qui n'est pas une autre chose.' And it is the same with a work of art, a cathedral, say; it's not 'a beautiful cathedral' but the cathedral of Amiens, 'au lieu où elle est echaînée au sol... avec la fatigue pour l'atteindre, par le temps qu'il fait, sous le même rayon de soleil qui nous touche, elle et moi'.

This is clearly related to that magical attitude to books we found in M. de Guermantes. And it is not just something theoretically endorsed by Proust, it forms the basis, however instinctive, of his entire aesthetics – his entire life. What the cathedral of Amiens, a girl suddenly glimpsed, the 'air' which detaches itself from the works of Balzac or Hardy have in common is that they fill the narrator with a sudden, inexplicable joy, which is akin to bringing him back to life. And they do this because they take him out of the world of habit and, touching him with their otherness, their uniqueness, make him realize that this world is made up of a million different worlds, and that he too is just such another, unique, himself and not another.

All Proust's criticism then is designed to explain, to himself as much as to his reader, why it is that a work of art should fill him with joy. But this joy, this 'being happy' of Proust's, is something quite different from Barthes' 'plaisir'. Having set up the opposition author/text, and having recognized that room needs to be made in the experience of reading for pleasure, Barthes has no other option open to him than to locate pleasure in the text itself. But since it cannot be in any ordinary reading of the text he is forced into a more and more perverse and hedonistic notion of both pleasure and pleasurable reading. Barthes was fond of saying that Brecht, good demythologizer that he was, was nevertheless fond of his cigar. In *Le Plaisir du texte* he develops an elaborate contrast between the anarchistic wildness of *jouissance* and the more restrained notion of *plaisir*, but both, he wants to insist, are of the body, not the mind. Proust too is suspicious of the mind, he also wants to talk about the body, but it is not a question with him of either *plaisir* or *jouissance*. Joy floods his body when habit drops away and he is opened to the world, and anything, a ray of sunlight on balcony railings, the turning of the pages of a forgotten novel, the sudden appearance of a woman at a street corner – anything can bring joy flooding back into his body. But this joy is not an indulgence of either the senses or the imagination; on the contrary, it is something that comes to him unexpectedly, from the outside, and it constrains him to attentiveness. As he grows attentive, as he strains to understand this world that has been revealed to him, he is made aware of himself as a body existing in time and space.

But again it is easy to misunderstand. There are few more joyful works than *A recherche du temps perdu*, but it is not made up of a series of epiphanies. Rather, the book is a *gradual* revelation of joy, as the narrator learns that such joy lies in the exploration of the relation between the epiphany and the waste sad time before and after, and comes to see that *the act of writing is precisely what makes such exploration possible*. The writing of the entire book then, from first word to last, is informed by that sense of potential release, of possibility realized, which is another name for joy. For Barthes, on the other hand, the world remains split between signs, which belong to the false world of ideology, of bad taste, and moments of pleasure which cannot be prolonged or meaningfully integrated into the rest of life, for the very reason that any such attempt would be, so he feels, to pull pleasure back into the false world of signs and so betray it.

III

Barthes' writing life began in the shadow of Brecht and Sartre; it ended in the shadow of Proust. Again and again in later life he referred to Proust's writings as a 'world' which formed the backdrop of his own life. Towards the end he even seemed quite deliberately to turn to the great Proustian themes of love and mourning. In these last books he was also moving away from criticism towards something which he called 'le romanesque' without the trappings of 'le roman' – character and plot.

Of course it is only a question of emphasis. In the late 1940s and 1950s he was, after all, writing essays in praise of Brecht, Butor, Camus, Robbe-Grillet and Queneau. But the attitude was generally bleak, the stance one of 'sarcasm'. Gradually, though, he moved towards an attitude of celebration, helped, as he said, by his stay in Japan, and I suppose also by the openness about his homosexuality which his growing fame and the more relaxed mores of the 1960s made easier. He even, at the end of his life, talked in public about eventually writing a novel himself. A Proustian novel, he would say.

But there's the rub. Proust himself would never have thought of writing a Proustian – or a Flaubertian – novel. The remark, though it mustn't perhaps be taken too seriously, is an index of the difference between the two. And it is a profound difference, made all the more acute by the many obvious similarities between them. An examination of just what it entails will help round out this sketch of two different attitudes to Balzac.

Barthes is such a good guide to instances of bad taste in our culture just because he realizes that we are all implicated. It is not just the editor of *Paris Match* or Mankiewicz or Poujade; it is you and me. *Fragments d'un discours amoureux* may not be about Barthes himself, it may be only a study of the typology of romantic discourse about love, but there is clearly a lot of Barthes himself in it. Here, for example, under the ironic heading 'Etre ascétique', is a description of the lover's bad faith:

Puisque je suis coupable de ceci, de cela...je vais me punir, je
vais abîmer mon corps...Je vais etre tres patient, un peu triste,
en un mot, *digne*...L'ascese...s'adresse à l'autre: retourne-toi,
regarde-moi, vois ce que tu fais de moi. C'est un chantage.[12]

At the heart of the book is the insistence on the fact that the lover
does not have a language at all. He can only say 'I love you', and
that is strictly *meaningless*. Such a lack of meaning is a sign of its
authenticity and the cause of his despair. Our culture tries to draw
love into its universe of discourse by the institution of the genre of
love stories. But a love story, however tragic, especially if tragic,
is society's last way of drawing love back into its orbit. But love is
atopos, it has no place. There is no element in a 'love story' that truly
comes before any other; all are there to be used by society if and
when it wishes. So Barthes writes his book as a series of little fragments laid out in alphabetical order. He does this because he wants
to maintain the integrity of his love, which means in the end keeping
it out of the mesh of language, of story, of plot, all of which belong
to society and not to him.

His last book, the study of photography which is in effect a study
of the place of death in our lives, is also built on an absolute dualism.
Barthes notes that most photos leave him cold, though he might in
certain moods find them 'interesting'; but a few, or the odd detail
in a few, seem to touch him to the quick. He develops this pheno-
menology by drawing a distinction between *punctum* and *studium*.
Studium, the realm of signs, is no longer seen as evil and corrupting,
as it had been in *Mythologies*, but merely as tedious, an aspect of
Proustian 'habit' and 'voluntary memory'. *Punctum* is no longer seen,
as in *S/Z* and *Le Plaisir du texte*, as leading to either *plaisir* or *jouissance*,
but as much more akin to Proustian involuntary memory. Photo-
graphy fascinates Barthes because a photo is not made up of discrete
signs – brush-strokes or words: it is a snapshot. What it has to tell
us then is both simple and almost impossible to grasp. It is that this
person whose photo I am looking at *once lived*. A photo is the result
of light bouncing off the body. That light has bounced off this
particular body is the guarantee that this body existed, stood under
this self-same sun. Such knowledge does not depend on the inter-
mediary of language or of any human set of signs; it is self-evident.
For that reason there is nothing to be said about it.

Seeing a photo of his mother as a little girl as he is going through
her belongings after her death, Barthes is struck down like the narrator in *A la recherche* bending to tie his shoe and suddenly, without

warning, feeling his grandmother alive and so for the first time really knowing her dead. The difference is that Proust has found a way of both staying true to the experience, to the way it seems to be outside any and every system of signs, *and* articulating it. Barthes can only reiterate his initial insight; he cannot move forward, since for him to talk is to betray.

Such blockage is of course something which all the great modern artists have encountered. We could say it was the essential impetus of modernism, this insight that to speak is to betray. It is what fuels the work of Kierkegaard and Nietzsche as well as that of Eliot and Kafka, Mallarmé and Beckett. It is of course at the heart of Proust's work. But the interesting thing is that in all these cases a way forward has been found which in the end does not betray the insight. That is not the case with Barthes.

Yet Barthes did, in his last book, come remarkably close to the Proustian insight. There, looking at the photo of his mother as a little girl, he suddenly feels her presence not as a subject of discourse, but 'telle qu'en elle-même'. And he calls this sense of presence *l'air*:

> L'air (j'appelle ainsi, faute de mieux, l'expression de verité) est comme le supplément intraitable de l'identité, cela qui est donné gracieusement, depouillé de tout 'importance': l'air exprime le sujet, en tant, qu'il ne se donne pas d'importance.[13]

And he adds, surprisingly, in view of his rather tedious earlier insistence on *jouissance*: 'Peut-être l'air est-il en définitive quelque chose de moral, amenant mystérieusement au visage le reflet d'une valeur de vie.' In these last meditations on his mother's photographs he rejoins the essential insights of Proust, which are that ethics and aesthetics can never be separated, that what moves me ultimately, when I catch sight of the sun on a wall or go to an exhibition of Vermeer or read the works of Balzac, is the double sense: how extraordinary that the world *is*, how extraordinary that *I* am.

Yet in the end Barthes can only fall back on his radical separation of the realm of signs and the realm of being: 'Telles sont les deux voies de la Photographie', he concludes. 'A moi de choisir, de soumettre son spectacle au code civilisé des illusions parfaites, ou d'affronter en elle le reveil de l'intraitable realité.' He can see no way of linking the two because process for him is irremediably tainted, it is a plunge into the false and treacherous realm of signs. For Proust signs, if properly read, point us to that unspeakable reality from which they emanate; the falsity of signs is the guarantee of the existence of others. And the artist, working, as he must, with signs, has to trust that through them reality will make itself manifest; not a reality on to which the book opens like a window, but the reality of the process of another person at work, making the book.

Barthes was, among other things, a great showman. His books are all meticulously planned so as to achieve the maximum effect. But he also worked that way because he knew that to write 'from the heart' was to surrender to the impersonal forces of language and (bad) taste. His works thus have to be objects, not outpourings, something over which he has to have control, not something control of which he would surrender to the unconscious. For, as he said in connection with the surrealists, there is nothing so predictable as the unconscious. But the high rhetorical polish which is a feature of all his books also has deeper roots, I suspect. In part it may have been a simple love of order, of making; but in part it must have been the result of a kind of fear, of a need for self-protection, a reluctance to let go.

To write fiction is to let go. It is to renounce the satisfaction of being totally in charge. But this need not lead to slovenly self-expression. On the contrary, *Contre Sainte-Beuve* is actually closer to Proust's own life than *A la recherche*. By the time he was working on the novel Proust had eliminated his brother and was in the process of transforming his mother into his grandmother. The exigencies of the fiction made it necessary for this to happen. Proust wrote himself out of subjectivity by trusting not his unconscious but the form itself. By contrast Barthes, in *Fragments d'un discours amoureux*, is somehow embarrassingly present. The alphabetical organization is in fact not rigorous enough. It only gives the impression of rigour, but the decisions as to what fragments to include, what letter to place at the head of each fragment (how to title it) are entirely arbitrary. And the result is that the fragments (and the titles) strike us as aggressive, as springing from the need simply to make an impression, to make us exclaim: 'How brilliant!' rather than 'How true!' There is here, as in so much he wrote, something *dandyish* about Barthes, a sense of wanting both to shock and to please at the same time. There is play here with letting go, but it remains only pretence. And Barthes is not alone in this. An even more striking example is Derrida's *La Carte postale*, where Derrida, trying to convey the freedom and randomness of an exchange of letters, gives us only an imitation of such freedom. There is nothing wrong with that, as Auden, for example, knew when he wrote his 'Letter to a Wound', but the problem with Derrida, as with Barthes, is that the artifice is insufficiently pointed, the rhetoric insufficiently acknowledged.

In the end we feel that Barthes and Derrida, like Lacan and Foucault, are always aware of the fact that they are addressing an audience. They are aware of the eyes of the audience upon them. However much they may seek to deny it, Barthes and Derrida live out their lives in the classroom; Proust and Auden do not. But with Barthes at any rate, I suspect it goes deeper than that. Even if he had written his novel I suspect he would always have had one eye on the effect he was making. There is a basic *trust* in Proust, in Kafka, in Beckett, a trust in the meaningfulness of time even ultimately in the moving hand which makes the marks on the page. Barthes lacks that trust.

Why should such trust exist in one person and not in another? Who can tell? Has it to do with the mother? The father? With childhood security? Why does one person become a novelist and another a critic? There are no answers to these questions.

Susan Sontag, in her moving obituary of Barthes, tells us that he was basically a melancholy man. And one can see why. He distrusted all the languages we use and all the gestures of renunciation we make. Proust, on the other hand, with many of the same doubts, seems never to have felt the need to impress. One of the most remarkable things about him is the way he suppressed *Jean Santeuil* when his family and friends were all putting pressure on him to give them proof that he was not entirely wasting his life. Had he published it, as Blanchot notes, he could never have written *A la recherche*. And although he was as aware as Barthes of the way we tend to lie to ourselves and others, of the half-conscious tricks we employ to make others think well of us, he was content to present Madame Verdurin and Monsieur Norpois to us and let us draw our own conclusions. He sensed that to get to the truth he would have to go by way of Madame Verdurin, of Sainte-Beuve, of the Goncourts; to find his own language he knew you had to go by way of the language of others. Barthes seems to have understood this theoretically at times, but been unable to act upon it. The more he tried to get free of false languages the more he locked himself up in a rigid set of postures. Yet it was he who best described what Proust had and he had not when he talked not about Proust but about another great French novelist of our time, Raymond Queneau:

Sa littérature n'est pas une littérature de l'avoir et du plein; il sait qu'on ne peut 'démystifier' de l'extérieur au nom d'une propriété, mais qu'il faut moi-même tremper tout entier dans le vide que l'on démontre; mais il sait aussi que cette compromission perdrait toute sa vertu si elle était *dite*, recupérée par un langage direct: La Littérature est le mode même de l'impossible, puisqu'elle seule peut dire son vide, et que le disant, elle fonde de nouveau une plénitude. A sa manière, Queneau s'installe au coeur de cette contradiction, qui définit peut-être notre littérature d'aujourd'hui: il assume le masque littéraire, mais en même temps il le montre du doigt. C'est là une opération très difficile, qu'on envie; c'est peut-être parce qu'elle est réussie, qu'il y a dans *Zazie* ce dernier et précieux paradoxe: un comique éclatant, et pourtant purifié de toute aggressivité.[11]

7 Text and Voice

'La question essentielle n'est plus aujourd'hui celle de l'*écrivain* et de l'*œuvre*, mais celle de l'*écriture* et de la *lecture*.'

Philippe Sollers

Oft of one wide expanse had I been told
That deep-browed Homer ruled as his demesne;
Yet did I never breathe its pure serene
Till I heard Chapman speak out loud and bold.

John Keats

Once upon a time it was easy. To the question: Who writes novels? the answer was obviously: a novelist. Today that is no longer the case. 'Nous pensons que ce qui a été appelé "littérature" appartient à une époque close laissant place à une science naissante, celle de l'écriture', writes the novelist and critic, Philippe Sollers.[1] And an American scholar asserts: 'It becomes futile – because radically inaccurate – to view a speaker as really beginning a discourse, still less as being its master... The relationship between discourse and speaker is governed by rules that antedate the speaker's appearance and postdate his disappearance.'[2] Instead of thinking of a novel as being written by someone – Dickens or Tolstoy, let us say – we must think of it as a *text*, something which exists in the world, but which is governed by its own laws, which will only be occluded by reference to the name on the title page. 'La notion de texte', writes Derrida, 'pensée avec toutes ses implications, est incompatible avec la notion univoque d'expression.'[3] And lest it be imagined that this kind of talk is confined to France or America, here is the end of a review of Joseph Heller's new novel which recently appeared in an English Sunday paper: '*Good as Gold*', the reviewer (admittedly an academic) says, 'is a good, busy, ambiguous text. But perhaps not, quite, good as gold.'

This substitution of the word 'text' for 'work' or 'book' is of course not a mere fad, though one may feel that it is in danger of passing into the select company of critical terms which function more as gestures than as useful tools, like 'rounded character' or 'stream of consciousness'. In France, at any rate, it is one symptom of the triumph of a revolution in thought which has been gradually acquiring momentum since the time of Mallarmé and Nietzsche, and which, in the course of the 1960s, burst with extraordinary force upon the general public. I believe that the assumptions which lie behind the use of the term – the assumptions embodied in the quote from Sollers – are both false and harmful, but that does not mean that I do not recognize and even to a large extent accept the implications of this larger revolution. Indeed, if we want to understand why such assumptions are false I think we have to take very seriously the movement of thought out of which they have grown. Thus, though this is a story that has often been told in recent years, it is necessary to sketch it in very briefly.[4]

With the gradual erosion of the notion of a Creator God, who made the world suddenly and out of nothing, the nineteenth century became increasingly concerned with the idea of origins. To trace something back to where it started was to explain what it meant. Everything must be traced back to its origins, man to the animals, modern civilization to primitive culture, a book to its author. Thus E.B. Tylor, in his article on Anthropology in the ninth edition of the *Encyclopaedia Britannica* (1875), could write:

> ANTHROPOLOGY: (The science of man . . .) denotes the natural history of mankind. In the general classification of knowledge it stands as the highest section of zoology or the science of animals, itself the highest section of biology or the science of living beings . . . It is undoubted that comparative anatomy and physiology, by treating the human species as one member of a long series of related organisms, have gained a higher and more perfect understanding of man himself and his place in the universe than could have been gained by the narrower investigation of his species by and for itself.[5]

This is to some extent true, but it also tends to appeal to analogy as a principle of explanation in a dangerously misleading way. Lévi-Strauss cites an example of this in another work of Tylor's: 'The bow and arrow is a species, the habit of flattening children's skulls is a species, the habit of reckoning numbers by ten is a species. The geographical distribution of these things, and their transmission from region to region, have to be studied as the naturalist studies the geography of his botanical and zoological species.' But to apply the principles of evolutionary biology in this naive way to the species *homo sapiens* can only result in error, as Lévi-Strauss points out:

Mais rien n'est plus dangereux que cette analogie. Car, même si le developpement de la génétique doit permettre de dépasser définitivement la notion d'espèce, ce qui l'a rendue et la rend encore valable pour le naturaliste, c'est que le cheval donne effectivement naissance au cheval, et qu'à travers un nombre suffisant de génerations, *Equus caballus* est le descendant réel d'Hipparion. La validité historique des reconstructions du naturaliste est garantie, en dernière analyse, par le lien biologique de la reproduction. Au contraire, une hache n'engendre jamais une autre hache; entre deux outils identiques, ou entre deux outils différents mais de forme aussi voisine qu'on voudra, il y a et il y aura toujours une discontinuité radicale, qui provient du fait que l'un n'est pas issu de l'autre, mais chacun d'eux d'un système de représentations.[6]

Thus a science which is concerned with the works of man will have to try and discover the specific laws governing such a system and avoid the temptations of analogies with other biological organisms.

Barthes makes a similar point when, in a splendid essay on Butor's *Mobile*, he invokes Mondrian and Webern, and reminds us that 'le discontinu est le statut fondamental de toute communication: il n'y a jamais de signes que discrets. Le problème esthétique est simplement de savoir comment mobiliser ce discontinu fatal, comment lui donner un souffle, un temps, une histoire.'[7] Classical rhetoric provided one kind of answer, the classical novel another – just as Dunstable found the means of writing large-scale works which differed from those of Monteverdi, which differed in turn from Bach's or Beethoven's or Wagner's or Stockhausen's. For all of them the word or the note remains the basic atom out of which the work is constructed.

This being the case, it becomes obvious that the task of literary criticism has barely begun. We possess a history but not a science of literature, Barthes points out,

> parce que, sans doute, nous n'avons pu encore reconnaître pleinement la nature de l'*object* littéraire, qui est un objet écrit. A partir du moment où l'on veut bien admettre que l'œuvre est faite avec de l'écriture (et en tirer les conséquences), une *certaine* science de la littérature est possible... Ce ne pourra être une science des contenus (sur lesquels seule la science historique la plus stricte peut avoir prise), mais une science des conditions du contenu, c'est-à-dire des formes...[8]

Such a science had already been envisaged by Northrop Frye, whose

work on Blake and Spenser had led him to see the need to draw up
a grammar of the forms of literature:

> In this book we are attempting to outline a few of the grammatical
> rudiments of literary expression, and the elements of it that cor-
> respond to such musical elements as tonality, simple and com-
> pound rhythm, canonical imitation and the like. The aim is to
> give a rational account of some of the structural principles of
> Western literature in the context of its Classical and Christian
> heritage.[9]

This way of looking at literature has had very beneficial consequences for criticism. Instead of sterile debates about influence and
origins we have seen a rehabilitation of that rhetoric which after all
guided the creation and appreciation of literature from the time of
Homer till the Romantics, and a new impetus has been given to the
study of the largely anonymous literature of the middle ages and
the formal literature of the Renaissance. In the wake of Barthes and
Lévi-Strauss critics have come to see the value for their work of the
developing sciences of linguistics and semiology, and have learned
the value of the experiments of the Russian Formalists carried out
in the twenties. Developments have in fact been so rapid that today
Frye's elaborate formal schemes have the nostalgic charm of a Heath
Robinson machine. For now we find books appearing with such
titles as *Problèmes de la structuration du texte*, in which Julia Kristeva
asserts: 'Ce qu'on a pu appeler "objet littéraire" ne serait pour la
sémiologie qu'un type de *pratique signifiante* sans aucune valorisation
esthétique ou autre.'[10] And Mieke Taat sums up recent developments
thus:

> Chaque texte particulier constitue lui-même son propre code et
> l'on peut étudier les écarts que le texte opère lui-même à ce code.
> Ce qui distinguerait alors un roman d'un autre, un roman mod-
> erne d'un roman plus ancien, ce serait aussi bien le type de code
> que chacun instaure à l'intérieur de son texte, que la manière d'y
> faire infraction.[11]

Perhaps, though, criticism has moved a little too fast and too
confidently. The last two quotations in particular suggest that critics
have chosen to forget the problematic status of the traditional novel
in this whole change of climate. For one way of describing the
critical revolution which has taken place is to say that we have managed to escape from certain dominant critical attitudes which saw
the novel as the archetypal form of literature. When Barthes, for

example, in the passage I quoted earlier, made the point that 'le discontinu est le statut fondamental de toute communication', he was concerned to defend a modern piece of narrative fiction (Butor's *Mobile*) which functioned according to norms other than those of the traditional novel. His point was that one of the things the novel did was to develop an unprecedented power of concealing this truth that works of art are made, not born. The traditional novel – to some extent like the classical symphony – functions by giving the *impression* of naturalness, continuity, unity. In his early work Barthes was concerned to make accessible writers like Robbe-Grillet and Butor, who might not be getting through to a public brought up on Mauriac and Montherlant; but more recently he has turned his attention to the traditional novel itself, approaching it, as one would expect, as an object made by joining up discrete elements rather than as a given whole. Outlining his approach in *S/Z* he says:

> Ce que l'on cherche, c'est à esquisser l'espace stéréographique d'une écriture (qui sera ici écriture classique, lisible). Le commentaire... ne peut donc travailler dans le 'respect' du texte: le texte tuteur sera sans cesse brisé, interrompu sans aucun égard pour ses divisions naturelles (syntaxiques, rhétoriques, anecdotiques); l'inventaire, l'explication et la digression pourront s'installer au coeur du suspense, séparer même le verbe et son complément, le nom et son attribut; le travail du commentaire, dès lors qu'il se soustrait à toute idéologie de la totalité, consiste précisément à *malmener* le texte, à lui *couper la parole*. Cependant, ce qui est nié, ce n'est pas la *qualité* du texte (ici incomparable), c'est son 'naturel'.[12]

This may appear to be a purely neutral and 'scientific' attitude to take, but Barthes cannot always keep out of his commentary a note of disgust which a work of this kind evokes in him – he talks, for example, of 'life' in such a work becoming 'un mélange écoeurant d'opinions courantes, une nappe étouffante d'idées reçues'.[13] And this should not surprise us, for the traditional novel plays in his thought a rather similar role to that played in the thought of Marx and Kierkegaard by Hegel's historiography. We have to remember that the modernist revolution, in its widest sense, is not the product of simple scientific 'advance', but is the result of a series of polemics, directed by artists and thinkers as different as Nietzsche, Marx, Monet, Mallarmé, and Kierkegaard against the established views of the time. And these views are recognized by the early revolutionaries as being rather intimately connected with the ways people normally think or see or read. Proust began by attacking the biographical reductionism of Sainte-Beuve in what at least started out as a critical essay; but it soon became clear to him that to defeat Sainte-Beuve he would have to plunge into a full-scale work of *imaginative* literature: only *A recherche du temps perdu* is an adequate refutation of what Proust felt to be the false ways of reading literature. In the same way, as Barthes noted, Robbe-Grillet's novels were quite inseparable from his critique of the traditional novel: whether it welcomes the position or not, art since 1850 is polemical or it is nothing.

In fact, as we would expect, it is the writers who have thought hardest about the implications of the modernist revolution, and it is to them rather than to critics or scholars that we should turn if we want to understand the full implications of that revolution. It so happens that there took place in Cerisy in 1971 a conference under the general title 'Nouveau Roman: Hier, Aujourd'hui'. What gave it its historical importance was the fact that it brought together not just academics and critics interested in the *nouveau roman*, but some of the key novelists themselves: Sarraute, Robbe-Grillet, Pinget, Simon, Ollier, Ricardou. The papers delivered at the conference have been published, along with the ensuing discussions, in two volumes which provide a fascinating insight into the way certain novelists are thinking about their art today and into the general climate of criticism in France.[14]

The leading light of the conference was undoubtedly Jean Ricardou. In 1967, in the wake of two novels, he had published a marvellous book of essays, *Problèmes du nouveau roman*, and this was followed in 1971 by *Pour une théorie du nouveau roman* (the change from 'problèmes' to 'théorie' was, as we will see, emblematic). These two books established him, in succession to Robbe-Grillet, as the main theorist of the new novel. At the Cerisy conference he was forever leaping up and berating speakers for lacking theoretical or terminological rigour and reminding them of his own precise formulations. His remarks, especially the pithy saying that the novel is no longer 'l'écriture d'une aventure' but 'l'aventure d'une écriture', were repeated with awe by many of the speakers, and, as we will see, Robbe-Grillet himself paid him a surprising tribute.

What then is Ricardou's message? What does it mean to say that writing is 'l'aventure d'une écriture'? In his opening paper Ricardou laid down the basis of his position:

L'originalité, on le sait, est la superstition vers laquelle sont irrémédiablement conduits tous ceux qui prétendent concevoir le distinctif selon le fallacieux schéma d'une doctrine de l'Expression. Pour le dogme expressif, éminemment romantique, le text ne saurait jamais être que la sortie d'une substance antécédente dont l'auteur serait en quelque façon le propriétaire.[15]

Instead, he goes on, we must realize, that 'C'est dans et par le texte que se produit le texte. Plutôt que d'imagination, il vaudrait mieux parler dès lors d'opérations génératrices qui ont l'avantage d'être spécifiques dans un processus de production précis.'[16] Such 'generative operations' are to be found in Roussel, for example, who, as he explained in a famous essay, would start a story with one phrase ('La peau verte de la prune un peu mûre'), and devise a plot that would lead him to the same phrase at the end, but with a single letter changed ('la peau verte de la brune un peu mûre'). Ricardou himself, explaining how he set about writing *La Prise de Constantinople*, says that he wished to start from nothing, realized that no novel started from nothing since before the first word there is always the title page with the author's name and the name of the publisher, so took off from there: Ricardou has five letters in common with Villehardouin, who wrote about the crusades; the fourth crusade stopped at Constantinople, the name Jean Ricardou breaks down into four plus eight, midnight would figure in the book, and also stars (the star on the title page of Edition de Minuit books), and so on and so forth.

The process is much more rigorous than this sketchy summary suggests, but it does make clear what Ricardou is up to. One way of summing it up is to say that he has pushed Proust and Joyce from the centre of the modernist pantheon and replaced them with Roussel. Robbe-Grillet, for one, is in no doubt that things have changed since the 1950s and that it is Ricardou who has helped to change them:

Le Nouveau Roman a considérablement evolué depuis ses débuts et, en particulier, grace à vous, Ricardou. Nos premiers écrits ne représentaient certainement pas le même degré de modernité que nos écrits actuels: moi-même et Nathalie Sarraute encore plus que moi, prêtions sans cesse le flanc à des interprétations référentielles. On a dit que *Le voyeur* avait eu comme premier titre *Le voyageur*, c'est inexact: son premier titre était *La vue*, en hommage au livre de Raymond Roussel. Mais, en même temps, sentant peut-être le terrain terriblement mal préparé, j'ai fourni moi-même à cette époque des interprétations référentielles qui allaient jusqu'au significations psychologiques. Quand on me disait: 'votre réalisme, n'est pas objectif', au lieu de répondre: 'c'est la notion de réalisme qui a fait faillite', je répondais: 'non, mais c'est un réalisme sub-jectif, c'est comme cela qu'est le monde à l'intérieur de nos têtes.'[17]

There are two important points here. The first is Robbe-Grillet's claim that Roussel had always been his ideal but that he had not in the early days known how to realize his Rousselian insights; the second is the implied belief that *either* a work is 'psychological', having to do with what goes on in people's heads, *or* it is Rousselian. I do not believe these are the real alternatives, but let us postpone that discussion for a moment and follow Robbe-Grillet a little further. There has been, he says, a change in the general climate of opinion, a change largely associated with the name of Michel Foucault, and this has coincided with a change within the *nouveau roman* itself:

> Je ne suis pas arrivé les armes de la modernité toutes forgées dans ma tête quand j'ai commencé à écrire... Peu à peu, par l'exercice de l'écriture, s'est accomplie cette révolution...; et il est exact que, pour moi, c'est *Dans le labyrinthe* qui constitue la charnière, à tel point que j'irais maintenant jusqu'à présenter *Les gommes, Le voyeur, La jalousie,* comme une espèce de trilogie appartenant encore à cette première moitié du XXe siècle, alors que nous sommes maintenant, avec vous Ricardou, dans la deuxième.[18]

All his earlier theoretical discourse, he says, served to place his work 'dans cette perspective... dont Joyce et Proust ne songeaient pas à s'ecarter'. However,

> Quand, peu à peu, par la pratique de notre écriture au sein du contact sensible avec le monde, nous nous sommes trouvés non plus hantés par une profondeur mais de plein-pied avec des sur-faces, une comparaison s'est imposée entre ces surfaces et les cartes à jouer. Vous savez que les jeux se font avec des signaux plats: derrière une dame de pique, il n'y a rien: pour une cartomancienne il y a quelque chose, mais pour un joueur de bridge il n'y a rien: c'est à lui de créer sa signification. On lui distribue des cartes et ces cartes sont de pures surfaces. Contrairement à ce que les adver-saires du jeu prétendent, cette superficialité n'empêche pas du tout la liberté. On vous distribue les cartes et vous commencez à les organiser en ce qu'on appelle une main; et ce seul ordre donné à des figures plates commence à projeter votre intervention dans le monde, ce qu'on peut appeler votre parole... En somme, le jeu est pour nous la seule manière possible d'intervenir dans un monde dorénavant privé de sa profondeur.[19]

It is a satisfying thing to find oneself in step with the times, and Robbe-Grillet's view both of art in general and of the history of the *nouveau roman* would elicit nods of agreement from France's leading thinkers; it certainly emerged as the new orthodoxy at the Cerisy conference. It is true that one irate lady was compelled to remark: 'il suffit de regarder Robbe-Grillet pour voir qu'il est autre chose qu'un mot', but no one paid very much attention to her. There were, however, two more substantial voices raised either in direct protest or in implicit criticism of the prevailing view, and these were the voices of Nathalie Sarraute and Robert Pinget.

In her own paper Nathalie Sarraute went over ground familiar to her readers when she talked about those

> régions silencieuses et obscures où aucun mot ne s'est encore introduit, sur lesquelles le langage n'a pas encore exercé son action asséchante et petrifiante, vers ce qui n'est encore que mouvance, virtualités, sensations vagues et globales, vers ce non-nommé qui oppose aux mots une résistance et qui pourtant les appelle, car il ne peut exister sans eux.[20]

This, one might have thought, would have been entirely acceptable to the author of *Le Voyeur* and *La Jalousie*, but the new, Ricardianized Robbe-Grillet will have none of it. When you start to write, he asks her, do you feel that your world already exists or is it through language that you bring something new into the world? No, says Sarraute, there is neither a fully-fledged world in her mind before-hand which simply needs to be got down on paper, nor does she simply start with the words on the page: 'ça n'existe pas sans le langage mais le langage sans ça ne peut pas exister.' But Robbe-Grillet will not let go. Believe me, he says, there are only two fundamental positions which the writer can hold, 'celui qui arrive dans un monde qui existe déjà et dont il va parler et celui qui arrive dans un monde qui n'existe pas encore et qu'il va créer par son propre langage'. And in your case, he tells her, as in mine, what clearly interests you 'c'est la création d'un monde qui n'existe pas encore'. Yes, agrees Sarraute, 'mais ce monde est créé à partir de quoi, pas uniquement à partir du langage?' To which Robbe-Grillet unconvincingly replies: 'Au commencement était le Verbe...'[21]

Sarraute thus tries to drive a wedge between the alternatives proposed by Robbe-Grillet and Ricardou. To hold that the novelist does not come with his plot ready-made and simply pours it out on paper does not mean, for her, that he starts with the first words. Sarraute, of course, was, like Beckett, welcomed by the early *nouveaux romanciers* as a precursor; at this conference she is regarded as limited and old-fashioned in her insistence on depth, interiority and mystery. The case of Pinget is rather different. *Passacaille*, published in 1969, is hailed as belonging to the new, purified *nouveau roman*, along with *La Maison de rendez-vous*, Simon's *Les Corps conducteurs* and Ricardou's *La Prise de Constantinople*. It is, says one speaker, a work where we have 'une variation de points de vue dont la motivations ne peut être que compositionelle et non psychologique'.[22] Pinget's own remarks, however, seem closer to Sarraute, and even to Proust and Joyce, than to Ricardou. In a modest and witty paper wittily and modestly entitled 'Pseudo-principes esthétiques' he says things no one else at the conference was prepared to say and which none of those present quite knew what to do with.

He begins by pointing out that though there may perhaps be something 'modern' or even 'valuable' in what he writes, he has never aimed at either modernity or at value. All he has ever been interested in is one thing: 'seul capte mon intérêt la *voix* de celui que parle'. The ear is as powerful a registering organ as the eye, but

> notre ton habituel, celui que l'on a par exemple avec soi-même ou avec ses proches, est une sorte de composé des divers tons, outre les héréditaires et ceux des livres, enregistrés par nous depuis notre enfance... C'est dire que jamais je n'ai tenté de rendre objectivement, tel un magnétophone, le son d'une voix étrangère, j'ai bien assez à faire de la mienne.

And he goes on:

> Je dis *la voix de celui qui parle*, car le travail préalable consiste pour moi à choisir parmi les composantes de la mienne celle qui m'intéresse sur le moment et de l'isoler...[23]

This work takes place in the dead period between one book and the next, and there is always the temptation to use again a tone he had already used, because not to write is painful and he is always anxious to get back to work, to the making of something. But it is a temptation which must be resisted, for it is precisely in the 'périodes creuses' that this essential 'mûrissement' takes place. And even then it is hardly a straightforward task:

> Inexact aussi de dire que le ton est trouvé du premier coup. Ça m'est arrivé exceptionellement. Plutôt une tonalité au début, ou la confiance en une certain tonalité, qui se precise par le travail, donc au cours du livre, et qui devient finalement un ton, peut-être

à la dernière page... Une chose est certaine, c'est que jamais au départ je ne sais ce que je vais dire. J'ai longtemps cru qu'il s'agissait là d'une faiblesse, mais pas moyen de l'éviter puisqu'elle est ma seule force, celle qui me fait poursuivre.[24]

Two important conclusions flow from this. First of all:

En ce qui concerne mes livres, je me suis aperçu que le futur y régit le passé. Ce n'est pas un paradoxe. Le fait de me lancer à l'aventure, sans matériau préalablement étiqueté, sans but que de découvrir en écrivant celui que je me propose, c'est choisir de ne compter que sur l'avenir, sur le futur qui est le temps de la découverte.[25]

For the new Robbe-Grillet as for Ricardou, doubt and failure are as meaningless as they would be for a card-player and hint at an interiority they deny. But, denying interiority, they also deny time. Because Pinget starts from doubt, confusion, uncertainty, he can only go on by trusting in the future, a beneficial time. However, he has not yet done, and he ends on a note Proust would have understood well: 'Il s'agit donc de ne pas ignorer que de quelque façon qu'on aborde un problème, la façon contraire est pareillement efficace pour aboutir à ce lieu commun que la vie nous échappe dans son essence et qu'on ne peut la retenir passagèrement que dans un acte d'amour arbitraire, celui de la création.'[26]

So far we have remained at the level of theory. But writers can be notoriously wrong about their own work, and it is important to test the views of Robbe-Grillet and Pinget against their own novels. Of course one can only skim the surface in an essay of this length, but even that may help us to see a little more clearly what the issues really are and how literary theory relates to practice. I would like to look at the opening pages of two novels: *Dans le labyrinthe*, which, as we have seen, Robbe-Grillet regards as a turning-point in his own work, and *Passacaille*, published ten years later and seen by the conference as a fine example of what came to be called, in the course of that week at Cerisy, the *nouveau nouveau roman*.

Here is how *Dans le labyrinthe* starts:

Je suis seul ici, maintenant, bien à l'abri. Dehors il pleut, dehors on marche sous la pluie en courbant la tête, s'abritant les yeux d'une main tout en regardant quant même devant soi, à quelques mètres devant soi, quelques mètres d'asphalte mouillé; dehors il fait froid, le vent souffle entre les branches noires dénudées; le vent souffle dans les feuilles, entraînant les rameaux entiers dans un balancement, dans un balancement, balancement, qui projette son ombre sur le crépi blanc des murs. Dehors il y a du soleil, il n'y a pas un arbre, ni un arbuste, pour donner de l'ombre, et l'on marche en plein soleil, s'abritant les yeux d'une main tout en regardant devant soi, à quelques mètres seulement devant soi, quelques mètres d'asphalte poussiéreux où le vent dessine des parallèles, des fourches, des spirales.

Ici le soleil n'entre pas, ni le vent, ni la pluie, ni la poussière. La fine poussière qui ternit le brillant des surfaces horizontales, le bois verni de la table, le plancher ciré...[27]

From the opening words an opposition is set up between 'here', the place where 'I am', and 'outside', where 'I am not'. As the novel progresses inner and outer, here and there, converge and merge and replace each other, though the boundaries between them are never abolished. But the important thing to note here is how easily we read this apparently baffling paragraph, with its series of unexplained contradictions. We are lulled by the rhythm, borne along by it and by the confidence it gives us in the 'je' who speaks. 'Ici' brings 'dehors' in its wake, and so we are led outside and a number of descriptions are 'floated' before, at the start of the second paragraph, the larger rhythm carries us back into the room. But now the dust of the street, which had been generated by the narrator's search for a description of 'dehors', migrates into the room. And in its wake will migrate all those parallels, forks and spirals, though this time as the shapes left by objects which had once lain on the dusty desk-top inside the room: 'Sur le bois verni de la table, la poussière a marqué l'emplacement occupé pendant quelque temps...par de menus objects, déplacés depuis, dont la base s'inscrit avec netteté pour quelques temps encore, un rond, un carré, un rectangle, d'autres formes moins simples...'[28] It is impossible to reconstitute the objects which have left these traces with any certainty, though one may guess at them: 'On dirait une fleur, le renflement terminal représentant une longue corolle fermée, en bout de tige, avec deux petites feuilles latérales au-dessus...Ce pourrait être aussi un poignard, avec son manche séparé par une garde de la forte lame obtuse à deux tranchants...'[29] But it is just because of this ambiguity that the object retains a haunting importance for us. Had the narrative simply opted for a flower or dagger we would have assimilated it to our general impression of the room and not given it another thought. Or rather,

for such is the way novels tend to function, we would have thought
little more about it if it had been a flower, but a dagger, because it
is a bit more unexpected, and because of our past experience with
novels, would have warned us of bloody business ahead. The
ambiguity, however, leaves us waiting, receptive, curious.

Now the rhythmic swing from inside to outside and back begins
to accelerate, as the dust in the room is transformed into the snow
outside. The narrative will settle for snow as the main element of
the weather, clearly because snow is so tangibly there and yet vanishes when it is picked up, and because, though it registers traces
very clearly, it soon wipes them out. A footstep in the snow is much
like a thought or image in the mind or words on a white page,
quickly turned.

> Un croisement, à angle droit, montre une seconde rue toute
> semblable... Au coin du trottoir, un bec de gaz est allumé, bien
> qu'il fasse grand jour... Au lieu des perspectives spectaculaires
> aux-quelles ces enfilades de maisons devraient donner naissance,
> il n'y a qu'un entrecroisement de lignes sans signification, la neige
> continue de tomber, ôtant au paysage tout son relief, comme si
> cette vue brouillée était seulement mal peinte, en faux-semblant,
> contre un mur nu.
>
> A la limite du mur et du plafond, l'ombre de la mouche, image
> grossie du filament de l'ampoule électrique, reparaît et poursuit
> son circuit... C'est encore le même filament, celui d'une lampe
> identique ou à peine plus grosse, qui brille pour rien au carrefour
> des deux rues, enfermé dans sa cage de verre...[30]

Once the rhythmic swing has done its job of creating both an inside
and an outside, it is time to annul the division between them. But
of course this can never quite happen. It is precisely our sense of
them as distinct, closed versus open, shelter versus cold and danger,
which makes the continual contamination of the one by the other
so disturbing.

It is characteristic of this narrative that it cannot keep still, that
each return to an earlier point involves drawing into the orbit of the
fiction some new element, which then in turn draws in another, and
so on. This happens to particularly good effect the next time round,
as the street lamp is described:

> Contre la base conique du support en fonte, évasée vers le bas,
> entourée de plusieurs bagues plus ou moins saillantes, s'enroulent
> de maigres rameaux d'un lierre théorique, en relief: tiges ondulées,

feuilles palmées à cinq lobes pointus et cinq nervures très apparentes, où la peinture noire qui s'écaille laisse voir le métal rouillé. Un peu plus haut, une hanche, un bras, une épaule s'appuient contre le fût du réverbère. L'homme est vêtu d'une capote militaire...[31]

The speaker, alone in the room, by the simple fact of saying he is there, seems to have set in motion a mechanism which leads inexorably to the appearance of the soldier. And it is he who will now take over from the speaker, become the prime focus of our attention, until, near the end, out of the soldier's adventure, a doctor is created, and this doctor becomes, at the very end, the narrator who is in the room. The last paragraph reads in part:

Dehors il pleut. Dehors on marche sous la pluie en courbant la tête... Ici la pluie n'entre pas, ni la neige, ni le vent; et la seule fine poussière qui ternit le brillant des surfaces horizontales... la seule poussière provient de la chambre elle-même... mais la vue se brouille à vouloir préciser les contours, de même que pour le dessin trop fin qui orne le papier des murs... le vestibule obscur où la canne-parapluie est appuyée obliquement contre le portmanteau, puis, la porte d'entrée une fois franchie, la succession des longs corridors, l'escalier en spirale, la porte de l'immeuble avec sa marche de pierre, et toute la ville derrière moi.[32]

In commenting on this novel I have talked about the narrative wanting to do this or that, rather than about the author or the hero. This is because that seems to be what does indeed happen. We feel that it is the narrative which gropes its way forward precisely because the rough lines, the early sketches, the false directions, are left in. The adventure, to go back to Ricardou's words, is that of the transformation of 'Je' into 'moi'. But is this the adventure of 'une écriture'? Or of something else, more mysterious, less easy to define?

In all Robbe-Grillet's early novels, up to this one, we are faced with a double process, a double pressure: the pressure to conceal and to reveal. In *Le Voyeur* and *La Jalousie*, the pressure is enormous, overwhelming, and it is located within the fiction, in the need of the hero to hide murder or jealousy from himself. In *Dans le labyrinthe*, on the other hand, the pressure is, as it were, evenly distributed and constant, a state of clarity / exhaustion which is reflected in the psychological state of the soldier, who no longer has anything either to hide or to show, only a necessary task to perform. In this novel, even more than in the previous ones, a limited, finite series of elements is permutated steadily and relentlessly, gradually secreting meaning.

The narrative gropes its way forward metonymically, via words like *poussière, mur, lampe, chemin,* searching for a way forward which will also be the way towards a point of final rest.

In the early novels the experience of the hero is somehow coterminous with that of the narrative. In *Dans le labyrinthe* there is no longer a central character, for character too starts to partake of this perpetual transformation. In the novels that have followed transformation is paramount, and there is no longer any pressure. We no longer have the sense of the repression or displacement of desire – in fact desire, wish, impulse, have gone. But as a result the transformations themselves lose any interest for us. Because it is only when we can enter the world of the fiction that its denial makes any impact upon us. It is only because we immediately feel with the 'I' in the room that his migration into the body of the soldier and then into that of the doctor affects us as it does (though of course in this novel there is never anything to hold on to, only the perpetual lure of a holding, a fullness, a final understanding).

Robbe-Grillet, I suspect, is wrong not only in his assessment of the relative value of his own novels, but also in his understanding of how they function. *Poussière, mur, lampe, chemin,* do not function as words on the page. They function in the much more mysterious space of the narrative, which is neither on the page nor in my head nor in the world, but which exists for me as I read. It is not the word *poussière* which does the trick, but the notion, what is evoked for the reader by that word. One of the central themes in Proust's *A la recherche,* it will be remembered, is the struggle with the magical power of names and even of words. Marcel's education consists in large part in discovering that the word and the thing are not one and the same, that the same name may clothe many different people. But the point is that this is not a discovery which he can make once and for all. It has to be perpetually remade. But Robbe-Grillet, in the novels that have followed *Dans le labyrinthe,* seems to be asserting that once we have realized that word and thing do not coincide we can be free to concentrate on the play of words. This is not going beyond the outdated epistemology of Proust and Joyce, but making a simple mistake about how language – and the novel – functions.

Out of the continuous search for fullness, for stasis, in *Dans le labyrinthe,* emerges something which is to be defined in terms neither of realism nor of abstraction, neither of psychology nor of construction. It is the sense of a voice. Since Pinget explicitly talks of seeking for a voice in his writing, it is likely that we will be able to find this in *Passacaille* as well.

Here is how that novel opens:

Le calme. Le gris. De remous aucun. Quelque chose doit être
cassé dans la mécanique mais rien ne transparaît. La pendule est
sur la cheminée, les aiguilles marquent l'heure.
    Quelqu'un dans la pièce froide viendrait d'entrer, la maison
était fermée, c'etait l'hiver.
    Le gris. Le calme. Se serait assis devant la table. Transi de froid,
jusqu'à la tombée de la nuit.
    C'était l'hiver, le jardin mort, la cour herbue. Il n'y aurait per-
sonne pendant des mois, tout est en ordre.
    La route qui conduit jusqua'là còtoie des champs où il n'y avait
rien. Des corbeaux s'envolent ou des pies, on voit mal, la nuit va
tomber.
    La pendule sur le cheminée est en marbre noir, cadran cerclé
d'or et chiffres romains.
    L'homme assis à cette table quelques heures avant retrouvé
mort sur le fumier n'aurait pas été seul, une sentinelle veillait, un
paysan sûr qui n'avait aperçu que le défunt un jour gris, froid, se
serait approché de la fente du volet et l'aurait vu distinctement
détraquer la pendule puis rester prostré sur sa chaise, les coudes
sur la table, la tête dans les mains.
    Comment se fier à ce murmure, l'oreille est en défaut.[33]

What is inside this world, what outside? Is the 'mécanique' which
is 'detraqué' the clock or the book itself? How do the tenses function
– at the simplest level, how are we to read a phrase like 'L'homme
assis à cette table quelques heures avant retrouvé mort sur le fumier'?
Who speaks these words? The old man dreaming? The watcher?
The narrator? But who is the narrator? What does it mean, in such
circumstances: to narrate?
    Pinget has gone well beyond even the most subtle *mise-en-abyme*
of Robbe-Grillet, yet the curious thing is how easy it is to read this
book. Once again, we are carried along by the rhythm established
at the start: 'Le calme. Le gris. De remous aucun.' But it would be
wrong to say we are reading something purely abstract, or even
something akin to a Mallarmé poem. We are somehow at once inside
the room and outside it, at once in sympathy with the solitary occupant and yet not quite at one with him. But that, strangely, is very
much how we feel in relation to ourselves: we grasp ourselves inter-
mittently, we inhabit more the surfaces of our bodies than their
insides, we always hope for insight, full understanding, but alas,
when it comes it is too late, we have changed, it is another person

who has understood... So, later in this novel, a will is mentioned, a judge, we feel that here is a source of supreme authority who will sort everything out, straighten out attributions, sequences, tenses. But nothing comes of it, the will is never found, or perhaps has not yet been written, there is only the murmur, the mumble, in the room, in our ears. In the end the narrative rises in despair: 'Je soussigné dans la pièce froide, ciguë, pendule détraqué, je soussigné dans le marais, chèvre ou carcasse d'oiseau, je soussigné au tournant de la route... Je soussigné sentinelle des morts, au croisement des routes, aux confins des terres si grises dans le carnet de notes...' before sinking back into resigned acceptance: 'Assis à cette table quelques heures avant retrouvé mort sur le fumier, une sentinelle veillait qui n'avait aperçu que le défunt un jour gris, froid, se serait approché de la fente du volet et l'aurait vu distinctement détraquer la pendule puis rester prostré sur sa chaise, les coudes sur la table, la tête dans les mains.'[34]

'La vie nous échappe dans son essence', Pinget had remarked, 'et [on] ne peut la retenir passagèrement que dans un acte d'amour arbitraire, celui de la création.' Like Eliot's magi we feel, as we put the book down, that we have witnessed something of vital importance, but whether it was birth or death it is impossible to tell. Though there is no 'je', no dramatized narrator, this very fact forces us to assume the burden, to try and hold this world together, make sense of it. It is we who become the protagonist of the book, our adventure that of reading it. But it is only an adventure because, as in *Dans le labyrinthe*, we are able, from the first word, to empathize, sympathize, make an imaginative leap. If the book did not first draw us in, it could not then push us away. Every paragraph here forces us to emerge from what had seemed to be a 'real world' and to reconsider it in the light of what follows. What drives the reader forward is the sense – shared by Proust's Marcel – that out of all these contradictions, the truth will emerge. Of course here, as in Proust's novel, truth does not emerge as something other, but only as the recognition of this condition, of our immersion, whether we like it or not, in a world without transcendance. And yet, strangely, the very struggle for transcendance, understanding, gives rise to something which *is* other than the book, and Pinget is right to talk about that something as a voice.

'Voice' has had a bad press in France recently. Jacques Derrida has made it almost his personal mission to free us from an unthinking positing of voice as in some sense primary in our experience. In his study of Husserl, *La Voix et le phénomène*, he makes the point which he is to repeat with growing insistence as he goes on, that voice is anything but immediacy, that the whole phenomenological tradition derived from Husserl has got it wrong, that to speak is to act in time, that speech brings difference and 'deferal' in its wake:

> Il s'agit de produire un nouveau concept d'écriture. On peut l'appeler *gramme* ou *différance*. Le jeu des différences suppose en effet des synthèses et des renvois qui interdisent qu'à aucun moment, en aucun sens, un élément simple soit *présent* en lui-même et ne renvoie qu'à lui-même. Que ce soit dans l'ordre du discours parlé ou du discours écrit, aucun élément qui lui-même n'est pas simplement présent. Cet enchaînement fait que chaque 'élément' – phonème ou graphème – se constitue à partir de la trace en lui des autres éléments de la chaîme ou du système. Cet enchaîne ment, ce tissue, est le *texte* qui ne se produit que dans la transformation d'un autre texte. Rien, ni dans les éléments ni dans le système, n'est nulle part ni jamais simplement présent ou absent.[35]

Derrida would seem to lend support to a developed theory of text as that which is a denial and an overcoming of voice. But I am not sure that what he says is actually so far from what I have in mind when I speak of voice.

What we get in the two novels we have examined is a sense of voice as both immanent and transcendent, as tied to the text and emanating from it, yet somehow more than the text, for the voice is constituted precisely by the gaps in the text, by the shifts from one partial or false voice to the next. This is why it is so misleading to speak of 'texts' and not 'works', and to insist, as Ricardou does, that the work of the novelist is done 'on words' and nowhere else. When Foucault quotes from Beckett's *L'Innommable*, 'Qu'importe qui parle, quelqu'un dit, qu'importe qui parle', or when, at the Cerisy conference, another phrase from that novel was quoted: 'Je suis en mots, je suis fait de mots', it is forgotten that this is not Beckett speaking but one of his characters. And the point about that character is that he is desperately seeking to name himself, to recover himself as *more* than words, to wrest a 'je' from 'quelqu'un dit'. It is in the tension between what can be said and what reality is that the novel exists, that the peculiar voice of *L'Innommable* emerges.

But is it not obvious that there is a voice in the classical novel? Is that voice not far more insistent in Dickens or Tolstoy or Hardy than it is in the modern novel? After all, Dickens meant his work to be read aloud; we know what pleasure he took in doing so himself. I do not think we need to spend too long on this question since the appearance of Barthes' *S/Z*. In that book Barthes demonstrated very convincingly, to my mind, the lack of unity of the 'voice' of the classical novelist, how it is made up of a whole range of different and at times incompatible voices glued together in haphazard ways. He isolates in Balzac the 'voice' of worldly wisdom, of social mores, of accepted symbolisms, of scientific 'truths' and so on. And though Balzac may well strike the English or Russian reader as unbearably crude or banal in comparison with Dickens or Tolstoy, there can be no doubt that Barthes has proved his main point:

> Dans le text classique... la plupart des énoncés sont originés, on peut identifier leur père et propriétaire: c'est tantôt une conscience..., tantôt une culture...La meilleure façon d'imaginer le pluriel classique est alors d'écouter le texte comme un échange chatoyant de voix multiples, posées sur des ondes différentes et saisies par moments d'un *fading* brusque...36

By contrast, he says, in the modern novel, 'le langage parle, c'est tout'. This isn't an altogether happy way of putting it, I think. For, if we are to believe Pinget, what the novelist is doing is trying to find the voice that is truly his out of the blur of jumbled voices which he has to make use of and which, in a sense, constantly make use of him.

To help define this a little more clearly it may be useful to turn to some English examples. Here is the ending of Virginia Woolf's *Mrs Dalloway*:

> 'I will come,' said Peter, and he sat on for a moment. What is this terror? What is this ecstasy? he thought to himself. What is it that fills me with extraordinary excitement?
>
> It is Clarissa, he said.
>
> For there she was.

'For there she was.' How little is conveyed by those words, how ordinary is the expression. And yet, coming as it does at the very end of the novel, the phrase is a sign of momentous event. After those four words the book is over. But we experience, for the first time – even if only momentarily – the central figure in her fullness. It is as if, when speech is over, there – just there, in front of us – *she* is. Notice too that 'I will come' is in inverted commas, but although the narrative adds that the penultimate phrase is said by Peter, it is not closed in inverted commas: *It is Clarissa, he said.* Clearly the last two phrases stand apart from the rest of the book; they are its sum-mation and, in a sense, both the cause and result of its being. It is an ending no classical novel would have been satisfied with, but here it releases at last the voice which had been felt straining to find itself in the two hundred pages which precede it.

The last few lines of any novel were always for Virginia Woolf that towards which she struggled in the course of her work. One can see this particularly clearly in the lay-out of *The Waves*, with a gap in the page and then, in italics, the single sentence: *The waves broke on the shore.* The italicization tells us what she was after: a voice that would be utterly impersonal, uncontaminated by any merely human hopes and desires. But the typographical solution here is perhaps a bit of a cheat, and a more interesting example is the ending of her very last book, *Between the Acts*:

> Isa let her sewing drop. The great hooded chairs had become enormous. And Giles too. And Isa too against the window. The window was all sky without colour. The House had lost its shelter. It was night before roads were made, or houses. It was the night that dwellers in caves had watched from some high place among the rocks.
> Then the curtain rose. They spoke.

The voice of the book starts when the voices of the book have come to an end. But, paradoxically, it is only because of the book that the voice is possible: *Then the curtain rose. They spoke.*

And here now are three very different examples from the work of another woman writer, perhaps almost as great as Virginia Woolf, but more ironic, cruel, elusive. First, the ending of Muriel Spark's *The Driver's Seat*: 'He sees already the gleaming buttons on the policemen's uniforms, hears the cold and the confiding, the hot and the barking voices, sees already the holsters and the epaulettes and all those trappings devised to protect them from the indecent exposure of fear and pity, pity and fear.' So much depends – in our understanding of the whole novel – on that strange inversion / repetition of the end. Who says this? Clearly not Muriel Spark (for she could say it much more simply), nor 'the language', nor 'the text'. What seems to happen is that the voice which speaks calls attention to itself, denies its absolute authority. And this throws us into confusion at the same time as it frees us from restriction. As the policemen are protected by their trappings, so we are usually protected by the narrative voice in a novel. To listen to that voice, telling us 'what happened', is to be freed from the responsibility of having to make choices, take decisions. Here the language opens up, so to speak, and through the cracks come not the soothing and expected words but the thing itself: fear because we sense that there is no safety anywhere in the world; pity because we recognize that this is our condition. Each by itself would be a falsehood; together they are a truth. A voice emerges from the action of the novel, speaks the words and then vanishes. The novel is finished.

Here is the opening of *Not to Disturb*:

> The other servants fall silent as Lister enters the room.
> 'Their life,' says Lister, 'a general mist of error. Their death, a hideous storm of terror. – I quote from *The Duchess of Malfi* by John Webster, an English dramatist of old.'

Lister appropriates Webster's words, as the narrative appropriates Lister's. We are aware at once of the clash of different registers, and the effect is disconcerting. The words are lifted out of their context and affect us as more than the mere carriers of meaning: they tell us something about Lister and something about what is about to happen or has happened in the novel, and about the way Lister understands that. Because of the way the quote is introduced – not as epigraph, not even indented and given correct line-endings, but embedded within the quotation marks of Lister's speech – the words give us a sense too of their *inappropriateness* to the uniqueness of the present case. We sense a gap between what is happening and how it is seen or described. Muriel Spark thus keeps the door of history open, so to speak, in the face of writing's perennial determination to close it off. In the clash of registers of this opening the theme of the whole book is not only stated but made tangible for the reader.

Even more complex is the opening of her next novel, *The Hothouse by the East River*. Here Muriel Spark presents us with one short sentence and then with a space on the page, before the book seems really to start. Is this then *The Waves* in reverse? No, for that of course is impossible: fullness of voice is not a given, it must be earned. Here is the opening sentence: 'If only it were true that all's well that ends well, if only it were true.' We sense at once that someone is speaking. But who? For in a sense this *is* a kind of absolute, it does stand outside the rest of the novel. As in *Not to Disturb* the embedded quote explodes here at the start and we get a kind of fall-out from it over the rest of the novel. And yet its status is queer, much queerer even than the Webster. It gestures towards fullness, inclusivity, objectivity, the confidence of the classical novelist, yet it does so nostalgically, as though cut off for ever from the source of authority.

What we get in Muriel Spark is that the narrator himself becomes part of the drama, but the narrator is never a persona, only that which speaks. It is as if the narrative feels that it can never speak simply, fully, never find 'its own voice', must always borrow and be hemmed in by someone else's way of putting things. By acknowledging this and dramatizing it, Muriel Spark conveys a sense of what a true narrative might be, a fully authoritative voice, 'the veritable small', as Stevens called it, and he went on, 'so that each of us / Beholds himself in you and hears his voice / In yours...' ('To an Old Philosopher in Rome').

Let us try and draw some of the strands of this argument together. First of all it is possible that I have been unfair to Robbe-Grillet. It is possible that my quarrel with him is only one more instance of the debate which always breaks out in the wake of abstraction (though the debate has till now tended to be confined to the world of painting.) We have heard my kind of argument in connection with Mondrian and Malevich and Ben Nicholson. It so happens that I prefer works which exist on the edge of the divide between the figurative and the abstract – Cubism, the art of Picasso and Klee, Bacon and Hockney. But the debate may not be a very meaningful one because different generations and even different individuals will see the divide in different places: many paintings by Monet, Klee and even Bacon could be regarded as abstract and thus open to all the objections I made earlier; while it could be argued that Ben Nicholson's white reliefs, for instance, are not abstract at all but still lives of a sort.[37] It is better therefore to point to the issue and withdraw.

In the case of critical theory, however, one's attitude must be different. It is easy to see how the notion of the disappearance of the author and the primacy of the text came about. I have tried to argue that what we loosely call structuralism is not only true to the facts but a great step forward in our understanding of ourselves and the world. Nevertheless it has built into it certain presuppositions which threaten, if allowed to go unchallenged, to impoverish us considerably. Barthes' remark that 'le problème esthétique est simplement de savoir comment mobiliser ce discontinu fatal, comment lui donner un souffle, un temps, une histoire' is in one sense true, but in another it is dangerously misleading. At a stroke it abolishes the dimension of history and of tradition. It does this of course in the interests of freeing us from a false history, a bogus tradition.

But this hatred of history (which is endemic to modernism, from Kierkegaard through Joyce to Robbe-Grillet) is something that should be treated with caution. Instead, as we know, it is greeted with cries of joy by critics and academics. And this is easy to understand. It is obviously easier to deal with a 'text' than with something as problematic as a writer or an alien culture. And the rise of 'great books' courses everywhere in the universities of the Western world has encouraged such an attitude. But of course in doing this the critics are falling into just the same error as the biographical critics they set out to demolish: they are removing the problematic from the work. For to cut a work off from its source is to cut it off from life. A work of literature is not an inert piece of matter which can be carved up on the dissecting table of the critic's desk. That is why I have stressed the centrality of the notion of voice. For it is a notion which avoids, so it seems to me, both the biographical and the textual temptations. And after all, when Keats read Chapman's translations of Homer he said:

> Oft of one wide expanse had I been told
> That deep-browed Homer ruled as his demesne;
> Yet did I never breathe its pure serene
> Till I heard Chapman speak out loud and bold.

Of course Keats never heard Chapman speak; he read his book. But it was not a text that he read; it was a voice that he heard.

Voice is something that the attentive reader hears but which always eludes the writer himself. He who thinks he has it, loses it; he who goes on groping for it, releases it. The situation, as between writer and reader, will always be asymmetrical. For the writer, as Henry James knew, it will always be the middle years, the time before, the time of failure, the time when it is necessary to start again. But for the reader the writer's middles are beginning and end, and in his work he sees the writer transformed, as Mallarmé said eternity transforms us, into himself: it always takes another to hear the voice.

I have said that the modern critic has succumbed to the temptation to close his ears to the call of that other, and I have suggested reasons for this. But what is mostly forgotten in talk of 'texte' and 'écriture' and 'structure' is that hearing this other voice come out of the past – or the present – is the source of the most profound joy (not pleasure, as a critic like Barthes, cut off by his demythologizing urge from any sense of time as beneficial, is forced to say). And nothing illustrates this better than a scene which occurs at the start of Dante's

Commedia, that great poem which begins in sleep before any voices can speak and ends with a vision that finally cuts off speech. The pilgrim Dante has been pushed back from his assault on the mountain of salvation, and turns disconsolate to find a figure coming towards him on the barren shore. He asks who he is and the other answers, simply, that he was a Mantuan, born under Caesar, in the time of the false and lying gods. For Virgil the meaning of his life is its failure and his own damnation. But for Dante it is far otherwise:

> 'Or se' tu quel Virgilio, e quella fonte,
>   che spandi di parlar si largo fiume?'
>   rispos'io lui con vergognosa fronte.
>
> 'O degli altri poeti onore e lume,
>   vagliami il lungo studio e il grande amore,
>   che m'ha fatto cercar lo tuo volume.
>
> Tu se' lo mio maestro, e il mio autore;
>   tu se' solo colui, da cu'io tolsi
>   lo bello stile, che m'ha fatto onore.'[38]

This is a father who does not crush his child but helps him to find his own words, gives him the confidence to discover his own voice. And as Virgil was to Dante, Dante was to Eliot, and so it goes on. Let us remember that before we are critics we are readers and before we are readers we are human beings. Art is there to remind us of precisely that.

8 *Perec's* La Vie mode d'emploi

Nothing in Perec's earlier work could have prepared one for *La Vie mode d'emploi*.[1] To open that book after reading even such fine novels as *Un homme qui dort* and *La Disparition* is to experience the same sense of shock and delight that one gets from turning to *Ulysses* after *A Portrait of the Artist* or to *A la Recherche du temps perdu* after *Pastiches et mélanges*. It is not just that it is a very big book (six hundred pages of text and another hundred of 'apparatus'). When English or American or Australian writers conceive of a Major Novel they can only think of it as an ordinary novel blown up (think of Burgess, Mailer, Carey). *La Vie mode d'emploi* is in quite a different category. It is encyclopaedic as *Ulysses* is encyclopaedic, though in its calmness and restraint it is more reminiscent of earlier encyclopaedic works, such as Dante's *Commedia* or Chaucer's *Canterbury Tales*. This is a large claim to make and I never thought to make it of any book written today. I hope that what follows will lend some credence to it, though inevitably it is a preliminary and tentative sketch, for the book was only published in 1978 and it will take us many years to catch up with it.

Serge Valène is dying. He has lived in the same building for close on sixty years (1919-1975), and he conceives the idea of a painting which will depict the entire building with its façade removed so that all the front rooms, the stairs, the entrance hall, and lift are visible. And, like those doll's houses in which are reproduced in miniature every detail of a normal house, his painting will include every picture on every wall, every carpet and every cat, every newspaper and hot-water-bottle and coffee-pot – as well of course as all the people who, at that moment, are sitting or standing or lying in these rooms.

As he thinks of his picture Valène lets his memory play on the objects and their owners and on the lives of those owners as he has observed them or as they have been told to him over the years. Each detail will be discrete, each room an entity; yet naturally, in a building where people have lived next to each other for a certain length of time, there will be links between the lives of the various inhabitants. A central place in Valène's memory, and thus in the book, is reserved for Percival Bartlebooth, an eccentric English millionaire. Early in life Bartlebooth came to the decision that he would use his fortune to live a perfectly planned existence. For ten years, from the age of twenty-five to thirty-five (1925-35), he would take lessons in water-colour painting (from Valène). For the next twenty years he and his manservant Smautf would travel round the world, taking in a differ-ent port or seaside resort every fortnight. Here Bartlebooth would paint a watercolour of the seascape and Smautf would dispatch the finished painting back to Paris where Gaspard Winckler (also living in the building) would turn it into a jigsaw puzzle consisting of seven hundred and fifty wooden pieces. These he would put in a box (supplied by another resident, Mme Hourcade), number the box, and put it away. Five hundred such boxes await Bartlebooth on his return, and he devotes the next twenty years (1955-75) to solving the puzzles they contain, also at the rate of one a fortnight. As each is completed it is passed to Morellet, an ex-laboratory assistant with a room in the attics next to Valène. His task is to bind the puzzle together in such a way that he is then able to lift off the original watercolour. This Bartlebooth immediately has sent to the place where it was painted, where a chemical dissolves the paint and the pristine sheet is sent back to him. In this way Bartlebooth will have lived from his twenty-fifth to his seventy-fifth year engaged in a pursuit that is totally absorbing and totally useless. He will have enjoyed himself, harmed no-one, and by the end will have left abso-lutely no trace of his fifty years of concentrated activity: 'Il voulait que le projet tout entier se referme sur lui-même sans laisser de traces, comme une mer d'huile qui se referme sur un homme qui se noie, il voulait que rien, absolument rien n'en subsiste, qu'il n'en sorte rien que le vide, la blancheur immaculée du rien, la perfection gratuite de l'inutile' (pp.481-82). The scheme of a madman perhaps, but also an image, lucidly conceived and unflinchingly carried out, of what we all do or do not do with our lives in an irredeemably secular world.

The book is thus presented to us under the aegis of two impera-tives. The first, found in the epigraph from Jules Verne, is 'regarde de tous tes yeux, regarde'. The second, found in the preamble, a meditation on jigsaw-puzzles (which is repeated verbatim at the start of the chapter on Winckler's workshop), has to do with the role of games in art and life. We could intuit from his other work, even if he had not been explicit about it in *Espèces d'espaces* (1974), that delightful meditation on the spaces we inhabit, that for Perec there is a moral dimension to both looking and game-playing. Sitting in a café gazing at a Parisian street he admonishes himself: don't just note the out-of-the-way, the peculiar; never use the word 'etcetera'. To learn to look is to learn to free one-self from one's prejudices and assumptions. Valéry, following Degas, had asked the painter to learn to see by drawing a lump of coal or a handkerchief dropped on to a table, whose folds and wrinkles would therefore be unique. Perec urges himself to be patient, to describe exactly what is going on in the street, just what sequence of movements is required to accomplish something as simple as taking the underground. And this is where play comes in: topological play, for instance. For left to our own instincts we would always walk the same streets, and probably in the same order. So: 'Essayer de calculer, en s'aidant de cartes et de plans adéquats, un itinéraire qui permettrait de prendre successivement tous les autobus de la capitale.' And then, naturally, follow it.

How does all this affect the novel? Here is an example, necessarily rather long. It consists of most of Chapter 19, 'Altamont 1', and the start of Chapter 20, 'Moreau 1'. The titles indicate that we are in the Altamont flat and the Moreau flat for the first time:[2]

Au second, chez les Altamont, on prépare la traditionelle réception annuelle. Il y aura un buffet dans chacune des cinq pièces en façade de l'appartement. Dans celle-ci... les tapis ont été roulés, mettant en évidence un précieux parquet cloisonné. Presque tous les meubles ont été enlevés; il ne reste que huit chaises en boix laqué, au dossier décoré de scènes évoquant la guerre des Boxers.

Il n'y a aucun tableau sur les murs, car les murs et les portes sont eux-mêmes décor: ils sont revêtus d'une toile peinte, un panorama somptueux dont les quelques effets de trompe-l'œil laissent penser qu'il s'agit d'une copie exécutée spécialement pour cette pièce à partir de cartons vraisemblablement plus anciens, représentant la vie aux Indes telle que l'imagination populaire pouvait la concevoir dans la deuxième moitié du dix-neuvième siècle: d'abord une jungle luxuriante peuplée de singes aux yeux énormes, puis une clairière aux bords d'un marigot dans lequel trois éléphants s'ébrouent en s'aspergeant mutuellement; plus loin encore des paillotes sur pilotis devant lesquelles des femmes en saris jaunes, bleu ciel et vert d'eau et des hommes vêtus de pagnes font sécher des feuilles de thé et des racines de gingembre cependant que d'autres, installés devant des bâtis de bois, décorent de grands carrés de cachemire à l'aide de blocs sculptés qu'ils trempent dans des pots remplis de teintures végétales; enfin, sur la droite, une scène classique de chasse au tigre....

Sur le mur de gauche, au centre, une vaste cheminée de marbre rose surmontée d'un grand miroir; sur la tablette, un haut vase de cristal, de section rectangulaire, rempli d'immortelles, et une tirelire mille neuf cent: c'est un nègre en pied, au large sourire, vaguement contorsionné; il est vêtu d'un ample ciré écossais à dominantes rouges, porte des gants blancs, des lunettes à monture d'acier et un chapeau haut-de-forme décoré de *stars and stripes* portant en larges caractères bleus et rouges le chiffre '75'. Sa main gauche...

Assis sur un tabouret entre le buffet et la porte qui donne sur le grand vestibule, le dos appuyé au mur, les jambes tendues et légèrement écartées, se trouve le seul personnage vivant de la scène: un domestique en pantalon noir et vest blanche; c'est un homme d'une trentaine d'années à la figure ronde et rouge; il lit avec un air de parfait ennui le prière d'insérer d'un roman sur la couverture duquel une femme presque nue couchée dans un hamac, un long fume-cigarettes aux lèvres, pointe négligemment un petit revolver à crosse de nacre en direction du lecteur:

'Dans *"La Souricière"*, le dernier roman de Paul Winther, le lecteur retrouvera avec plaisir le héros favori de l'auteur de *"Couche-la dans le sainfoin"*, *"Les Écossais sont en colère"*, *"L'Homme à l'imperméable"* et tant d'autres valcurs dûres de la littérature policière d'aujourd'hui et de demain: le Capitaine Horty, qui sera cette fois aux prises avec un dangereux psychopathe semant la mort dans un port de la Baltique.'

Chapitre XX. Moreau, 1.

Une chambre du grand appartement du premier étage. Le sol est couvert d'une moquette couleur tabac; les murs sont tendus de panneaux de jute gris clair.

Il y a trois personnes dans la pièce. L'une est une vieille femme, Madame Moreau, la propriétaire de l'appartement. Elle est couchée dans un grand lit-bateau, sous une courte-pointe blanche semée de fleurs bleues.

Debout devant le lit, l'amie d'enfance de Madame Moreau, Madame Trévins, vêtue d'un imperméable et d'un foulard de cachemire, sort de son sac à main, pour la lui montrer, une carte postale qu'elle vient de recevoir: elle représente un singe, coiffé d'une casquette, au volant d'une camionnette. Un phylactère rose se déploie au-dessus, avec l'inscription: *Souvenir de Saint-Mouezy-sur-Éon.*

A la droite du lit, sur la table de nuit, il y a... (pp.97-100)

What is so shocking about this? What is going on here that does not normally go on in novels? It is as well to proceed slowly in such circumstances, for narrative effects are difficult to pin down. Let us look first at the kind of description we find in an 'ordinary' novel:

> His apartment was small and stuffy and impersonal. He might have moved in that afternoon. On a coffee table in front of a hard green davenport was a half-empty Scotch bottle and melted ice in a bowl and three empty fizzwater bottles and two glasses and a glass ashtray loaded with stubs with and without lipstick. There wasn't a photograph or a personal article of any kind in the place. It might have been a hotel room rented for a meeting or a farewell, for a few drinks and a talk, for a roll in the hay. It didn't look like a place where anyone lived.

I have put 'ordinary' in inverted commas because of course no two novels are quite the same. This is a passage from Raymond Chandler's *The Long Goodbye* and it serves our purpose well. What is going on here is perfectly obvious. Marlowe has come to the flat to look for clues, and the apparently objective description in fact screams a message out at us: this is the kind of man Terry Lennox is or the kind of man he has allowed himself to become. The clues are laid before us as they are laid before Marlowe, and one look is enough to decipher them. As if that were not enough the author concludes by giving his explanation: 'It didn't look like a place where anyone lived.'

The passage perhaps serves our purpose too well. The description is strongly motivated, as it always is in novels. Rooms and people are as they are because of the role they have to play in the story. But thrillers by their very nature are more formal than 'normal' novels; for that reason they bring out their essence, but fail to show how well this essence is usually concealed. For, as we are beginning to learn, 'realism' is not something simple or monumental but the result of a series of subtle adjustments whose purpose is to confirm our belief in a background against which the events are played out and in the ultimate meaningfulness of those events which take place within that background.[3] But what of Perec's descriptions? After all, what *is* the story? Bartlebooth's 'story' certainly runs through the book, surfacing more frequently than any other, but if we look at the title-page we see that the book is subtitled *romans*, not *roman*. At the back, alongside the index, is a 'Rappel de quelques-unes des histoires racontées dans cet ouvrage', and there are over a hundred of these. Mme Moreau's life, for example, in no way overlaps with that of the Altamonts, except for a single acquaintance they have in common. Both their 'stories' simply co-exist within the covers of the same book.

Is Perec then a hyper-realist, only concerned to detail what is to be found in the average Parisian building around 1975? Or does he perhaps wish to tell us something about the characters through the descriptions? It is true that we learn that the Altamonts are wealthy and Mme Moreau bedridden. But why this particular wallpaper, why that particular postcard? Why tell us in detail what the servant is reading, and why is he reading just that? It cannot be to create an effect of realism, for the minute description of the money-box and the postcard would surely not be necessary for that. On the contrary. What we realize as we read this book is how very selective the ordinary novelist is and how Perec's method actually destroys the delicate balance of foreground and background on which novels depend for their effect of reality. But then this is in keeping with what new art always does: it does not render the old obsolete but helps to make us see the often hidden parameters and conventions of the old.

The selection of items to be described and the degree of detail with which they will be described is dictated to Chandler by two things: what *he* expects of a novel and what he knows his public expects. It is of course impossible to disentangle the two in even the most commercially-minded writer. But what is the writer to do who feels that the traditional motivation is inadequate? As we know, there are as many answers to this question as there are major modern works. But what of Perec? The feeling mounts as one reads that there are very good reasons why the descriptions are as they are, but that these reasons will always escape us. Perec has himself explained some of his main procedures in writing the book, and though his explanations do not of course tell us what the book is *like*, any more than a composer's programme note tells us what his music is like, they are certainly worth attending to. As long ago as 1972, he tells us, he had three distinct projects in mind: a novel about a jigsaw-puzzle-playing millionaire; a novel about a large Parisian building; and a novel based on the Graeco-Latin square of ten.[4] The present book took off when he realized that house and square could be one and the same, and that this was where the millionaire could live. As my plan shows, there are a hundred rooms in the front part of the house, including stairs and so on, corresponding to the hundred boxes of the square. Each room will have a chapter devoted to it and each chapter's contents will be dictated by the square's numbers. But to have gone through the rooms in sequence would have been tedious for both writer and reader (there are deeper reasons, as I hope to show); yet he could no more leave the moves from room to room to chance than he could leave the itemizing of the contents of the rooms. What he did was to adapt to his ten-by-ten square the sequence of moves known to amateurs of chess as the Polygraph of the Knight, whereby the chess Knight is made to cover the entire board without ever covering the same square twice. My plan shows how he did this, starting on the stairs, five from the right and five from the bottom, making his first move to third from right and fourth from bottom, and ending up in Bartlebooth's study, first on left and five from bottom.[5]

There are numerous other constraints operating in the construction of the book. In the descriptions of Hutting's twenty-four portraits in Chapter 59, for instance, Perec has set himself the task of embedding the names of all his friends and colleagues at OULIPO. And in the description of the 179 sequences Valène is going to paint round the painting of the building which he will paint himself painting, up in his attic room, first from right and second from top, each description takes sixty letters, the spaces between words counting as single letters. The last of these is, naturally, 'le vieux peintre faisant tenir toute la maison dans sa toile'.

Such devices help generate and control the material. They in no way guarantee the quality of the book. As David Roberts has remarked in an informative article on Peter Maxwell Davies's recent music, 'there is nothing magical about the employment of a magic square as an aid to composition. In the case of *A Mirror of Whitening Light* the use of the Mercury matrix...contributes to one of the composer's finest works; in the case of *Westerlings* the same matrix does nothing to prevent the work from being one of Davies's most disappointing'.[6] As we will see, one of the interesting things about Perec's novel is that it is an exploration of the implications of such procedures as well as an example of them. But first we must ask what the effect is on the reader as he experiences the book for the first time. And of course, as soon as we put it like that we realize that, as with all works of art, effect is never single. Let us try then to disentangle some of the many things that happen to us as we read this novel.

1/1 Honoré HUTT... ING 59	7/8 83	6/9 SMAUTF 15	5/10 SUTTON 10	10/2 ORLOWSKA 48	3/4 ALBIN 48	8/6 Morellet 7	2/3 Simpson PLASSAERT 52	3/5 Troyan S SA E 45	4/7 Troquet RT 54
8/7 ...ING 97	2/2 G 11	1/8 GRATIOLET 58	7/9 82	6/10 CRESPI 16	10/3 NIETO & ROGERS 9	9/5 Jérôme 46	3/4 Fresnel 55	4/6 BREIDEL 6	5/1 VALÈNE 51
9/6 Brodin-Gratiolet CINOC 84	8/1 60	2/3 DINTEVILLE 96	2/8 14	1/9 47	7/10 S 56	10/4 49	4/5 WINKLER 8	5/7 Jérôme 83	6/2 44
10/5 REOL Hourcade 12	9/7 98	8/2 R O R S 81	4/4 Gratiolet 86	3/8 et 95	2/9 T 17	1/10 28	3/6 Hébert FOULEROT 45	6/1 50	7/3 5
2/10 BERGER Speiss 61	10/6 85	9/1 13	8/3 Grifalconi 80	5/9 S CH A S SI M 87	4/8 A 79	3/9 94	6/7 Echard MARQUISEAUX 4	7/2 41	1/4 30
4/9 BARTLEBOOTH 99	3/10 70	10/7 26	9/2 80	8/4 Danglars 87	6/6 I 1	5/8 42	7/1 Colomb FOUREAU 29	1/3 93	2/5 3
6/8 ALTAMONT 25	5/5 62	4/10 Appenzzell 88	10/1 69	9/3 19	8/5 36	7/7 R 78	1/2 DE BEAUMONT 2	2/4 31	3/6 40
3/2 MOREAU 71	4/3 65	5/4 20	6/5 23	7/6 89	1/7 62	2/1 S 34	8/8 LOUVET 37	9/9 77	10/10 92
5/3 SERVICE ENTRANCE 63	6/4 MARCIA (S H O P) 24	7/5 66	1/6 73	2/7 CONCIERGE 35	3/1 ENTRANCE HALL 22	4/2 90	9/10 MARCIA MASSY 75	10/8 39	8/9 32
7/4	1/5 CELLARS 72	2/6 BUILERS 64	3/7 21	4/1 CELLARS 67	5/2 LIFT MACHINERY 74	6/3 38	10/9 CELLARS 33	8/10 91	9/8 76

11 RUE SIMON-CRUBELLIER

I have used the diagram Perec appended to his novel, but have defined more clearly the number of rooms occupied by each inhabitant. Previous inhabitants in lower case. The figures in the top left-hand corner of each square refer to the Graeco-Roman magic square as used by Perec. The figures in the bottom right-hand corner, referring to the chapter numbers, have been added for the reader's convenience.

Sometimes the effect of returning to a particular flat long after our last visit helps to fill out our picture of what is going on or to confirm or explain something that had been left hanging in the air. Thus the maths notebook of Chapter 2 is found in Chapter 40 to belong to one of the Breidel daughters, and the picture by Forbes in the Marquiseaux apartment is discovered later to have been given to the young couple by Mme Marcia; or the blind piano-tuner at work in Mme de Beaumont's salon in Chapter 2 is found much later to have been brought there by his grandson, who sits on the stairs, in Chapter 78, reading the fictionalized biography of Carel van Loorens, the famous explorer. Sometimes the 'story' of one character or family is merely suspended at the end of one chapter and taken up again when we next enter their flat. Sometimes such filling out brings a shock with it, as when the adorable Flora Champigny stuck in the lift in 1925 turns out to be the same as old Mme Albin who lives in one of the attic rooms; or as when, after hearing a great deal about Rémi Rorschash, about his fabulous wife the Australian child-star Olivia Norvell and her preparations for her fifty-sixth round-the-world tour, we come to Rémi's own room and learn that it will remain empty for ever, since he is dead. Such effects have something in common with those suggested by the authors of a book on Islamic design. 'These symmetries,' they write, talking of Islamic carpets, 'usually relate to the geometric grid upon which the whole carpet is based. The overall pattern, as with the arabesque, is arbitrarily defined by a border which is unrelated to the main field. This gives the observer the impression of looking through a trap-door to a section of the continuing pattern'.[7]

The pattern, though, rarely brings with it the sense of satisfying closure. On the contrary. Mme Nochère, the concierge, finds a packet on the stairs which is never claimed: 'L'énigme ne fut jamais résolue.' Even the knowledge that it was Mme Marcia who gave the Forbes painting to the Marquiseaux does not actually advance us at all: it remains one more fact to add to the ever-growing set of facts the book presents us with. In the attic room inhabited by Elzbieta Orlowska (la Belle Polonaise, as everyone calls her) a stool acts as a bedside table. It is covered with books:

un volumineux essai intitulé *The Arabian Knights. New Visions on the Islamic Feudalism in the Beginnings of the Hegira*, signé d'un certain Charles Nunneley, et un roman policier de Lawrence Wargrave, *Le juge est l'assassin*: X a tué A de telle façon que la justice, qui le sait, ne peut l'inculper. Le juge d'instruction tue B de telle

façon que X est suspecté, arrêté, jugé, reconnu coupable et exé-
cuté sans avoir jamais rien pu faire pour prouver son innocence.
Le sol est couvert d'un linoléum rouge sombre. (pp.334-35)

Who is Charles Nunneley? Why mention him? Why the odd English
of the title? Why summarize Lawrence Wargrave's book for us?
We are faced with the effect of enumeration, which is atomization.
Just as each chapter is distinct, so within the chapters the items fail
to link up. The intrusion of the detective-story plot into the description of the room, rather like the intrusion of the thriller cover into
the Altamont's drawing room or the postcard into Mme Moreau's,
has the effect of decentring the novel. Nothing comes together.
Everything moves away from everything else, asserting its own
right to our attention but then forcing us to ask why it should be
there at all as it does not seem to lead anywhere.

One result of this is humour. This is one of the funniest books
since *Watt* or *Zazie dans le métro*. Cinoc (Cinoque? Chinoque?
Tchinosse? No-one is sure how it should be pronounced) – Cinoc
is in his kitchen, 'un vieillard maigre et sec vêtu d'un gilet de flanelle
d'un vert pisseux'. For many years he worked on the Larousse dic-
tionaries, charged with the odd but presumably necessary task of
taking out obsolete words to make room for all the new ones:

Quand il prit sa retraite, en mille neuf cent soixante-cinq, après
cinquante-trois ans de scrupuleux services, il avait fait disparaître
des centaines et des milliers d'outils, de techniques, de coutumes,
de croyances, de dictons, de plats, de jeux, de sobriquets, de poids
et de mesures; il avait rayé de la carte des dizaines d'îles, des
centaines de villes et de fleuves, des milliers de chefs-lieux de
canton; il avait renvoyé à leur annonymat taxinomique des centaines de sortes de vache, des espèces d'oiseaux, d'insectes et de
serpents, des poissons un peu spéciaux, des variétés de coquil-
lages, des plantes pas tout à fait pareilles, des types particuliers
de légumes et de fruits; il avait fait s'évanouir dans la nuit des
temps des cohortes de géographes, de missionaires, d'entomo-
logistes, de Pères de l'Église, d'homme de lettres, de généraux,
de Dieux et de Démons. . . . Où étaient passés ces *abounas*, métro-
politains de l'Église éthiopienne, ces *palatines*, fourrures que les
femmes portaient sur le cou en hiver. . ., et ces *chandernagors*, ces
sous-officiers tout chamarrés d'or qui précédaient les défilés sous
le Second Empire? Qu'étaient devenus Léopold-Rudolph von
Schwanzenbad-Hodenthaler dont l'action d'éclat à Eisenühr avait
permis à Zimmerwald de remporter la victoire a Kisàszony? Et

Uz (Jean-Pierre), 1720–1796, poètie allemand...?   (pp.361–62)

Our laughter stems from pleasure and bewilderment. We admire the abundance but wonder; is he having us on? Did these people really exist? And how marvellously that low-style *ubi sunt* rises out of the simple description of an old man in his kitchen.

When Aristotle said that tragedy dealt with the probable he accurately defined the area in which the novel would operate. Perec's novel continually forces us to question our sense of what is probable and what is improbable but likely to be true. Interestingly, Western art as a whole is also committed to two other notions discussed by Aristotle in the *Poetics*: destiny and revelation. In Perec both of these are subverted. The effect of all those summaries of detective stories, for instance, is precisely to drain them of their inner forward momentum, and the same is true of the various stories that are recounted about the characters in the book. Their meaning emerges not from anything within them which is eventually revealed, but from their relation to all the other stories. There is thus no revelation but only pattern, and lives do not make any 'final sense' but are simply seen to take on certain shapes.

And there are so many lives, so many stories. Stories of the present inhabitants of the house and their families: Elisabeth Breidel, daughter of Fernand de Beaumont the archaeologist and Véra Orlova the singer and pupil of Schoenberg, as an au pair in England inadvertently kills a baby in her care and flees the vengeance of the father until flight becomes more unbearable than surrender and she writes begging him to come and kill her; Mme Moreau, the quiet little peasant who finds in her widowhood that she has an amazing business brain and makes a fortune selling do-it-yourself equipment to all the millions of Europeans now rich enough to own a weekend home but too poor to hire a professional to do it up for them; Léon Marcia who, as a servant in a luxury hotel in the Tessino, discovers in himself a voracious appetite for books and is given enough money by the clients of the hotel to go and study with Panofsky. Then there are the previous inhabitants, such as Fresnel, the cook bitten by the acting bug who ends up working in New York for the amazing Grace Twinker; Massy, the racing cyclist dogged by bad luck whose gangster brother-in-law has his marriage saved by plastic surgery; Helène Brodin, descendant of the first owner of the building, who coolly kills off the three thugs who murdered her husband before coming back to Paris to live quietly in the house for the rest of her life. There are the casual visitors, such as 'Hortense', the sex-change pop-star managed by the Marquiseaux and now waiting in their drawing room for them to emerge from their bath. And there are the characters who do not appear at all but are merely mentioned in connexion with someone else, such as Grace Twinker, who dreams of reviving her fabulous life in a Broadway musical which she will direct herself; or Lady Forthright and her clocks, whose tragic story is painted by the Newcastle artist Forbes; or Lord Ashtray and his ties and passion for three-dimensional geometry; or the atomic physicist Kolliker,

> qui avait perdu bras et jambes lors du bombardement de son laboratoire mais que l'on considérait comme le cerveau le plus évolué de son temps bien qu'il fût par surcroît sourd et muet: constamment entouré de quatre gardes du corps et assisté d'un ingénieur spécialisé qui avait suivi un entraînement intensif à seule fin de lire sur ses lèvres les équations qu'il transcrivait ensuite sur des tableaux noirs   (p.375);

or the hamster Polonius, bought by Rémi Rorschash for Olivia Norvell shortly after they had met:

> Ils avaient vu dans un music-hall de Stuttgart un montreur d'animaux et avaient été à ce point passionés par les prouesses sportives du hamster Ludovic – aussi à l'aise aux anneaux qu'à la barre fixe, au trapèze ou aux barres parallèles – qu'ils avaient demandé à l'acheter. Le montreur, Lefèvre, avait refusé, mais leur avait vendu un couple – Gertrude et Sigismond – auquel il avait appris à jouer aux dominos. La tradition s'était perpétuée de génération en génération, les parents apprenant chque fois spontanément à jouer à leurs rejetons. Malheuresement, l'hiver précédent, une épidémie avait presque entièrement détruit la petite colonie: l'unique survivant, Polonius, ne pouvait jouer seul et, qui plus est, était condamné à dépérir s'il ne pouvait continuer à pratiquer son passe-temps favori. Aussi fallait-il, une fois par semaine, le mener à Meudon chez le montreur qui, aujourd'hui retiré, continuait pour son seul plaisir à élever des petits animaux savants.   (pp.485-86)

The effect of all these *romans* and *romans* within *romans* and glimpses of other *romans* within those is not only funny. It also makes us conscious of the variety of life and of its ultimate mysteriousness. Why does Fernand de Beaumont commit suicide? Why does Grifalconi make no effort to stop his wife running away with Hebert? Why does Mme Fresnel hardly react to her husband's leaving her, go on living in the flat for most of her life and, when he does return, years later, show him the door and then leave for good herself, going to live (rather unhappily) with her son and daughter-in-law? Novelists usually provide answers to such questions; indeed, they only raise them in order to answer them. Perec on the other hand provides no answers, he merely allows the play of contrasting stories to reflect on each other. And the reason is plain: the characters themselves do not know why they do these things; they merely do them.

We realize, reading this book, how very linear the traditional novel is, and how this linearity goes hand in hand with the idea of destiny and discovery, which in turn is linked to a notion of character and anecdote. Even when a writer as boldly innovatory as Joyce wants to get away from the anecdotal and the linear he can only do it by trying to present Bloom as Everyman. Joyce, like Freud, was very often confused by his own instincts and interpreted his discoveries in terms of the nineteenth-century patterns of thought which these very discoveries were in the process of subverting. Thus 'Cyclops' and 'Ithaca' pull in one direction, centrifugally, while 'Circe' and 'Penelope', for all their flirtation with fragmentation and the dissolution of self, really affirm a rather old-fashioned view of character and archetypes. It is as though the discoveries Joyce made at the level of style he was not able to translate into any notion of overall form. That is why it will always be possible for Derridean readings of *Ulysses* to co-exist with readings which extol Joyce's 'classical temper', remind us of Joyce's debt to Ibsen, and make out a sound case for reading *Ulysses* as the last and greatest of nineteenth-century novels.

But there is no such thing as Everyman or Everywoman. There are only multiple possibilities, multiple things we can do with our lives, just as there are multiple things a gymnast (or a trained hamster) can do with his body. What man 'is' and what life 'is' can be understood only by moving amongst the many lives of men and looking not for an essence but for configurations, as Dante knew when he put these words at the very centre of his great poem:

> Ogne forma sustanzial, che setta
> è da matera ed è con lei unita,
> specifica vertute ha in sé colletta,
> la qual sanza operar non è sentita,
> né si dimostra mai che per effetto,
> come per verdi fronde in pianta vita.
>
> (*Purgatorio*, 18.49)

We realize, too, how narrow is the range of the 'probable' within which the novel usually operates. This book operates beyond the normal boundaries, at both ends. As far as time is concerned a whole life can flash by in three lines while many pages can be taken up enumerating the contents of Mme Moreau's different do-it-yourself packs or the dictionary of discarded words Cinoc is compiling. As far as action is concerned events veer between the wildly improbable and those which are so ordinary and trivial that novels no not usually mention them. There is plenty here that would find a place in the novels of Waugh or Amis. There, however, a figure like Hutting, with his 'mist-paintings' and his 'recipes' for generating pictures would be a figure of satire. But satire requires a firm ground from which to operate, and in this book there is no such ground. How we react to Hutting depends on how we react to the other figures in the book who turn life into art by the use of the imagination: Mme Trévins, Rémi Rorschash, Grace Twinker, Ursula Sobieski, Véra Orlova, Blanche Gardel.

In the traditional novel time is transmuted into meaning; this book is about the triumph of time. Helène Brodin has many years of ordinary living to do after her successful pursuit of her husband's murderers; the Breidel daughters grow up as quite ordinary girls despite their parents' dreadful end; after his wife's death Winckler still has thirty years to get through. Nowhere are we allowed the luxury of climax and revelation. Véra de Beaumont sets a detective to find the murderer of her daughter and son-in-law and does in fact succeed, but in the process learns that the truth would have emerged in time anyway. As with the three-line summaries of detective stories, the shape of the action is made clear but revelation is drained of impact. And what this means, ultimately, is that time and chance are allowed to emerge with the force they have in life but which the traditional novel, committed as it is to a metaphysic of destiny and revelation, is never able to convey. The final effect of this book is thus curiously moving and as curiously realistic. Surprisingly perhaps in view of its playful character and the often grotesquely unlikely tales which it parades before us, the book as a whole conveys that sense of individual life set within a larger rhythm which we find in the Old Testament, or in Proust and Wallace Stevens:

> It is a kind of total grandeur at the end,
> With every visible thing enlarged and yet
> No more than a bed, a chair and moving nuns,

The immensest theatre, the pillared porch,
The book and candle in your ambered room.[8]

It is time to turn to the life of the book. For Perec has not written
another version of Butor's *Mobile* or *Degrés* but a work in which
we are driven forward as compulsively as we are when we launch
ourselves in Dante's great poem.

The book opens, though we do not realize it at the time, with the
portent of the destruction which is to overtake all the characters,
the destruction of Time. It opens with a figure on the stairs. She is
an employee of an estate agency come to look over the empty flat
Gaspard Winckler once inhabited in order to see what improvements
need to be made to render it sellable or rentable:

> De ces trois petites chambres dans lesquelles pendant presque
> quarante ans a vécu et travaillé Gaspard Winckler, il ne reste plus
> grande-chose. Ses quelques meubles, son petit établi, sa scie
> sauteuse, ses minuscules limes sont partis. Il n'y a plus sur le mur
> de la chambres, en face de son lit, a côté de la fenêtre, ce tableau
> carré qu'il aimait tant.... La femme monte les escaliers. Bientôt,
> le vieil appartement deviendra un coquet logement, double liv.
> + ch., cft., vue, calme. Gaspard Winckler est mort... (p.22)

Valène remembers Winckler with something approaching love,
though in actual fact it had been Winckler's wife he had been secretly
in love with. But she died, giving birth to a still-born child. All this
we learn later, as we also learn of Winckler's reaction to this, his
sitting for days in silence, motionless, and then his careful, obsessive
destruction of everything connected with his memory, his gradual
withdrawal from the world, his last years as a virtual recluse. Now
every last trace of Winckler is to be rooted out, impersonally,
efficiently, without fuss. Up in his room Valène ponders on this
and, at other times, indulges in apocalyptic fantasies about the disappearance of the building, the street, the entire neighbourhood –
not as a result of a nuclear holocaust but of something much more
banal: redevelopment. After all, not so long ago neither street nor
building existed, so why should we think that they will last for ever
just because we happen to inhabit them?

A few chapters later we meet someone else on the stairs: in the
entrance hall, to be precise. It is the American novelist, Ursula
Sobieski, come to the building to try and acquire information from
Bartlebooth about his great-uncle, James Sherwood, a millionaire

who had made his fortune in America manufacturing cough drops
and who had later been involved in one of the most notorious frauds
of the century. Sherwood was known to collect *unica*, those objects
of which there is only one of each kind in the world. Two crooks,
playing on his passion, tricked him into believing he was on the trail
of the greatest *unicum* of them all, the Holy Grail, and eventually
sold him for a million dollars an earthenware pitcher picked up in
a North African *souk*. The entire documentary trail as well, naturally,
as the identity of the two men, turned out to be a fake. However,
there was a twist in the tail, for we are given a hint at the end of the
recounting of this story that the million dollars handed over by
Sherwood might themselves only have been as authentic as the vase.

It is Sherwood's fortune which Bartlebooth has inherited, along
with some of his furniture and his genial and curious temperament.
Even if he were in the position of being able to give the American
the information she wanted it is clear that he would not. For when,
some years previously, Rémi Rorschash had approached him with
the proposition of a film about his strange life Bartlebooth had
politely shown him the door. After all, the whole point of his project
was that it should have no impact whatever on the world. Though
in one sense it is a game, it has behind it a religious, a Kierkegaardian
response to life. Each man's life is unique. To turn it into art is to
deny that uniqueness, to multiply it in the interest of worldly fame.
Naturally Bartlebooth refuses. But Rorschash is not to be deterred
and decides to go ahead with his project anyway. Unfortunately for
him he is important enough in the TV hierarchy to be listened to
with respect, but not quite important enough for his ideas to be
implemented; so the scheme languishes.

But the insidious poison cannot be kept out for ever. Two large
hotel chains decide to merge in a bid to outdo their rivals. They
plan a kind of mad *summa* of modern consumer society, a series of
twenty-four super-luxury hotels in as many parts of the globe. Each
will naturally be magnificently equipped, but the real originality of
the enterprise is this: by booking in at any one hotel a guest will
acquire the possibility of making use (within reason) of any other.
Thus the wealthy tourist in search of pleasure, culture, and variety
will have his life greatly simplified:

Si, pour prendre un exemple simplifié, un client arrivé à Safad
cochait en vrac des événements tel que: ski, bains ferrugineux,
visite de la Kasbah' de Ouarzazate, dégustation de fromages et
vins suisses, tournoi de canasta, visite du musée de l'Ermitage,

dîner alsacien, visite du château de Champs-sur-Marne, concert par l'orchestre philharmonique de Des Moines sous la direction de Lazslo Birnbaum, visite des Grottes de Bétharram..., la direction, après s'être mise en rapport avec l'ordinateur géant de la compagnie, prévoirait immédiatement un transport à Coire (Suisse) où auraient lieu les séances de ski sur glacier, la dégustation de fromages et vins suisses..., les bains ferrugineux et le tournoi de canasta, et un autre transport, de Coire à Vence, pour la visite des Grottes Reconstituées de Bétharram.... A Safad même pourraient prendre place le dîner alsacien et les visites du musée et du château assurées par des conférences audiovisuelles permettant au voyageur, confortablement installé dans un fauteuil-club, de découvrir, intelligemment présentées et mises en valeur, les merveilles artistiques de tous les temps et de tous les pays. Par contre, la Direction n'assurerait le transport à Artesia, où se dressait une réplique fabuleuse de la Kasbah' de Ouarzazete, et à Orlando-Disneyworld, où l'orchestre philharmonique de Des Moines avait été engagé pour la saison, que si le client s'inscrivait pour une semaine supplémentaire, et suggérerait en éventuel remplacement la visite des authentiques synagogues de Safad (à Safad), une soirée avec l'orchestre de chambre de Bregenz... ou une conférence du Professeur Strossi, de l'université de Clermont-Ferrand, sur *Marshall McLuhan et la troisième révolution copernicienne* (à Coire). (pp.522-23)

This consumer paradise where the unique has been effectively abolished by money and technology is of course still in the planning stages. One per cent of the enormous budget is to be devoted to art works to adorn the hotels, and the company entrusts this sum to the famous art critic Beyssandre, giving him an entirely free hand. In the first few heady days he calculates that with this (still notional) budget he could buy fifty Klees, nearly all the Magrittes, about five hundred Dubuffets, roughly twenty of the best Picassos, a hundred de Staels, nearly all the Frank Stellas, nearly all the Kleins, nearly all the Klines, all the Rothkos, all the Huffings in the Fichtwinder Donation, and all the Huttings of the 'période brouillard'.

News of Beyssandre's new purchasing power, however, wreaks havoc in the art markets of the world and makes it practically impossible for the poor man to set foot in an art gallery any more. As a result he changes tack. Reading in a newspaper interview with Rorschash about Bartlebooth, Beyssandre becomes obsessed with the idea of acquiring Bartlebooth's watercolours. A battle of wills then ensues, with the Englishman deftly fending off every move of the art critic. But Beyssandre finally succeeds in stealing the four-hundred-and-thirty-eighth watercolour as it is being delivered back to its place of origin. His triumph, however, is short-lived. New calculations show that the time required for the completion of the hotels is to be six years and two months, not the four years and eight months originally envisaged, and the backers withdraw their money. The entire scheme promptly collapses, and Beyssandre is never heard of again.

Nevertheless the blow to Bartlebooth is considerable. Already almost blind, he now feels that all his carefully planned privacy has been fatally breached. But would his project not have foundered anyway on the reef of purely internal contradictions? To answer this question we have to step back for a moment and draw some of the threads of this book together.

St Augustine divided mankind into two categories, those motivated by *amor sui* and those motivated by *amor dei*. In Perec's world there is also a radical division. On the one hand there are those, like Sobieski and Rorschash, who would turn everything into art. An attitude like Bartlebooth's makes no sense to them. They belong without qualm to present-day Western culture, and whether we describe that culture as capitalist or consumer does not much matter. Their natural allies are tourist agencies, hotel chains, house agencies, and those ordinary citizens for whom life is simply a matter of acquiring as much wealth or territory or fame as they can. The Plessaerts are a good example of the type. Starting out with a couple of rooms in the attic, they are gradually enlarging their flat by buying up the adjacent rooms as they become vacant. This of course means seeing that the occupants of those rooms are evicted at the slightest excuse. The Plessaerts are not wicked; they could even be said to be exemplary citizens, since Troquet is practically a tramp who doesn't pay his rent regularly and Morrelet seems likely to set the building on fire with his chemical experiments. The Plessaerts are in fact doing everyone a service by seeing that they are thrown out. They are ordinary decent bourgeois whose lives are fuelled by nothing but greed.

Opposing such people (or rather, standing, in the economy of the book, over against them, since opposition as such is not in their nature) are all those, like Morrelet, Jérome, Simpson, Winckler, Bartlebooth, and Valène himself, who have too much leisure or too much imagination for their own good. Marcel Appenzzell, who once occupied the Altamont flat, is a good example of this type.

As a pupil of Malinowski's Appenzzell had gone off as a young man to Sumatra to study a tribe called the Kubus. He returned five years later a changed man. He seemed lethargic, unable to work, cut off in some way from colleagues and friends. A few days before he was due to deliver the paper in which he would report on his experiences with the Kubus he burned all his notes and vanished, leaving a brief word to say that he was returning to Sumatra and did not feel he had the right to divulge anything concerning the tribe he had gone to study. Gradually disciples and students pieced together the few shreds of evidence and tentatively reconstructed the story of those five years in the field. It seemed that the Kubus were not nomads, yet whenever the young ethnographer caught up with them he found them in the process of packing their few belongings and moving on. For months he followed, trying to understand the reasons for their ceaseless migrations, but he could get nothing out of them. Eventually he understood: he alone was the reason.

Appenzzell's experience is in a sense an allegory of the ethnologist's problem. But it also has a general application. To understand anything you cannot remain on the outside, looking in. Yet to enter is to cut yourself off from those outside. After that there is no choice but to leave your old life behind you forever. Or, to put it another way, we can achieve our ends so long as we keep ourselves closed off from any real contact with life. But in that case those ends are nothing but dust and lies. On the other hand to open yourself to life is to become extremely vulnerable, and not many can survive that.

Elizabeth Breidel successfully evades her avenger for many years. It is only when she briefly comes out into the open at the moment when she finally decides to get married that he gets on to her track, and after that she is doomed. So for her, as we see in retrospect, it was a matter of either not really living or else, in accepting to live a normal life, effectively signing her death warrant.

Or take the case of Grégoire Simpson. We would not be entirely on the wrong track if we were to relate him to Kafka's Gregor Samsa or to the anonymous hero of Perec's own *Un Homme qui dort*. Like the latter he is a student who lives in an attic bed-sitter, finds himself with too much leisure on his hands, and begins gradually to drift away from other people. He takes to wandering the streets of Paris, amusing himself with meaningless games such as counting all the Russian restaurants of the XVIIIᵉ and planning an itinerary which would link them all without his ever having to recross his path. Eventually he ceases even to go out and lies motionless on his bed all day. Once his neighbour Troyan comes in to ask if anything is the matter, but Simpson only tells him to go to hell and turns his face to the wall. Then one day he vanishes.

Or M. Jérome, who had once occupied Winckler's flat. As a brilliant young historian he had carried off the defence of his doctoral thesis on the Medieval Spice Route with great panache:

> Désireux de démontrer que l'introduction en Europe de ces petits piments séchés que l'on appelle 'piments oiseaux' avait correspondu à une véritable mutation dans l'art de préparer les venaisons, il n'hésita pas, lors de sa soutenance, à faire goûter aux trois vieux professeurs qui le jugeaient, des marinades de sa composition. Il fut évidement reçu avec les félicitations du jury.   (p.264)

Named cultural attaché to Lahore, he leaves Paris. Thirty years later he returns and takes a room in the attic of the building in which he had once lived. But he who had been 'un Normalien prestigieux et sur de lui, plein d'enthousiasme et de projets' is now 'un homme méconnaissable, élimé, éliminé, liminé'. He earns a meagre living translating children's primers and never tells anyone what happened to him in India. Once, though, without being asked, 'il dit que ce qu'il avait vu de plus beau au monde, de plus éblouissant, c'était un plafond divisé en compartimentes octogones, rehaussés d'or et d'argent, plus ciselé qu'un bijou'.

It is as though the question 'what does one do with one's life?' had proved too much for these people. Too imaginative to live according to the limited goals others set themselves (buying a better bed, enlarging their flat, writing a novel or a TV script), they are also too weak to live with the knowledge imagination brings.

The most striking of these wounded figures is Gaspard Winckler himself. In an earlier book, *W ou le souvenir d'enfance*, Perec had interwoven two stories, one a strict account of his own childhood, the other an adolescent fantasy about a community whose existence is organized entirely around the notion of sport. The central character of the second story is the deaf-mute child, Gaspard Winckler, or (further complication) someone who has taken over his name when he was drowned at sea. Clearly, again, there is a link with a character outside the book, that other deaf-mute Gaspard whose case has haunted the European imagination since he was found in the late eighteenth century. Gaspard Winckler and Gaspard Hauser are not one and the same, nor is the Gaspard Winckler of *W* the same as that of the later novel, but they are clearly related.

Winckler's workshop was in the room just below Valène's. It

creates a gap in the painter's life when one day Winckler decides he has had enough and the gentle whine of the fret-saw is stilled forever. Already the death of his wife had wrought a change in Winckler, and, once he has finished his twenty years' work for Bartlebooth, it is plain that he will not find it easy to go on. The book begins not just with the final dispersal of his last remains but also with another, more mysterious, comment: 'Gaspard Winckler est mort, mais la longue vengeance qu'il a si patiemment, si minutieusement ourdie, n'a pas encore fini de s'assouvir.' What is the nature of this vengeance?

The game of jigsaw is a game played between cutter and solver. For the true player the challenge lies in the way the cutter will have anticipated his reactions and will have set traps for him: he in turn will try to avoid the traps, see them before he falls into them, always keeping his mind open for the possibility that even here the cutter may be a step ahead of him. On his return from his twenty-year absence Bartlebooth is very much his old self, confident, courteous, kindly, enthusiastic. He goes out to dinner, meets old friends, even occasionally asks new ones in to see his puzzles. But gradually he too starts to change. The puzzles seem to get harder and harder to solve and his struggles with each one become desperate affairs, leading him from the depths of despair to the heights of exaltation. At times he experiences, before the puzzles, that sense of charged neutrality which we are told the great chess players or Zen masters experience. But his is a losing battle, and in the end he is defeated, not by Rorschash or Beyssandre, not by his blindness, not even, quite, by Winckler. What Winckler does is merely to make him recognize the impossibility of his ever successfully carrying out his bet with fate.

For at the moment that Ursula Sobiesky is consulting the list of names of the inhabitants of the building, at the moment when the thousand and one things Valène will paint are taking place in the different rooms, Bartlebooth is sitting in James Sherwood's swivel chair with the four-hundred-and-thirty-ninth puzzle almost complete in front of him. It shows the port of the river Meander, a kind of city of the dead. Only one piece is missing, for there is an X-shaped hole left on the board. But the piece which the blind Bartlebooth is holding in his hand is a W. And Barthlebooth is dead.

Bartlebooth is the type of the fin-de-siècle aesthete. Perfectly lucid about what life has in store for him, he makes his plans accordingly. He is a warm and likeable man, a friend to the ill-fated Fernand de Beaumont, tolerant of Smautf, kind to Valène, fond of Elzbieta Orlowska. But it is as though the effort to keep up his challenge to

life were taking a greater and greater toll of him. The last time
Valène sees him is in 1972, when they pass each other on the stairs:

> Il portait son habituel pantalon de flanelle grise, une veste à car-
> reaux, et une de ces chemises en fil d'Écosse qu'il affectionnait
> tellement. Il l'avait salué au passage d'une trés bréve inclinaison
> de la tête. Il n'avait pas beacoup changé; il etait voûté, mais mar-
> chait sans canne; son visage s'était légèrement creusé, ses yeux
> était devenus presque blancs; c'est cela qui avait le plus frappé
> Valène: ce regard qui n'était pas arrivé à rencontrer le sien, comme
> si Bartlebooth avait cherché à regarder derrière sa tête, avail voulu
> traverser sa tête pour atteindre, au dela, le refuge neutre de l'es-
> calier.... Il y avait dans ce regard qui l'évitait quelque chose de
> beaucoup plus violent que le vide, quelque chose qui n'était pas
> seulement de l'orgeuil ou de la haine, mais presque de la panique,
> quelque chose comme un espoir insensé, comme un appel au
> secours, comme un signal de détresse.   (p.166)

For in the end the wager must be lost. Time cannot be turned into
a game. The sense Valène has of confronting a panic-stricken animal
comes from the fact that Bartlebooth, despite all his plans, feels
creeping up on him that which is utterly other, that which will,
sooner or later, take him away from himself.

It is this, it seems to me, which Winckler is trying to tell him:
you cannot do it, you cannot totally plan your life, even if it is for
the must unselfish of ends. There will always be an X-shaped hole,
even in the most perfectly organized existence, even when there is
all the money in the world to help you, even if you are the most
self-effacing of people. The W is an index of pain in this book, as
in *W*, of a pain which cannot be spoken because it is itself the root
of all speech, the pain of living itself.

The novel ends with the image of Bartlebooth dead in his swivel
chair. But there is an epilogue. There we learn that within two
months Valène himself was dead. In his small attic bedsitter, and
taking up most of the space in the room, stands the large canvas he
had been at work on when he died. It has been neatly divided into
squares, but otherwise it is totally blank.

It is a curious fact that neither music nor painting can exist in the
conditional but that literature can. The novel, in a sense, is always
in the conditional, for it only 'happens' inside the heads of writer
and reader. But I cannot think of another major novel which accepts

its condition, its conditionality, as fully as this one. Valène is dead, his great project not even begun, yet *La Vie mode d'emploi* is there, it exists, as much or as little as any work of literature, even though it purports to be only the description of a non-existent painting. More than most works, though, it sets us meditating on the relation between imagination and reality, possibility and actuality.

Amidst all the images of silent despair and decay, of the failures of hope and of the effort required simply to keep going, two stand out as particularly monstrous, perversions of the good as frightening as anything in Dante. The first is the vision in one of the rooms in the mysterious flat, third right, which seems to be occupied by ghostly figures without names. The scene described is the aftermath of a party and the chaos, the mingling of different elements of consumption in a broken and disorderly mess, is in its way a vision of Hell. The other is the description of a room in the attics once occupied by the cook Fresnel. Again the present occupant is nameless, but this time he is also naked: 'La chambre est aujourd'hui occupée par un homme d'une trentaine d années: il est sur son lit, entièrement nu, à plat ventre, au milieu de cinq poupées gonflables, couché de tout son long sur l'une d'entre elles, en enserrant deux autres dans ses bras, semblant éprouver sur ces simulacres instables un orgasme hors pair.' (p.331) These are visions of horror because they are visions of unredeemed despair: the life of the spirit is entirely gone and there is only a wallowing in the confusion of the physical and the imaginary.

By contrast the lives of even the saddest of the other occupants has about it a dignity and even the possibility of joy. Winckler, for example, never talks about his past to Valène when, in the last years, the painter occasionally drops in to see him. Yet once, 'avec une chaleur soudaine', he starts to speak of the man who taught him his trade, a M. Gouttman, maker of articles of piety which he would hawk round the towns and villages. One day he sets out but never returns. 'Winckler apprit plus tard qu'il était mort de froid, au bord de la route, en forêt d'Argonne, entre les Islettes et Clermont.' Valène asks him how he had come to Paris and met Bartlebooth. 'Mais Winckler répondit seulement que c'était parcequ'il était jeune.'

The skills Gouttman taught him have clearly been a joy to Winckler, and this joy stands in the book alongside the young Jérome's pleasure in historical research, Raymond Massy's in his cycling ability, and Bartlebooth's when he feels the solution of a puzzle coming. But it would be wrong to see it as leading in some way to Winckler's 'salvation'. Salvation belongs to a metaphysic which this book turns its back on. It belongs to a view of life as a movement forward and upward, by way of revelation. Here there is no revelation, there are only lives to be lived. And there is no absolute distinction, between the man in Fresnel's room and Winckler or Valène or Bartlebooth. Winckler's suffering at his wife's death, his silent lonely end, the way his tools and belongings are cleared out of the space he occupied for so long, and the way even his memory will gradually disappear as those who knew him die in their turn – all this is as real, no more and no less, than his youthful enthusiasm for his craft, his admiration for M. Gouttman, or his love for his wife.

And for the author too there is no final triumph or salvation. For Bartlebooth's failure is his failure too. If one piece will not fit then the whole game was misguided and nothing whatever fits. It is worth recalling that the earliest depiction of a magic square in Western art is to be found in Dürer's *Melancholia I*. That engravinng, as Panofsky has pointed out, was meant by Dürer to be seen alongside his *St Jerome in his Study* of the same year, 1514. St Jerome is here a figure at ease within tradition, seated at his desk at work on his Bible translation, his animals dozing beside him. By contrast the Melancholia is an image of anxiety: 'Winged yet cowering on the ground – wreathed, yet beclouded by shadows – equipped with the tools of art and science, yet brooding in idleness, she gives the impression of a creative being reduced to despair by an awareness of insurmountable barriers which separate her from a higher realm of thought.'[9] She is an image of the artist who, with the loss of an assured tradition to guide him, has found himself cut off from meaning. He can either scribble away meaninglessly like the putto in the engraving, or sit staring out in impotent frustration like the Melancholia. The artist who has taken the message of that picture to heart must acknowledge despair because while he recognizes that the only way to create now is to make his own rules, he also recognizes, as Bartlebooth for so long refuses to do, that rules which he has made himself will never totally sustain him. Yet, paradoxically, he can triumph after all, if only precariously, by incorporating this painful knowledge into his work. When that happens, as it does in *La Vie mode d'emploi*, something infinitely precious is given to the world, a hope on the other side of despair, as Zeitblom said of Lerverkühn's work, and, for us, a sense of human potential realized, not squandered.

W ou le souvenir d'enfance tells the story of Georges Perec or Peretz (how then are we to pronounce it? Peretch? Peresse? Pereque?), a Polish Jew whose father was killed in the first year of the war, fighting for the French, and whose mother was deported to Auschwitz. Writing of his parents he says there: 'J'écris parcequ'ils ont laissé en moi leur marque indélébile et que la trace en est l'écriture; l'écriture est le souvenir de leur mort et l'affirmation de ma vie.' And again: 'Écrire: essayer méticuleusement de retenir quelque chose, de faire survivre quelque chose.' Apart from that he never wrote about the war or the camps, and rigorously avoided the temptation of turning his life and that of his parents into art. In its lack of sentimentality and its playful awareness of limitation his work is a burning indictment of all those who have grown fat and famous by their ceaseless chatter about those events. Yet in one sense his books are about nothing else. As Robert Bober, who made the film *Récits d'Ellis Island* with Perec, has said, *La Disparition* is a book which in effect demonstrates the following: just as a book can be written without the most indispensable letter of all, the *e*, so Perec showed what sort of a life could be lived without the most indispensable thing of all, a mother and father. One *can* live in such circumstances, says Bober, only it's a different sort of life. A book *can* be written, only it's a different sort of book.

Georges Perec died of cancer on 10 March 1982. He was forty-six. One cannot help wondering as one reads the terrible catalogue of deaths which forms the climax of *La Vie mode d'emploi* whether, in writing it, he knew his own death was so near. It is absurd to speculate, but it is also impossible to read the book in quite the same way once one knows. Yet though he died tragically in mid-career he cannot have failed to recognize that he had produced a remarkable book. Like the greatest work of Dante and Chaucer, Joyce and Proust, it could never have been predicted. Utterly original and deeply embedded in tradition, it makes nonsense of the barriers we erect between languages and cultures and renews our sense of the wealth of possibilities which are always there, waiting to be tapped.

Just as Winckler sent a message to Bartlebooth by way of the puzzles, so Perec sends us a message through the puzzles which form his book. It is a message about tradition and individual talent. Mme Moreau had asked her interior designer, Henry Fleury, to produce a set of rooms for her where she would be able to entertain with equal facility Japanese businessmen, French politicians, Italian bishops, and artists and intellectuals from all over the world. In the smoking-room-library, among other items, we find une maison de poupée, parallélépipédique, haute d'un mètre, large de quatre-vingt-dix centimètres, profonde de soixante, datant de la fin du xixᵉ siècle et reproduisant, jusque dans ses moindres détails un typicque cottage britannique: un salon avec baywindow (ogives à double lancette), y compris le thermomètre, un petit salon, quatre chambres à coucher, deux chambres de domestiques, une cuisine carrelée avec fourneau et office, un hall avec placards à•linge, et un dispositif de rayons de bibliothèque en chêne teinté contenant l'*Encyclopaedia britannica* et le *New Century Dictionary*, des panoplies d'anciennes armes médiévales et orientales... un perchoir avec son perroquet, et plusiers centaines d'objets usuels, bibelots, vaisselles, vêtements, restitués presque microscopiquement avec une fidélité maniaque.   (p.135)

This doll's house is no more 'original' to Perec than any of the other elements which make up the book. It is taken from the end of the penultimate chapter of *Ulysses*, where it forms part of Bloom's fantasy of his 'ultimate ambition'.

La Vie mode d'emploi is a homage to tradition, the storehouse of possibilities. In particular it is a homage to Joyce, the man who above all others made it possible. And by that I mean made the book as it stands possible, but also made possible the pleasure which work on the book no doubt gave to Perec. And it is a typical and beautiful touch that the passage Perec chose to quote and transpose should be not a piece of spectacular Irishry, but Joyce / Bloom's own homage to the land which had after all given him the language he used to such good effect, and to those *petit-bourgeois* values he despised so much but which he also knew must form an indispensable ingredient in the life and character of every ambitious artist.

Writing and the Body

THE NORTHCLIFFE LECTURES
1981

To George Craig

'It seems so dreadful to stay a bachelor, to become an old man struggling to keep one's dignity while begging for an invitation whenever one wants to spend an evening in company, to lie ill gazing for weeks into an empty room from the corner where one's bed is, always having to say good night at the front door, never to run up a stairway beside one's wife, to have only side-doors in one's room leading into other people's living-rooms, having to carry one's supper home in one's hand, having to admire other people's children and not even being allowed to go on saying: "I have none myself", modelling oneself in appearance and behaviour on one or two bachelors remembered from one's youth.

That's how it will be, except that in reality both today and later, one will stand there with a palpable body and a real head, a real forehead, that is, for smiting on with one's hand.'

KAFKA

'What is yours to bestow is not yours to reserve.'
SHAKESPEARE

Preface

In the summer of 1979 I was invited to deliver the Lord Northcliffe Lectures at University College, London, for the 1980-81 session. What follows is substantially the lectures as I gave them, though the exigencies of time forced me to shorten one or two of them slightly when I delivered them.

The invitation was to give four lectures on 'whatever you happen to be working on'. I was embarrassed to admit that I was not 'working on' anything, and that all I could imagine myself at work on in a year's time would be a novel or play. Clearly I was not being invited to read from that kind of work in progress. At the same time, as far as I was concerned, the invitation had come at a most appropriate moment. I had just finished a novel on which I had been working with great intensity for fifteen months, and one's spirits are never so low as in the immediate aftermath of such an effort. One feels as if one has been talking for as long as one can remember into an unpeopled void, and whatever enthusiasm buoyed one up at the start of the enterprise has evaporated by the end; one is left only with the sense of waste, frustration and failure. To be asked at this juncture to talk to a group of interested people about a subject of my choice was an unexpected tonic. I immediately accepted.

But what subject should I choose? I had not realized till then how difficult this sort of assignment could be. To give a single lecture on a subject of one's choice is not too difficult; to give four lectures on a specific subject is also relatively easy. But to be asked to give four lectures on any subject one wants raises very real problems. For what *did* I want to talk about? What did I want to spend the next year thinking and reading about?

I realized early on that I was faced with at least one clear set of alternatives: I could either look at an apparently extremely limited subject in considerable detail in order to show that even this raised problems for reading and criticism which four lectures would be only just sufficient to bring out into the open (the relation of background to foreground in the first paragraph of *A la recherche*, and the nature of the gaps in Eliot's poetry were topics that came to

169

mind); or I could tackle a subject so vast that though a book might seem pretentious and impossibly ambitious, four lectures could be seen as a personal and preliminary set of moves, designed more to raise questions than to provide answers. The special constraints of the lecture form – no more matter than can be comfortably delivered in one hour –; but also its special privileges – direct contact with an audience, and thus the audience's constant awareness of the subjective and personal nature of the discourse – made the second option all the more attractive, and this is what I finally chose.

There was naturally a strong temptation to tinker with the lectures after they had been delivered, to try and fill out and develop some of the themes prior to publication. But to have succumbed to the temptation would have led the reader to ask, and rightly: Why have you stopped there? Why have you not rewritten the whole thing? Why have you not dealt with this aspect of the subject, or that? And then I would have been landed with just what I had wanted to avoid. I would have found myself in the position of trying to defend a thesis against all possible attack, instead of merely exploring certain issues which had seemed important to me. Since I believe no thesis is ever fully defensible, and since I am not sure if I even have a thesis (it feels more like a set of nagging worries), I have resisted the temptation and left the lectures as I wrote them to be delivered.

But to return to the question of subject. A series of four lectures clearly requires a degree of commitment not demanded by one lecture. It cannot be built round a passing or peripheral interest; it must be concerned with something of absolutely central interest. As I thought about what I might like to speak about, I began to wonder if *any* subject would be able to claim my commitment in this way. Why spend a year on a reconsideration of the *nouveau roman*, on the strengths and weaknesses of recent critical theory, on the striking parallels between the *Commedia* and *A la recherche*? These were all important and fascinating subjects, subjects I had given some thought to and about which I felt I might have something of interest to say. They were *all* fascinating, *all* worth while. That was the problem. And by the same token none was so utterly absorbing that I felt I absolutely *had* to tackle it.

Was it simply a case of my inability to make up my mind? Was I being lazy, just wanting to defer any decision which would force me to get down to work? Or did the trouble perhaps lie with the subjects I was hesitating over? Was there not perhaps something I *really* wanted to write about, behind all of these, but which somehow I was not clear-headed enough to discern? Of course in such situations one can never be sure, but something told me I should trust my instinct, and my instinct told me it was not just a personal difficulty I was facing. And then it began to dawn on me that my subject might lie not on the other side of the confusion, of the thicket of conflicting desires in which I seemed to be caught, but in the nature of the confusion itself. My subject was not another topic, but the nature of choice itself, of the act of commitment to one subject rather than another.

As I began to understand what it was I might be after I also became aware of the fact that this rather precise question about the subject-matter of a series of lectures overlapped with something I had often been vaguely aware of but which I would never have previously thought of dignifying with the name of problem or topic. This was something which concerned the writing of fiction. While one is at work on an extended piece of fiction (and I imagine it is the same with painting and music) one has no desire to see anyone or to read anything. Everything seems to be an intrusion. It is not so much that one is afraid the book might be damaged by such contact – though that comes into it – as that nothing interests one except what one is working on. This total absorption is a blessing. But it is also a tyranny. As one nears the end of such work one longs for other voices, for the company of one's friends, of books. One feels one has been away from the world too long and one wants to integrate oneself with it, to 'live' again. But this is very curious. One leaves the world because one feels the need to write in order to come fully alive, and then one is glad writing is coming to an end because in the later stages it was starting to feel more like death than life. Does the act of making on which the artist is engaged bring him more fully in touch with his real self and with the world, or does it take him further away from both?

At this point I happened to read again Yeats's great poem, 'Ego Dominus Tuus'. It is a dialogue between the two parts of the self, *Hic* and *Ille*, that which is near and that which is far. The poem asks what activity leads to true self-knowledge and self-fulfilment, and it takes the form of a debate between the claims of introspection and rhetoric, meditation and the making of images. *Hic* accuses *Ille* of never facing up to himself but of always escaping into the creation of yet one more image; *Ille* defends himself by saying that meditation and introspection do not lead to true self-knowledge but only to dreamy self-satisfaction or self-laceration. The poem does not come down on either side, but only shows up the dangers and weaknesses of both. Like all true dialogues, it has no end.

But it is not just about the choices each human being and each artist has to make; it is also concerned with the contrast between epochs, between the art of the past and that of the present. 'I would find myself and not an image', says *Hic*, whereupon *Ille* replies:

> That is our modern hope, and by its light
> We have lit upon the gentle, sensitive mind
> And lost the old nonchalance of the hand;
> Whether we have chosen chisel, pen or brush,
> We are but critics or but half create,
> Timid, entangled, empty and abashed...

This is the argument between Classicism and Romanticism, between an art based on the principles of rhetoric and one based on the principle of sincerity. One of the exciting things about the poem is the way Yeats restates these old oppositions in an entirely fresh way and shows that, far from belonging to the mere history of art, the issues are as fresh and alive today as they ever were.

Yeats's poem, as well as confirming me in my feeling that I had a genuine subject on my hands, also alerted me to the fact that that subject had a historical dimension. If I was going to do it justice I would have to try and explore the assumptions and the limitations of both the ancient rhetorical tradition and the tradition of sincerity which replaced it with the rise of the novel and the coming of Romanticism. This is what I have tried to do in the second and third lectures.

Once I started work on the lectures they took on a logic of their own, and I discovered that the real centre of debate was not quite where I thought it was. In the end the Yeats poem disappeared entirely and was replaced even in the epigraph, where it had lingered almost to the end, by a quotation from Kafka. This quotation, an entire 'story' from one of the few collections Kafka published in his lifetime, manages in a few lines to bring out what I finally saw to be the elusive theme for which I had been searching from the moment I accepted the assignment: the relations between writing and the body.

It remains to add that by the time I had finished I had learnt something else. This is that writing and thinking discursively about this subject, however, tempting it may seem while one is engaged in the process of making, is itself an unsatisfactory compromise. The maker, however much he wants to, cannot understand himself and what drives him to make; he can only be honest to his inspiration and hope history will vindicate him. This is actually the theme of the closing sections of the third and the whole of the fourth lecture. As I wrote them I realized that I was writing against myself, and that what I was arguing for was the inadequacy of the mode of argument itself. But then that is one of the miracles of language, that it allows us to do just that.

I am grateful to the Provost and Fellows of University College, London, for inviting me to give the lectures in the first place, and to Professor Karl Miller for his unfailing courtesy and kindness.

I am also immensely grateful to my audiences, and to those friends and colleagues who took time off from their own work to read what I had written and comment upon it: Rosalind Belben, David Esterly, Dan Gunn, John Mepham, Roger Moss, Tony Nuttall, Alan Sinfield, Gerry Webster, Allon White. Without them these lectures would have been a poorer thing. My greatest intellectual debts are to Bernard Harrison and George Craig. They read and commented on the entire typescript and gave me encouragement when the whole project seemed either impossibly ambitious or impossibly vague. Their friendship over the past fifteen years has helped to save me from the cynicism and despair which sooner or later threatens to overcome all those who venture to teach the humanities. Finally, as always, my mother read and commented on nearly every draft, and was critical and encouraging in just the right doses.

I *The Body in the Library*

1. Let me begin with a few words about the general theme and title of these lectures.

Our bodies are, in a sense, more familiar to us than our closest friends; and yet they are – and will remain – mysterious and unfamiliar until we part from them. They are all we have – yet can we really be said to have them?

In these four lectures I want to try and explore these paradoxes and to examine the role which language, writing and books play in our lives, the lives we live with our bodies.

These are difficult matters. When I first began to think about them I was appalled at my inability to follow through any clear line of argument. But then I began to realize that if this was in part a personal weakness, it was also related to something inherent in what I was trying to say. And I realized why I instinctively felt that I should call the lectures '*Writing* and the Body' and not '*Literature* and the Body'. For the term 'literature' abstracts and idealizes; it suggests unity, coherence, a subject lying there waiting to be examined. Writ-*ing*, on the other hand, suggests a process, something that is happening; something too that is uncertain, insecure, liable to come to a stop at any moment as the result of cramp, boredom, despair, or any one of a hundred unforeseen circumstances. For writing and speaking – unlike 'art' and 'literature' – are at the crossroads of the mental and the physical, the orders of culture and of nature.

But notice how strong is the temptation to reify, to unify. When I say: Writing is this or that; or, Writing must be opposed to litera-ture; or, simply, these writings – I am turning writing itself into a concept, a noun, evading its verbal force and problematic nature. To avoid such temptations – or perhaps, as I have said, because that is the only way I myself can work – I will proceed in these lectures not so much by way of argument as by the exploration of certain pieces of writing. Story and example, rather than rigorous abstract argument, will be the order of the day.

And yet there is an argument of sorts in what I will be saying, one which is partly historical and partly what would probably be called phenomenological. I will not press it too hard, but I hope it will emerge as these lectures proceed.

2.   Today I want to explore some simple and perhaps not so simple facts about writing and reading. I have called this lecture 'The Body in the Library' because I want to draw your attention to what a very odd thing it is to read or write. A child, looking at an adult engaged in either activity, is bound to feel baffled. Apart from the movement of the hand, continual but slight in the one case, occasional in the other, the person might as well be dead... And this brings me to the second aspect of the title. I want to suggest that there is no clear line of demarcation between highbrow and lowbrow literature that our excitement at reading the title: 'The Body in the Library' on the spine of the book, our wanting to know: Which body? How? Why? – that these are not questions we should be embarrassed about. On the contrary, they are central to our quest.

3.   But first we need a specific body in a specific library.

In one of his finest stories Borges recounts an incident that is purported to have taken place during the First World War.[1] A Chinese spy in England in the pay of the Germans learns that the Allies are about to launch a bomb attack and that their munitions are concentrated for this purpose in the French town of Albert. At the same time he learns that his cover has been blown and that the dread Captain Richard Madden, an Irishman working for the English, is at his heels. If only he could communicate the name of the town to his chief before being caught. But how? 'My human voice was very weak. How might I make it carry to the ears of the Chief?' Suddenly he hits on a solution. He looks up the name 'Albert' in the telephone directory and takes a train to a nearby town, where a certain Stephen Albert lives. He finds him in the library of his house, and in the few minutes before Madden catches up with him, they talk. The conversation is metaphysical in the extreme, for Stephen Albert, it turns out, is, amazingly, a Sinologist, and one, moreover, who has cracked a famous puzzle of Chinese intellectual history. Finally, catching sight of Madden entering the garden, the Chinaman kills Albert and thus accomplishes his task: the Chief gets the message. Nevertheless, we know from the opening paragraph of the story what the protagonists do not: that the bombing of the town of Albert by the Germans made no difference to the course of history, for it only delayed the Allied attack by a few days, a delay which the history books now attribute to the torrential rains which fell at about that time. On the other hand Stephen Albert's death is, for the Chinaman, an irrevocable act for which there can be no pardon in the tribunal of his conscience.

4.   In this context it is worth remembering the old dream, revived in the Renaissance and positively haunting the seventeenth century, of a universal language, a language that would be understood at once by all and that would tell no lies. The dream never dies, and if in logical circles it reached its apotheosis in Whitehead and Russell's *Principia Mathematica* and was then dealt its death blow by Wittgenstein's *Tractatus*, it is one whose roots, I want to suggest, go much deeper than mere intellectual curiosity. We all, always, long for a language that will take over from 'my very weak human voice'. Recall another post-Renaissance dream of total communication, Swift's description of the men of the Academy of Lagado, who carried every possible object on their backs and then instead of talking needed only to point.[2] We laugh at the absurdity of it, but late in life Stravinsky, in an interview, recalled the incident.[3] 'What did you mean, a moment ago, when you declared your disbelief in words?' asked the interviewer. 'Is it a question of their inexactness?' 'They are not so much inexact as metaphorical,' answered Stravinsky, and he added: 'Sometimes I feel like those old men Gulliver encounters in the *Voyage to Laputa*, who have renounced language and who try to converse by means of objects themselves.'

5.   Is Borges suggesting that a communication *beyond words* can only be bought at the price of a death? And is a library without a body in it doomed to be a library of Babel?

In order to move closer to an understanding of what is at issue here I would like to look in more detail at one particular book, written in the mid–eighteenth century, but sending its roots back to the Renaissance while also pointing forward to Borges: Sterne's *Tristram Shandy*. And so that you may see at once why I have chosen this particular book, here are two passages from it. The first is from Chapter 14 of Volume III:

> It is a singular stroke of eloquence (at least it was so, when eloquence flourished at Athens and Rome, and would be so now, did orators wear mantles) not to mention the name of a thing, when you had the thing about you, *in petto*, ready to produce, pop, in the place you want it. A scar, an axe, a sword, a pinked doublet, a rusty helmet, a pound and a half of pot-ashes in an urn, or a

three-halfpenny pickle pot, – but above all, a tender infant royally accoutred. – Though if it was too young, and the oration so long as Tully's second Philippic, – it must certainly have beshit the orator's mantle. – And then again, if too old, – it must have been unwieldy and incommodious to his action, – so as to make him lose by his child almost as much as he could gain by it. – Otherwise, when a state orator has hit the precise age to a minute, – hid his Bambino in his mantle so cunningly that no mortal could smell it, – and produced so critically, that no soul could say, it came in by head and shoulders, – Oh, Sirs! it has done wonders. – It has opened the sluices, and turned the brains, and shook the principles, and unhinged the politics of half a nation.

These feats however are not to be done, except in those states and times, I say, where orators wore mantles, – and pretty large ones too, my brethren, with some twenty or five and twenty yards of good purple, superfine, marketable cloth in them, – with large flowing folds and doubles, and in a great stile of design. – All which plainly shews, may it please your worships, that the decay of eloquence, and the little good service it does at present, both within, and without doors, is owing to nothing else in the world, but short coats, and the disuse of *trunk-hose.* – We can conceal nothing under ours, Madam, worth shewing.

The second passage comes from Chapter 17 of Volume IV:

It is not half an hour ago, when (in the great hurry and precipitation of a poor devil's writing for daily bread) I threw a fair sheet, which I had just finished, and carefully wrote out, slap into the fire, instead of the foul one.

Instantly I snatched off my wig, and threw it perpendicularly, with all imaginable violence, up to the top of the room – indeed I caught it as it fell – but there was an end of the matter; nor do I think anything else in Nature, would have given such immediate ease . . .

6.   It has often been observed that the theme of castration and impotence runs strongly through *Tristram Shandy*. The book opens with a conception which is frustrated in its natural flow, and it ends with an impotent bull. Between the desire and the act, between the act and its effects, falls the shadow. Mrs Shandy's one-track mind weakens, if it does not altogether stop, the natural flow of Walter's semen; Susannah's faulty memory leads to Tristram's being wrongly named; the events surrounding the person of Dr Slop lead to Tristram's

nose being crushed in birth, and if this castration is purely symbolic, the same cannot be said for the later incident of the sash-window. And that incident is itself the result of Toby's castration, symbolic or otherwise, on the field of Namur, and his compulsive replaying of that moment on the bowling-green, which leads to Trim's taking the weights off the sash-windows to use for guns, which leads to the windows not staying up when they ought... Nor is Walter himself exempt from the general blight: the hints are strong that all is not well with his sexual performance either.

7.   What is the reason for this? 'Unhappy Tristram!' laments Walter,

> child of wrath! child of decrepitude! interruption! mistake! and discontent! What one misfortune or disaster in the book of embryotic evils, that could unmechanize thy frame, or entangle they filaments! which has not fallen upon thy head, or ever thou camest into the world...   (IV.19)

This, we feel, comes as near to describing the book as we could get. And it makes us see that the impotence and failure which blights all the characters is *reduplicated* at the level of the narrative. Tristram sets out grandly to write his 'Life and Opinions', and what do we get? One cock and bull story after another. How often he is in despair! There are too many unfinished bits and pieces on his hands, too many loose ends that refuse to be tied up, he is constantly frustrated by misadventures, such as throwing the clean copy instead of the rough into the fire, his papers getting used as hair-curlers by unknown women, and so on and so forth – or, as Swift's Grub Street Hack would say, 'Etcetera the Elder and Etcetera the Younger.' Nor can he seem to keep any story going once he has started it: Slawkenbergius's tale, his narrative of his journey to France, the story of Toby's amours – these start off well enough, but all soon peter out. And everyone else in the book seems to be afflicted with the same inability to keep going: remember Walter's impressive openings, or poor Trim's attempts at story-telling.

As everyone knows, the disease seems to have attacked Sterne as well. In the end *Tristram Shandy* itself is all digression and no straight line. And just as Tristram's nose is put together by Dr Slop with 'a piece of cotton and a thin piece of whalebone out of Susannah's stays', so the book is contrived out of an old sermon of Sterne's, the name of a character who is already only a skull in Shakespeare, some typographical tricks, and bits and pieces out of a variety of sixteenth and seventeenth century authors.

Is the book then an unmitigated disaster? The answer, of course, is that it is nothing of the sort. But to understand why it is a triumph and not a disaster, and to understand what *sort* of a triumph it is, we need to take the theme of failure and impotence, of frustration and confusion, as seriously as Tristram himself does.

Note though that the frustration and impotence are never absolute. Tristram, after all, does get born, the sash-window does not actually castrate him, what it does, it is suggested, is more to circumcise him; a novel – of sorts – does get written. We cannot ignore the pressures of impotence, but, in spite of everything, something struggles into existence where before it did not exist. Yet the book, like Tristram himself, exists only as a series of failures, of negations: it is not a straight line, it does not tell a proper story properly, it is not, perhaps, finally, either a novel or not a novel. Yet, like Tristram, it is indubitably there. What then, as the riddles have it, is *it*?

8. I want to suggest that Sterne, standing at the threshold of the modern world, recognizes that the old rhetoric, which had upheld Cicero and Shakespeare, Ronsard and Spenser, will no longer work. The novel is the form of the future. But the novel too, Sterne realizes, has its built-in contradictions. It is these he proceeds to make manifest.

To begin at the beginning. Robinson Crusoe, in the first paragraph of his story, tells us who he is and where he was born. If we ask him: But who are you? He will answer: 'Men call me, nay, I call myself Robinson Crusoe.' For some, that is a sufficient answer. For others, including Sterne, it is nothing of the sort.

Kafka's letter to his father is relevant here. What Kafka is exploring in that extraordinary work is the relation of himself to his father, in an attempt to answer the question Crusoe never asks: Yes, but who is this Franz Kafka? Looked at from his father's point of view – and Kafka is adept at looking at things from the other person's point of view – he is weak, impotent, unmarried, a failure. Instead of his father's strength and confidence, his will to get on in the world, beget children, make a success of his business, use his religion cannily as a tool for security and social advancement, Kafka is filled with doubts, lacking belief in the meaningfulness of work, unable to marry, unable even to bring to a successful conclusion any writing he might wish to do. But looked at from another point of view everything changes. What is the relation between the sexual act and the child one fathers? A meaningless biological activity leads to its inevitable biological result: a child is born. All this is wrapped round and dignified with cultural signs: marriage, naming, teaching the child one's language, etc. etc. Kafka's reluctance to marry could just as well spring from his too great respect for the meaning of life and for the nature of sacrament; just as his inability to get any of his novels finished could spring from his too great respect for art and for truth. 'Why should I do it this way if I might just as well do it that way?' is not just a preliminary question. It is the first question and the last one too. For it is another way of asking: By what authority do I do what I do? Unable to find the conviction to do it by his private authority, he nevertheless cannot find an external authority to which he can unconditionally submit – and if submission is not unconditional then it is nothing.

Like all Kafka's writing, his letter to his father – which he never sent – is genuinely ambiguous. Its power and its despair spring from the same source: the author does not have the confidence even to adjudicate between the two points of view, that of his father and of himself. He can only move forever from the one to the other and back.

9. Here now is the opening of *Tristram Shandy*:

I wish either my father or my mother, or indeed both of them, as they were in duty both equally bound to it, had minded what they were about when they begot me; had they duly considered how much depended upon what they were then doing...

Pray, my dear, quoth my mother, *have you not forgot to wind up the clock?* – Good G–! cried my father, making an exclamation, but taking care to moderate his voice at the same time, – *Did ever woman, since the creation of the world, interrupt a man with such a silly question?* Pray, what was your father saying? – Nothing.

We are here at the start of the book. Also at the moment of the creation of a child. We are reminded too of the creation of the world. But the making of a book is not at all the same thing as the making of a child. As Lévi-Strauss puts it:

[T]he horse does effectively give birth to the horse, and... through a sufficient number of generations, *equus caballus* is the true descendant of *Hipparion*. The historical validity of the reconstruction of the naturalist is guaranteed, in the last analysis, by the biological link of reproduction. On the other hand, an axe never engenders another axe; between two identical tools, or between two tools which are different but as near neighbours in form as one could wish, there will always be a radical discontinuity, which comes from the fact that the one has not issued from the other, but both from a system of representations.[4]

The classic novel implies that the making of the novel and the making of the hero are one and the same. Novels are called *Robinson Crusoe, Tom Jones, Humphry Clinker, Clarissa*. Sterne too writes a novel with the name of the hero in the title; he too is determined to write in such a way that book and hero are inseparable. But, unlike his fellow-novelists, he is only too aware of the fact that the issue is problematic. Yet he is also aware of the fact that any such tidy distinction as Lévi-Strauss's simply will not hold either where works of art and not objects of use are being considered. For a book *is* in one sense produced biologically, in the same way as a laugh or a scream has biological roots. But a book is also, of course, like an axe, the issue not of biology but of a system of representations. But could the same not be said of human beings? Sterne's book is not 'about books' while those of other novelists are 'about people'. Because it takes people seriously, *Tristram Shandy* takes books seriously. Both Tristram himself and the novel, *Tristram Shandy*, hover uneasily between the two orders, of nature and of culture. That is the source of the book's humour and of its poignancy.

10. An axe has a function in the culture which produces it. What function has a novel?

Consider the end of Volume V:

> – Didst thou ever see a white bear? cried my father, turning his head round to Trim, who stood at the back of his chair: – No, an' please your honour, replied the corporal. – But thou couldst discourse about one, Trim, said my father, in case of need? – How is it possible, brother, quoth my Uncle Toby, if the corporal never saw one? – 'Tis the fact I want, replied my father, – and the possibility of it is as follows.

And Walter proceeds to show how it is done, with a sprightly demonstration of the possibilities of rhetorical *amplificatio*. We could be witnessing a dramatization of a fragment of Erasmus's *De copia*.

There is no need to go over the benefits which a training in rhetoric gave to the great Renaissance writers, from Rabelais to Shakespeare. However, as I suggested some years ago, and as Terence Cave has recently demonstrated with marvellous skill and scholarship,[5] the legacy of *copia* is two-fold. On the one hand it is a valuable expressive tool; on the other its very richness leads the more thoughtful writers to question its essence: If I can say anything, then what is the status of what I say? If I can talk about bears or beguines or beeswax or birth at the drop of a hat, and then go on to cats, clouds, coprophilia and cucumbers, then what is the point of talking about any of them? And, if I start, where am I to stop?

For Cicero such questions do not arise, since his rhetoric serves a specific forensic function. But for the writer who is pleading no one's cause, not even his own, the questions become insistent. Or, should I say, for some writers, since they clearly do not trouble Defoe or Richardson. But they do trouble Sterne. Indeed, more perhaps than any other writer, he makes his book out of precisely these questions. The novel form, after all, comes into being as the possibility of questioning the old assumptions about epic and genre. Sterne is merely carrying this critical tendency a little further, until the assumptions underlying the apparently innocent new form are themselves brought out into the open.

11.   The making of a work of art, in which, after all, artists pass the greater part of their lives, has, strangely, been largely occluded from our culture, though the product – the finished work – assumed a new centrality in the Renaissance, which it has really never lost. *Tristram Shandy* constantly reminds us – or rather, scarcely lets us forget – that someone is there, biting his pen, scratching his ear, throwing his wig into the air, someone alone in his study, someone who, like us, grows tired, is not always in control of his movements, forgets, gets excited, gets bored – someone is making this book that we are reading. And, as with all made objects – at least those made by men, not God or nature – it is put together out of bits and pieces, attached to each other by dint of hard work, skill, guile and sheer preservative instinct. But at the same time we are made strongly aware of the maker of this book: of his desires, choices, decisions – ultimately, of the darkness and silence out of which such decisions spring.

This is done by making the reader himself shoulder the task of the making. For this patchwork, piecemeal object, is also a mouse-trap, designed to catch the reader. The more he withdraws, tries to establish himself in a safe position above the action, retreats to the safety of his seat in the library, the more enmeshed he becomes in the toils of the book. Once he has started reading this novel, there is no escape for him: he is made to give up many of the assumptions he held before he started, and the process is one not just of loss but also of discovery.

How is this done?

12.   I see three main strategies on Sterne's part, though naturally they overlap. The one most frequently commented on is the direct address to the reader. Yet even this simple gesture involves us in something quite complicated. When Sterne peremptorily sends a female reader back to the previous chapter, our own exemption from this command (whether we be male or female) makes us fleetingly aware of ourselves as guilty of the very fault for which he is criticising her:

> I have imposed this penance upon the lady, neither out of wantonness nor cruelty, but from the best of motives; ... – 'Tis to rebuke a vicious taste, which has crept into thousands besides herself, – of reading straight forwards, more in quest of the adventures than of the deep erudition and knowledge which a book of this cast, if read over as it should be, would infallibly impart with them... – But here comes my fair Lady. Have you read over again the chapter, Madam, as I desired you?   (I.20)

13.   This leads us straight into the second strategy: the play on the reader's curiosity.

We don't like to admit it, but it is curiosity which drives us to reading novels – both picking them up in the first place and then reading them through to the end. And it seems to me that it is probably just the same kind of curiosity as that which makes us go on reading a letter addressed to someone else which falls into our hands, or makes us eager to listen to gossip. The satisfaction of curiosity is the chief reason for the popularity of the novel – the *new*.

Curiosity drives us forward, but its satisfaction nearly always involves disappointment. It is thus important for the novelist to keep us curious for the duration of the book, and make us believe against the odds that this time we will not be disappointed. Strangely, we are only too willing to co-operate in this confidence trick. Why?

'The reader will be content', writes Sterne at the end of the second volume, 'to wait for a full explanation of these matters till the next year, – when a series of things will be laid open which he little expects.' When Sterne says that the reader will be content, he makes us aware of the fact that we will *not* be content. He plays here with our desire for *fullness, openness.* We are not content to wait; *we want to know, now, as soon as possible.*

Even more interesting is the end of Volume I:

> What these perplexities of my uncle Toby were, – 'tis impossible for you to guess; – if you could, – I should blush; not as a relation, – not as a man, – nor even as a woman, – but I should blush as an author; inasmuch as I set no small store by myself upon this very account, that my reader has never yet been able to guess at any thing. And in this, Sir, I am of so nice and singular a humour, that if I thought you was able to form the least judgement or probable conjecture to yourself, of what was to come in the next page, – I would tear it out of my book.

Though Sterne / Tristram denies that he would blush as a man, the very denial arouses our expectations, which the context reinforces: what Volume II will reveal will have something to do with Toby's sexual life. Blushing as a man and as an author then may not be such separate things; it may be that curiosity in the sense in which I have been describing it is nearly always sexual curiosity.

14.   Earlier critics, who objected to Sterne's dirty mind, are not to be lightly dismissed. The book abounds in sexual innuendos. But I think the reason is not simply or only Sterne's prurience or his realization that such things would sell his books – though both probably played a part.

Look at this example of innuendo. Sterne / Tristram is dismissing Locke and doing one of his typical Swiftian dramatizations of a theory in order to descredit it. It is a brilliant piece of work, but part of its brilliance rests on a pretty low sort of come-on:

> – Call down Dolly your chamber-maid, and I will give you my cap and bell along with it, if I make not this matter so plain that Dolly herself should understand it as well as Malebranch. – When Dolly has indited her epistle to Robin, and has thrust her arm into the bottom of her pocket hanging by her right side; – take that opportunity to recollect that the organs and faculties of perception, can, by nothing in this world, be so aptly typified and explained as by that one thing which Dolly's hand is in search of. – Your organs are not so dull that I should inform you – 'tis an inch, Sir, of red seal-wax.   (II.2)

Tristram Shandy is, among other things, a wonderful study of the close links that exist between pornography and the novel. Just read Slawkenbergius's tale again, or, for a more compressed form, Chapter 21 of Volume IX. The strip-tease strategy is the same in both cases, and so ubiquitous is the pattern in this book that we must sooner or later be led to ask: Why cannot the thing be said straight out? For indeed it seems that it cannot. At the slightest hint of talk of the sexual organs we are presented with a row of asterisks – as if the one thing this chatterbox of a book could not do was speak directly on this point. Why?

15.   Consider Uncle Toby. He has been wounded in the groin at the Battle of Namur, and the Widow Wadman is surely not the only one to wonder if the word 'groin' is not perhaps a euphemism. The idea of Toby having children is inconceivable to Walter, and, indeed, to us, not so much because of any natural deficiency as because *he seems to be perfectly happy as he is.* And what does he do with his time? He relives, via a model – first a map and then, when that proves inadequate, a three-dimensional reconstruction – he relives the moment when his wound occurred *in order to make sense of it.* The compulsion is obviously there – the opening of Volume II makes that clear – but his way of coping with it is clearly entirely pleasurable. And we realize that, were the Widow Wadman successful in her campaign, that would be the end of Toby's game, of his innocence and of his happiness.

But Toby, like Walter, only develops to extremes one aspect of the writer's own situation. Tristram too has made *his* game out of the playful exploration of his own compulsive concerns with the primal scene, a scene of both birth and death, gain and loss. Indeed, it is as if the game could not be elaborated unless there were loss, castration; and unless that loss were coped with by being *displaced.*

We can now make a tentative stab at an explanation of the innuendo I began with, the narrator's remark that our present orators are no match for the ancients because they have nothing under their short tunics. They are, we may tentatively say, only orators *because* they have nothing under their tunics.

17.   For the reader, no less than for the Widow Wadman, it becomes a matter of dire necessity to know what is under Toby's tunic. Yet that is the one thing Sterne will not tell him. And it is not just a matter of leading him on and then turning away. Sterne goes shallower than that.

Listen to this passage:

> – 'My sister, mayhap,' quoth my Uncle Toby, 'does not choose
> to let a man come so near her ****.' Make this dash, – 'tis an
> Aposiopesis. – Take the dash away, and write *Backside*, – 'tis
> Bawdy. Scratch Backside out, and put *Covered Way* in, 'tis a
> Metaphor; – and, I dare say, as fortification ran so much in my
> uncle Toby's head, that if he had been left to have added one
> word to the sentence, – that word was it.

Something extremely complicated is happening here. It is not just
that we are being made aware of the fact that there is really no Mrs
Shandy, no Toby, no Walter – that they are made up of rhetorical
conventions, words and letters – that is, ultimately, so many straight
and curved black lines on white paper. No. The fiction is too powerful for that. It is that they are 'real people' for us by this time (we
are half way through the second volume), alive for us as characters
in fiction can be – *but also, suddenly, mere words*. We want to move
forwards, get on with the story, inwards, to an understanding of
their motives, *and we are frustrated*. Not because the fiction stops,
but because, before our eyes, it turns into something else, into
another kind of discourse. Or rather, since the characteristic of the
classical novel is that the fiction conceals its status as discourse, we
seem to move, as in a Möbius strip, from inside to outside without
any apparent hiatus, and the harder we try to get back in, so to
speak, the more resolutely we find ourselves shut out.

And this is characteristic of the book as a whole. The paragraph
immediately following the one I have just quoted reads:

> But whether that was the case or not the case: – or whether the
> snapping of my father's tobacco-pipe so critically, happened
> through accident or anger, – will be seen in due time.

'Due time' is comforting. It is so as to have all explained in due time
that we read on. But in this book time is never due. Incident is added
to incident, word to word, and we seem to move further and further
from meaning within a world of mere extension.

Consider the following, even more mind-boggling passage:

> – ANALOGY, replied my father, is the certain relation and agree-
> ment, which different – Here devil of a rap at the door snapped
> my father's definition (like his tobacco-pipe) in two, – and, at the
> same time, crushed the head of as notable and curious a disserta-
> tion as ever was engendered in the womb of speculation... (II.7)

The definition, like the tobacco-pipe, is snapped in two. But that
of course is not all. We have already had a hint of what is going to

happen to Tristram's nose as he is brought into the world, though the actual incident will only be recounted later. But we are suddenly made to ask ourselves: Which engenders which, the reality the metaphor or the metaphor the reality? The answer must be that neither comes first; they lie alongside each other, affecting each other by a kind of metonymic contamination. The effect is eerie. Which is an analogy for which? Are they both perhaps analogies for something else? When we later learn of Tristram's head being crushed in his mother's womb we feel for him, putting ourselves in his place – even that place – as we always do when reading fiction – but at the same time we half-sense that this may not really be happening, that it may all be metaphor or analogy, that Tristram himself may be an analogy, and so that we too, who thought ourselves so solid, may only be... what?

18.   We begin to see that our wish to get at the 'real' meaning of the book is more than a matter of idle curiosity. Perhaps curiosity is never idle. A great deal seems to be at stake for us as readers in its satisfaction. But can curiosity ever be satisfied?

> I define a nose as follows [writes Tristram] – entreating only beforehand, and beseeching my readers, both male and female, of what age, complexion and condition soever, for the love of God and their own souls, to guard against the temptations and suggestions of the devil, and suffer him by no art or wile to put any other ideas into their minds, than what I put into my definition. – For by the word *Nose*, throughout all this long chapter of noses, and in every other part of my work, where the word *Nose* occurrs, – I declare, by that word I mean a Nose, and nothing else, or less.   (III.31)

But it is a characteristic of speech and writing that meaning cannot simply be circumscribed in this way. If a nose is the centre of a story we are bound to ask why. And if the answer cannot be given in terms of verisimilitude – and even here there is something puzzling, unaccounted for – then the thing must have another meaning. Walter, at any rate, is convinced of this, and a little later we find him studying Erasmus on noses:

> Nature had been prodigal in her gifts to my father beyond measure, and had sown the seeds of verbal criticism as deep within him, as she had done the seeds of all other knowledge, – so that he got out his pen-knife, and was trying experiments upon the

> sentence, to see if he could not scratch some better sense into it. – I've got within a single letter, brother Toby, cried my father, of Erasmus his mystic meaning. – You are near enough, brother, replied my uncle, in all conscience. – Pshaw! cried my father, scratching on, – I might as well be seven miles off. – I've done it, said my father, snapping his fingers. – See, my dear brother Toby, how I have mended the sense. – But you have marred a word, replied my uncle Toby. – My father put on his spectacles, – bit his lip, – and tore out the leaf in a passion.

It seems to be a law here that we urgently desire to get to the heart of meaning, yet that to get there is to mar all. Indirection is the order of the day, in *Tristram Shandy* just as much as in *A la recherche du temps perdu.*

19. It is here that what I will call the collage elements – black pages, marbled pages, asterisks, pointing fingers, even the relative lengths of the dashes which eighteenth-century printers were willing to supply but the use of which we have now lost[6] – here that what I will call the collage elements come into play. They do not all function in precisely the same way, of course, and it would be interesting to analyse the different effects on the reader of a black and a marbled page. The invitation of the first is to go behind, to lift up the stone of the tomb and behold Yorick lying beneath, so to speak; the effect of the second is to make us trace patterns in an effort to discover meaning. Again, a pointing finger makes different demands from the twirling trajectory of a walking stick. But by and large we can say that the collage elements seem to give us the thing itself, which mere words have been unable to do. But at the same time as they give, they take away. A pointing finger remains only an icon of the human hand, its silent presence in a book even more ludicrously uninformative than words. So we hurry back from the collage elements, back to the words which will, perhaps, after all, yield up the secret – but of course they never do.

20. We can now see that the ultimate play with the reader still involves curiosity, and that this curiosity is still sexual, if we are prepared to recognize that the domain of sex is as large as Freud suggested – that is, that what is at stake is the desire to discover the meaning of one's body.

This curiosity, in Sterne, is forever being frustrated. And as this happens we come to realize that to read 'deeply' and to read 'frivolously' amount to the same thing. Both rest on the assumption that ultimately, either 'beneath' or 'in the end', there is a 'real truth' or 'real centre', which we can reach. But Sterne demonstrates that though this is a perfectly natural mistake to make, it is a mistake nonetheless: there is no Father at the start, disseminating meaning. no virile bull at the end. There is only an absence, a lack – no cock and no bull, but only a cock and bull story.

And yet that 'only', though it is in one sense an admission of failure, is also the precondition of triumph. I want now to suggest that the book's recognition of its poverty, of the way it is merely stuck together by a kind of *bricolage*, of its lack of cock – that this is not merely a sign of its greater honesty, but also that which allows it to be more than the vehicle for Sterne's 'terribly weak human voice', and to affect us where it most matters: in our very bodies.

21.   I began by reminding you of Walter's despair at what Fortune had done to make his child quite other than he might have wished. But perhaps Tristram is only the child of misfortune and disaster because Walter's expectations are so Utopian. In fact, for Walter, his son is only one more *idea*. ' "Were I an absolute prince," he would say, pulling up his breeches with both hands, as he rose from his arm-chair, "I would appoint able judges..." '. But just as Gonzalo's dreams serve to define the reality of Prospero's island, so Walter's Utopian fantasies, the more they are indulged, the more they help us see the reality of the Shandy household. (And are not Defoe and Crusoe really Walters, though Walters who are indeed absolute princes on their own islands?)

In *Tristram Shandy*, the more Walter treats Tristram as a mere idea, the more Tristram's resistant corporality is borne in on us. The opening of Volume III is particularly interesting in this respect. We have got used to the fact that Tristram is not yet born – and then suddenly he is there, and we realize that he has actually been there for some time. Sterne's refusal to pander to our expectations of being present at the birth, so to speak, is rather like Proust's killing off of Swann in a subordinate clause. The continuous talk about everything under the sun that goes on while birth is taking place elsewhere in the house makes that silent (unspeakable) event present to us in ways description of it never could. Again, in the discussion of the Tristrapaedia, the excess of mere words and their lack of relation to the living child brings that child's reality poignantly home to us. As in Proust once more (a point beautifully brought out by George Craig in a recent essay)[7], the overt direction of the pointing finger helps alert us to the silent unseen object away from which the finger points. Tristram is: all that which is other than words, all that which his father cannot speak.

But how? you will say. Is not Tristram before us the whole time? Are not his words all that we see and hear?

Yes. But he is not an object submitted to our gaze; he is a source of potential. He is not described and defined by the words in the book; rather, he is present in and through them.

22.   But could one not say this of any first person narrator? I think not.

Earlier I compared Toby's innocent games on the bowling green with Tristram's games in the study at his writing-table. Now I have contrasted Walter and Tristram. And it is true that of the two Toby is more like Tristram than Walter. But there is another sense in which both seem to exist in stark contrast to Tristram. They are types of the man of action and the scholar, and neither has any doubts about the validity of either his calling or his philosophy of life. Yet this very lack of doubt gives their lives a quite unreal air; they exist happily ensconced in their own cocoons, and neither engages with reality at any point. It is Toby whistling away what is uncomfortable, Walter talking it away, who are the children of this book, and not even the children but the babies, clinging for all they are worth to the Pleasure Principle, and perpetually denying reality. By contrast Tristram's struggles to get his book written, and even the continuing saga of the failure of Walter's ideals where he is concerned, are signs of a response to reality which can only be called creative.

To understand just why this should be so we need to understand a little more clearly the role of interruption in this novel. Walter, you will remember, described his son not just as a child of wrath and decrepitude, but as a child of interruption. And I suggested that interruption was characteristic of the novel as a whole. So far we have looked at it in its negative aspect, so to speak, as a denial of the reader's desire to move forward to a fullness of truth. Now we need to examine its positive role.

Walter Benjamin has acutely observed the function of interruption in Brecht's theatre:

> The task of epic theatre [he says] . . . is not so much the develop-
> ment of actions as the representation of conditions. This does not
> mean reproduction as the theoreticians of Naturalism understood

it. Rather, the truly important thing is to discover the conditions of life... This... takes place through the interruption of happenings... Epic theatre is by definition a gestic theatre. For the more frequently we interrupt someone in the act of acting, the more gestures result.[8]

Robinson Crusoe and *The Praise of Folly* are, in their different ways, comfortable works to live with. They establish a convention or distance at the start and remain faithful to it throughout the work. But *Tristram Shandy* is a story of interruptions, a story made up of multiple gestures, and that is much more exciting, amusing and disturbing.

The classic novel exists in time in ways in which even the longest epic cannot be said to do. That is, it both takes time to read and it is unconcerned with the passing of time. But, curiously it seems quite unable to register the actual effects of time. Or perhaps we should say that in the classic novel time exists as a beneficient deity, one who will bring forth whatever is in her womb. Its other name is plot.

Plot, in the sense in which it exists in George Eliot or Dickens, does not exist in *Tristram Shandy*. That novel's movement is all sideways, never forwards towards the final revelation inherent in plot. *Tristram Shandy* thus seems to stand in the same relation to the classic novel as, according to Benjamin's 'Theses on the Philosophy of History', historical materialism stands to historicism. This is how Benjamin puts it:

A historical materialist cannot do without the notion of a present which is not a transition, but in which time stands still and has come to a stop. For this notion defines the present in which he himself is writing history.[9]

The present in the classic novel is always a transition; in *Tristram Shandy* time, as we have seen, keeps standing still, and this precisely defines the present in which the story is trying to get written. Historicism inevitably culminates in universal history, but

Universal history has no theoretical armature. Its method is additive; it musters a mass of data to fill a homogeneous, empty time. Materialist historiography, on the other hand, is based on a constructive principle. Thinking involves not only the flow of thoughts, but their arrest as well. Where thinking suddenly stops in a configuration pregnant with tensions, it gives that configuration a shock...

When that happens the present is suddenly seen as 'the time of the now', which, says Benjamin, is 'shot through with the chips of Messianic time.'

These aphoristic formulations, terse and compressed as they are, nevertheless help us to see the source of the power of Sterne's novel. From this perspective not only the play with time but the whole bag of tricks associated with the novel take on a new significance. By interrupting an action Sterne makes us aware of the potential of actions; by fragmenting, changing direction, never allowing us to relax in a distance established once and for all between ourselves and the novel, he brings the world alive for us.

23.   Can we be more precise about this?

I have already given numerous examples of how Sterne refuses to let us settle into the comfort of accepting the book either as rhetoric or as history. We cannot read it as we do most novels, for it keeps flattening out into rhetoric (an interruption is merely an aposiopesis). On the other hand we cannot read it as a rhetorical game, for it maintains connections with lived reality, it works on us as novels always do work, bringing the characters and events alive for us as they would be were we to receive a letter about them from a friend.

The unsettling, double quality of this book is manifested most clearly in its dealings with time.

Traditional story-telling has always taken place in a special time.[10] The community gathers round and listens to one of their number, specially gifted with memory and eloquence, who repeats for them the stories they have so often heard before. While he talks, usually in the long evening hours when it is no longer possible to work in the fields or out at sea, the women may well get on with the work of their hands, basket-weaving or rope-making, while the children fool around or drop off to sleep. In that way time passes. But time, the history of the community, is also re-affirmed, in the story and by the very gathering of its members to listen to the story. A novel, on the other hand, is read by each of us alone, in bed, in an armchair or in a library. We do nothing with our hands while we read. Our hours with the book help us to pass the time and allow us to escape from our own meaningless lives into the meaningful and purposeful life of the hero.

Sterne will have none of that. He is at pains to remind us that telling stories *takes up time*, ordinary common or garden time, and so does listening to or reading them. As in Cervantes, the action keeps breaking off while people gather round to listen to someone tell a story. But here, unlike Cervantes' novel, whose author, with one part of himself, still tries to believe that he lives in a world of oral story-telling, here there is always the sense that they should be doing something else, that the time they are spending *here* is time they are wasting *there*. And if this is true of the characters of the book, it is true, willy nilly, of Tristram himself, of Sterne, and of the reader.

'I like to hear Trim's stories about the captain,' says Susannah. And then 'Susannah, the cook, Jonathan, Obadiah, and corporal Trim formed a circle about the fire; and as soon as the scullion had shut the kitchen door, – the corporal begun.' But instead of giving us the corporal's story, for which we are now as keen as the servants, the next chapter begins: 'I am a Turk if I had not so much as forgot my mother.' We too had forgotten Mrs Shandy and must, reluctantly, turn from the corporal's tale to attend to her.

Partly what this does is to reinforce the Puritan sense that it is wrong to listen to stories, that time must be used well, not idled away.[11] ''Tis commonly observed,' wrote one reformer in 1704, 'that the first step to wickedness is idleness; and indeed there is little hopes of anyone being a good man or a good Christian, who has no care of his time.' In a chapter entitled 'Of Spending Time', in his *Advice to an Only Child* (1693), the Presbyterian Oliver Heywood offered the following typical counsel:

> Never do anything merely to pass the time away. Neither make any visits, nor set upon any thing called recreation, barely on that account. Time is too precious a jewel, too valuable a treasure, to study how to get rid of it, as some do of an old commodity that lies on their hands, that they cannot tell what to do with. God never gave us the least pittance or moment of good to trifle away...

But one does not have to invoke historical explanations. The reformers may have no doubts as to how one *should* spend one's time, but Tristram and Sterne certainly do. To begin with the novel shows us how we use stories in order to protect ourselves from the consequences of time. Remember, for example, how the assault on the Widow Wadman is delayed and delayed while Trim goes through the complicated ritual of starting a story, eagerly abetted by Toby. Both of them know that a successful assault on the Widow (and any assault on that lady is likely to be successful) will spell the end of the happy life they have lived up to then. Telling stories is an excellent way of postponing that moment.

Time spent telling stories and listening to them, time spent writing and reading, is time not spent elsewhere. And for the characters in this book elsewhere is not better but worse than here. Elsewhere is in fact the place where time passes and death is seen to come a little nearer every second.

All talk of *Tristram Shandy* as a game with the reader, a brilliant rhetorical exercise, founders on this rock. For if the book is, as I have suggested, like Toby's games, a way of deflecting sexuality and making it manageable, it is also, quite simply, an ultimately hopeless flight from death. Tristram writes for all he's worth, but there is no privileged time for writing, no chamber sealed off from time and the world in which the writer can settle at his ease. That is why Volume VII is placed where it is. It is the necessary complement to Volumes I-II and VIII-IX, the volumes which deal respectively with birth and love.

24.   Volume VII brings all the issues of the book together: the nature of verisimilitude; the relations of fiction to pornography; of writing to sex and death.

The tone does not change, but that makes it all the more painful to read. Is Tristram's journey to France to try to escape Death a real journey or only a metaphor or analogy? But what does 'real' mean here? Volume VI, for example, begins:

> – We'll not stop two moments, my dear Sir, – only, as we have got through these five volumes, (do, Sir, sit down upon a set – they are better than nothing) let us just look back upon the country we have passed through. –

A common enough metaphor. But suddenly we find that this is a journey we too are embarked on, and one we cannot conveniently escape from merely by putting down the book:

> Now there is nothing in this world I abominate worse, than to be interrupted in a story – and I was that moment telling Eugenius a most tawdry one in my way, of a nun who fancied herself a shell-fish, and of a monk damned for eating a mussel, and was shewing him the grounds and justice of the procedure –
>   '– Did ever so grave a personage get into so vile a scrape?' quoth Death. Thou hast had a narrow escape, Tristram, said Eugenius, taking hold of my hand as I finished my story –
>   But there is no *living*, Eugenius, replied I, at this rate, for as this *son of a whore* has found out my lodgings –

– You call him rightly, said Eugenius – for by sin, we are told, he entered the world – I care not which way he entered, quoth I, provided he be not in such a hurry to take me out with him – for I have forty volumes to write, and forty thousand things to say and do, which no body in the world will say and do for me, except thyself; and as thou seest he has got me by the throat (for Eugenius could scarce hear me speak across the table) and that I am no match for him in the open field, had I not better, whilst these two spider legs of mine (holding one of them up to him) are able to support me – had I not better, Eugenius, fly for my life? 'Tis my advice, my dear Tristram, said Eugenius – Then by heaven! I will lead him a dance he little thinks of – for I will gallop, quoth I, without looking once behind me, to the banks of the Garonne; and if I hear him clattering at my heels – I'll scamper away to mount Vesuvius...

The writer who senses the possibilities of his craft is in control of the reader of this book; he can play with time in it, stop, move off in a different direction, turn round suddenly and pounce on the reader from behind. But even as he does that time is passing. It cannot be spoken, for to speak it is to deny it; it can only be felt. And, as I suggested we felt Tristram's presence in the area of silence which surrounds him, so we feel death as the book draws to its end, a spectral presence which had in fact been there from the start. It was this, unknown to us and to him, which led to his desperation at not being able to get his story off the ground. Now it pervades everything as, four hundred pages and so many years later, still nothing meaningful has been achieved.

25.   Plot and metaphor suggest a triumph of the artist over time. It is not surprising that aestheticians, concerned to replace religion by art, have made so much of these things. *Tristram Shandy* enacts the effort to achieve them and the failure of that effort. The book is all extension and no meaning, all analogy and metonymy and no metaphor or plot.

Writing and reading take place in time. They cannot escape it. This novel does not try to. Again, as with *A la recherche*, it temporarily frees us from the compulsion of both sex and time by making us recognize them for what they are. Though Proust flirts with a Platonic solution in *Le temps retrouvé*, in the end he remains faithful to his profoundest insight: that we are given back time by recognizing that it is what inevitably passes. We are really in it, and what is happening to us is really going by as it happens, the future is not at a distance, but is always becoming the present, and there is no graspable shape to our lives except this process. To avoid recognition of this is to avoid recognition of one's own body. To accept the one is to be given back the other.

In Borges' story, with which I began, the narrator makes an amazing discovery:

> Through the window I saw the familiar roofs and the cloud-shaped six o'clock sun. It seemed incredible to me that that day without premonitions or symbols should be the one of my inexorable death. In spite of my dead father, in spite of having been a child in a symmetrical garden of Hai Feng, was I – now – going to die? Then I reflected that everything happens to a man precisely, precisely *now*.

In Stephen Albert's library the other side is presented to him:

> In all fictional work, each time a man is confronted with several alternatives, he chooses one and eliminates the others; in the fiction of Ts'ui Pên, he chooses – simultaneously – all of them... Sometimes, the paths of this labyrinth converge: for example, you arrive at this house; but in one of the possible pasts you are my enemy, in another, my friend.

It is not surprising that commentators have seized on this latter aspect of Borges at the expense of the former. That everything happens to a man precisely *now*, that death is not something I can ever tame by the use of the imagination, is not an easy notion to grasp, since to grasp it the imagination must somehow recognize its own limits. In fact, it can only be grasped by realizing its opposite: because I grasp that there are alternative lives I could live, I could have lived, I am able to understand why the one I do live and have lived is necessary.

26. In Chapter twelve of Volume I we are told of Yorick's death. We are told that he lies under a plain marble slab, upon which is inscribed the legend: 'Alas, poor Yorick!' The name is in capitals, followed by an exclamation mark, and the legend has a black line round it. A few lines later the phrase is repeated. Again it is placed on a separate line, but this time it is not bounded. We are asked to imagine the words sighingly spoken by those who pass by: 'Alas, poor Yorick!'

If we try to unpack the effect of this on us we get something like friend was broke; he squeez'd his hand,——and then walk'd softly out of the room, weeping as he walk'd. *Yorick* followed *Eugenius* with his eyes to the door,----he then closed them,—— and never opened them more.

He lies buried in a corner of his church-yard, in the parish   5 of————, under a plain marble slabb, which his friend *Eugen-ius,* by leave of his executors, laid upon his grave, with no more than these three words of inscription serving both for his epitaph and elegy.

> Alas, poor Y O R I C K !

Ten times in a day has *Yorick*'s ghost the consolation to hear his monumental inscription read over with such a variety of plaintive tones, as denote a general pity and esteem for him;——a foot-way crossing the church-yard close by the side of his grave,—not a passenger goes by without stopping to cast a look upon it,——and sighing as he walks on,

Alas, poor Y O R I C K !

The end of Vol. I, ch. 12 of *Tristram Shandy*

this. An epitaph may be quaint or amusing, but it has to be essentially true: 'Here lies X or Y' is something we do not question. But of course there is no body underneath the page we are reading. A novel is not a tomb, the words inscribed on its cover do not function in the same way as does an epitaph. On the other hand if we imagine it does, the book will indeed become a kind of tomb. Yet if we simply read it as a 'story' we will somehow miss the body which does lie behind it. What happens as we read this page of the book is that we react to the tone, a tone by turns sentimental and prurient. But the tone forces us to laugh at the absurd combination of funerary inscription and exclamation mark, at the uneasy mixture of the hieratic and the demotic, the eternal and the evanescent. And if we have doubts about the epitaph, what about the repetition of the phrase? Can it really be what people feel about Yorick? Have we not heard it somewhere before, in rather less reverential a context?

We recognize the strength of our feelings – we *want* to feel for Yorick. But we are only made aware of them because they are deflected. After all, the phrase is not Tristram's, or that of Yorick's friends, it is a quote from the most famous play in the language. So, if it is not Yorick's fate which moves us here, what is it? Is it that of Tristram, for whom we feel *through* the uneasy language? But no, it is not that either, for Tristram himself, we feel, is the product of Sterne's imagination. Ah, so it is Sterne who moves us. But who is Sterne? An eccentric eighteenth-century clergyman? Yes, but it is not he who moves us either. The Sterne we experience as we read is the Sterne who wrote – no, the Sterne who *writes*. As he writes he comes alive, and as he writes he dies a little more each day. The recognition of the latter is what makes the former possible.

By exploring the multiple possibilities, their inevitable limitations and final disappearance, Sterne returns us, his readers, to the primal world of polymorphous perversity, *and simultaneously* makes us realize that a condition of such an exploration is that such a world has gone for good and that soon we too will be no more. As he does so the dead bones of his body and of ours begin to live. It is, as far as I am concerned, the only possible resurrection.

Stephen Albert is killed that the message may be conveyed more powerfully than it could ever be through merely human speech. Tristram is born for the same reason. The seventeenth-century dream of a universal language was doomed to failure, but that other late Renaissance discovery, the novel, in the right hands, would provide such a language: not in the words, not in the story, not in the book as an object, but in the book *as it is read*: a living body.

II *Everything and Nothing*

1.   I spoke last week about some of the implications of writing and reading fiction, and also about Sterne's nostalgia for a time before, a time when orators had something to hide under their cloaks. In Tristram's mind this golden age seems to have been associated with Yorick, and it may be that in Sterne's own mind it was associated with Yorick's creator, the writer who could so unselfconsciously have his hero exclaim: 'Alas, poor Yorick!'

It is about that writer and that golden world that I wish to speak today. I will follow the pattern of my last lecture and start with a story by Borges. This one is called 'Everything and Nothing', and it begins like this:

> There was no one in him; behind his face (which even in the poor paintings of the period is unlike any other) and his words, which were copious, imaginative, and emotional, there was nothing but a little chill, a dream not dreamed by anyone. At first he thought everyone was like him, but the puzzled look on a friend's face when he remarked on that emptiness told him he was mistaken and convinced him forever that an individual must not differ from his species.[12]

He goes to school, grows up, marries, moves to London:

> Instinctively, he had already trained himself in the habit of pretending that he was someone, so that it would not be discovered that he was no one. In London he hit upon the profession to which he was predestined, that of the actor, who plays on stage at being someone else. His playacting taught him a singular happiness, perhaps the first he had known; but when the last line was applauded and the last corpse removed from the stage, the hated sense of unreality came over him again.

So he turns to dreaming, and then to writing about the heroes of his dreams.

> Twenty years he persisted in that controlled hallucination, but one morning he was overcome by the surfeit and the horror of

being so many kings who die by the sword and so many unhappy lovers who converge, diverge, and melodiously agonize... That same day he disposed of his theatre. Before a week was out he had returned to the village of his birth, where he recovered the trees and the river of his childhood; and he did not bind them to those others his muse had celebrated, those made illustrious by mythological allusions and Latin phrases. He had to be someone; he became a retired impresario who has made his fortune and who interests himself in loans, lawsuits, and petty usury...

The story goes that, before, or after he died, he found himself before God and he said: 'I who have been so many men in vain, want to be one man: myself.' The voice of God replied from a whirlwind: 'Neither am I one self; I dreamed the world as you dreamed your work, my Shakespeare, and among the shapes of my dream are you, who, like me, are many persons – and none.'

Perhaps we feel that this is slightly sentimental; yet Borges has, I think, touched on a central factor in our experience of Shakespeare. He is not, like the nineteenth-century Shakespearians, trying to give us a spiritual biography of the dramatist; rather, like Coleridge and Ruskin, he is highlighting what Frank Kermode has called Shakespeare's patience, his ability to absorb all our questions.[13] Indeed, Kermode, at the end of his fine centennial lecture called 'The Patience of Shakespeare', quotes from a poem by Delmore Schwartz, which ends in a very similar vein to Borges's story:

> ... sweet prince, black night has always descended and has always ended.
> ... prince of Avon, sovereign and king
> With all the sweetness and all the truth with which you sang anything and everything.

2. It is not difficult to recognize the truth of such remarks; but it is difficult to know where to go, critically, from there. We don't seem to have the critical vocabulary to deal with the notions of patience and allied concepts. Our critical vocabulary directs us to open up, explore, understand. The criticism of Shakespeare which wants to go in a different direction is usually reduced to the reiteration of platitudes.

No one has done more to help us break out of this impasse than Northrop Frye. In his marvellous lectures on the comedies, *A Natural Perspective* (1965), he points out that

It is curious that we can think of impartiality only as detachment, of devotion to craftsmanship only as purism, an attitude which, as in Flaubert, turns all simple life into an enormously intricate still life, like the golden touch of Midas. We can hardly conceive of an imagination so concrete that for it the structure is prior to the attitude, and prescribes the attitude. Shakespeare's impartiality is a totally involved and committed impartiality; it expresses itself in bringing everything equally to life.

This is a vitally important insight, and I will return to it from a different angle in the next lecture. But it is not an easy notion to grasp, so let us try to follow Frye as he fleshes it out.

'Of course all art is conventionalised,' he says, 'but where the convention is most obvious and obtrusive the sense of play, of accepting the rules of the game, is at its strongest.' For Shakespeare 'does not ask his audiences to accept illusion: he asks them to listen to a story.' In this he is quite different from Jonson, who wants to teach and correct, and who 'strives in his art to create an unbreakable illusion.' Frye suggests that 'Shakespeare's plays bring us close to the oral tradition, with its shifting and kaleidoscopic variants, its migrating themes and motifs, its tolerance of interpolation, its detachment from the printed ideal of an established text.' He points out that in Jonson the complexity of the drama tends to be teleological, directed towards an end in which all will be resolved, while in Shakespeare it is often processional and contrapuntal. If we think of the miracle plays, of *Tamburlaine*, we see that English drama before Jonson tends towards the processional, and that Shakespeare never loses his fondness for this right up to *Henry VIII*.

What all this suggests to Frye is that if we see the comedies rather than the tragedies as central to Shakespeare's output, then he is found to have affinities with older and non-Western drama and with opera, whereas Jonson initiates a tradition which is still dominant today, though less obviously so than in the nineteenth century, the tradition of what we might call the well-made play. Frye reminds us of Chinese plays of the Sung period, which cannot readily be distinguished from opera, for music plays a crucial role in them, keeping the *plot* always subordinate to the *rhythm*: 'Plots of operas are often more uninhibited than plots of plays, because the driving force of the opera is provided by the music.' Thus

In *Figaro* we have a comfortable feeling that no doubt all the complications will work out as they should, but in the meantime something more important, like 'Voi che Sapete' or 'Dove sono' is likely to turn up at any time and claim our main attention.

It is thus to *Figaro* and *The Magic Flute* that Frye turns when looking for parallels to *Twelfth Night* and *The Tempest*, and to operatic terms when trying to describe individual works, remarking perceptively about *Pericles*, for example, that

> Gower provides a narrative continuity, like *recitativo*, while the main action dramatizes the central episodes. In the imagery music is practically the hero of the play: it is to the action of *Pericles* what Prospero's magic is to the action of *The Tempest*.

3. Frye's insistence on the story-telling elements in Shakespeare, on his affinities with medieval drama, Chinese music-drama and opera seems to me wholly justified and very illuminating. And anyone who reads through the thirty-six plays is bound to feel that Shakespeare is here exploring the possibilities of dramatic form in very much the same way as Bach and Mozart explored the possibilities of the musical forms they inherited. 'Then learn this of me,' Touchstone says to William, 'To have is to have; for it is a figure in rhetoric that drink, being poured out of a cup into a glass, by filling the one doth empty the other.' Shakespeare pours from cup to glass to mug, but the cup is always full, for we are in a world where giving only makes us discover how much we have. That is why our pleasure in him is so immeasurably enhanced when we start to become familiar enough with his plays to note the repetitions and permutations. And here I am not thinking only of the storms at sea, identical twins, heroines disguised as boys, retreats into forests and disappearing rulers. I am thinking also of the way contrasts emerge more sharply through our awareness of similarity. Thus, to take *Othello* as a purely arbitrary focus, we note that both Iago and Macbeth are described as 'honest' when we first meet them, but with Iago it is a plain case of mistaken identity, while with Macbeth it is at least partly true. And we may wonder whether, if Iago and not Othello had been the centre of the dramatist's attention, we might not have discovered the same to be true of him. Again, Othello and Leontes have much in common, but where all Shakespeare's skill went into motivating the jealousy of the former, having done that, he now wants to focus on the aftermath of jealousy and so makes the motivation as perfunctory as possible. Or, if we see Iago as a manipulator, organizing the action, and Othello as a slow-speaking, clumsy, good-hearted non-European who is taught a new kind of language by Iago in which curses figure prominently, we

may suddenly feel that we are not all that far from the Prospero-Caliban relationship.

These examples, however, perhaps alert us to an unease we may feel with Frye's argument. Profound and salutary as it is, it is noticeably more successful in dealing with the comedies than with the tragedies. And you will I am sure have noted too that it only takes up one aspect of Borges's little story. For what Borges suggests of course is that the very strengths we have been outlining are also, for Shakespeare, a source of deep anxiety. Borges would not be justified in making this claim – or rather, we would not register it as at least partly true – if it were not for the fact that Shakespeare himself seems concerned with it. For what else is *Richard II* but a play which explores the relationship of what a man says and does to what he is? And *Hamlet* of course derives a large part of its power from the fact that it dramatizes the very dilemma with which Borges is concerned: Who am I? What is the relationship between myself and the roles I am called upon to play? What action is the right action? What is the right way for *me* to die?

Shakespeare, I suspect, holds the place he does in our literature – and our affections – just because he both exists in the same world as the Sung dramatists and the writers of the miracle plays, and because he is close enough to the decline of that world to ask himself questions about it. In that he is like Mozart, who also holds an ambiguous and pivotal position in the history of his art.

But it is not just a matter of *when* Shakespeare and Mozart lived and worked. It is not just that Mozart is more classical than Beethoven, more romantic than Haydn, or Shakespeare more medieval than Milton, more modern than Spenser. It has something to do with the fact that, facing as they do in both directions they seem to be aware of the *cost* of committing themselves wholeheartedly to either. Milton and Beethoven seem so confident of the rightness of what *they* have to say: Haydn and Spenser seem so confident of what they have to *do*. But Borges's story – like Kierkegaard's essay on *Don Giovanni* – is disturbing because it hints at an ambivalence at the heart of Shakespeare. Frye is right to see that compared to Jonson Shakespeare is an upholder of the old, oral, story-like kind of play, where Jonson is moving towards a new, teleologically oriented drama, with an insistence on plot and the creation of an unbreakable illusion. But Frye perhaps does not appreciate enough what the tension between the two forms is, or how difficult it is for 'story' to survive the temptations of 'plot'.

But if Shakespeare wrote *everything*, he must have written this as well. I would like to suggest that he did, and that we find it in the play of his that comes closest to a well-made nineteenth-century drama, *Othello*.

4.   Before turning to *Othello*, however, I would like to glance very briefly at a slightly earlier play which seems to be intimately connected with it, *Twelfth Night*. This will also help us to see that our sense of Shakespeare's plays as being like the *Art of Fugue* or the *Goldberg Variations* should not, as it too easily can, be taken as implying purely formal variations and transpositions.

Twelfth Night is an ideal example of what Frye means by 'a totally involved and committed impartiality', by the sense of play being at its strongest where the conventions are the most intrusive. It is a play in which everyone plays, and those to whom our sympathies go out are those who are most aware of the game they are playing and are least concerned to establish a self in the face of the world: Feste and Viola. On the other hand Olivia, Orsino, Sir Andrew and Malvolio, in roughly descending order, exhibit the vices of these virtues, and the play demonstrates with wonderful virtuosity the errors of self-regard and the need for a willingness on the part of each of us to play the roles life requires of us in full awareness of what we are doing, without self-pity or self-seeking.

Yet to put it like this is to put it far too blandly. As always with any commentary on the comedies, one loses the speed and lightness, the breathtaking assurance of the thing itself. As Terence Cave has recently pointed out, what makes it so difficult to talk about Shakespeare is that the plays are quite prepared to comment on themselves and alert us to their reliance on convention, but such comments are themselves part of the convention. Cave concludes a discussion precisely of *Twelfth Night* by remarking:

> If one wanted to invent an allegorical schema for its interpretation, one might say that *Twelfth Night* dramatizes various kinds of misreading. Those characters who are deceived by the parade of figures, or who are devoted to the literal sense (which may well amount to the same thing), are misled and, according to their status, mildly teased and chastised or mercilessly baited.[14]

However, he is quick to point out,

> This reading is itself, no doubt, a misreading; but that only serves to make more palpable the fact that the play is resistant to critical formalization. For all its linguistic and theatrical self-consciousness,

Twelfth Night provides few openings for critical discourse to begin its work; and those openings may themselves prove deceptive, so that the critic risks finding himself in the middle of the stage, smirking and sporting his yellow stockings and cross-garters for the amusement of the public.

This modest conclusion is actually, of course, a critical gain. And yet may not even this refusal of the critic to rest in any one position be itself a position of rest? Or, to put it another way, may not our placing of ourselves with such certainty *above* Malvolio be itself an example of a Malvolio-type attitude?

Frye had noted that Shakespeare 'seems never to have addressed his audience with any other attitude than that expressed in the last line of *Twelfth Night*: "We'll strive to please you every day."' This may be true, yet neither we nor Shakespeare can forget the very real horror and humiliation to which Malvolio has been subjected: shut up in darkness and told he is mad – the ultimate nightmare of solipsism. *His* last words, we recall, are: 'I'll be revenged on the whole pack of you!'

Othello could well be called *Malvolio's Revenge*.

5.   'I look down towards his feet – but that's a fable.' Yet Iago, if not the Prince of Lies himself, is very like him. For, like the serpent in Eden, he brings division where before there was none; and he does so simply by speaking the way he does. For if language is the prerogative of man, part of its mystery lies in the fact that it can also be used against his humanity. And from the very first scene of the play we see Iago using language apparently neutrally (just as the serpent merely asked: 'Yea, hath God said, Ye shall not eat of every tree of the garden?'), but in actual fact sowing discord; waking our buried dreams and fears and then using them for his own ends.

Everyone knows the opening lines of *Twelfth Night*. The first words of *Othello*, if less memorable, are just as significant:

Roderigo: Tush! Never tell me?...
Iago: 'Sblood, but you'll not hear me!
            If ever I did dream of such a matter,
            Abhor me.

We are used to being told things at the start of a play. In scene two of *The Tempest* Miranda notoriously does nothing but ask leading questions. Here too Roderigo seems to be asking for information, and Iago supplying it, *for our benefit*. But this is not in fact what is going on. We grasp that what has happened just prior to the opening of the play is that Iago has *refused* to say something. And this initial stance of blockage is one we will grow familiar with in the course of the play. It is Iago's chief ploy.

Let us examine it a little more closely. I entertain a visitor in my room. There are two doors, the one through which he has just come, and another, in the opposite wall. He may, at slack moments in our conversation, wonder where this second door leads, but the question will remain latent for him – unless, that is, I back up against it and say: 'I'm sorry, you can't go through that door.' It doesn't need Freud to explain that that 'can't' has introduced the possibility of 'can', which did not exist before that moment.

So it is with Iago. 'I will not speak,' he keeps asserting, and then, when pressed, 'All right then, if you insist...'. But why should he speak in the first place? There are two sorts of answer. The first is: 'Because he wants to achieve his ends and speech is his chief weapon.' The second is: 'Because in a play everyone must speak.' When someone doesn't, on stage, this is so curious a state of affairs that it becomes the centre of the plot and the play is called *The Silent Woman*. The two answers, it will be seen, treat the work from two quite different perspectives. The first remains within the fiction of the play while the second stands back from it and looks at the dramatist's role in the presentation of that fiction. *Othello*, as we shall see, forces these two perspectives into far greater tension than plays which overtly try to relate them, such as *Hamlet* and *The Tempest*.

But to return to that first scene. Roderigo and Iago approach Brabantio's house and Iago suddenly breaks the silence of the night with a shout: 'Awake! What ho, Brabantio! Thieves, thieves, thieves! Look to your house, your daughter, and your bags!' The comic mode of lovers escaping the jurisdiction of the heavy father is here inverted – not just *Twelfth Night* but *The Merchant of Venice* stands behind *Othello* as its ironic mirror. Iago's call, moreover, will ring through the seventeenth century: not look *at*, but look *to*.

And what does Iago say when Brabantio appears? 'Are your doors locked?' The question, which, with variations, is the one he will plague Othello with, is the crucial one, splitting as it does inner and outer, public and private, bringing, like the serpent's question to Eve, a sense of division in what had previously been the smooth envelope of reality. But Iago has many weapons in his armoury. When Brabantio answers: 'Why, wherefore ask you this?' he is ready for him:

Zounds, sir, Y'are robbed! For shame. Put on your gown! Your heart is burst, you have lost half your soul. Even now, now, very now, an old black ram is tupping your white ewe.

We talk too easily perhaps about the richness of Shakespeare's language. It is, of course, overwhelming. Virginia Woolf, no mean user of language herself, jotted down in her diary:

> I never yet knew how amazing his stretch and speed and word coining power is, until I felt it utterly outpace and outrace my own, seeming to start equal and then I see him draw ahead and do things I could not in my wildest tumult and utmost press of mind imagine. Even the less known and worser plays are written at a speed that is quicker than anybody else's quickest; and the words drop so fast one can't pick them up . . . Evidently the pliancy of his mind was so complete that he could furbish out any train of thought; and, relaxing lets fall a shower of such unregarded flowers. Why then should anyone else attempt to write. This is not 'writing' at all. Indeed, I could say that Shakespeare surpasses literature altogether, if I knew that I meant.[15]

Yet I think Eliot was right to be worried by Shakespeare's ease with language, and to contrast his way of writing (with just a hint of disapproval) with Dante's economy and directness. But the point is that Shakespeare too is worried by it, and *Othello* is his most significant examination of its implications. It is the measure of his greatness that he needed to understand all the implications of the extraordinary instrument at his command. Starting his career by imitating the bombast of Peele and Marlowe, he very quickly came to see that the best way to master it was to parody it, as he does in *Love's Labour's Lost* and *Henry IV*. Yet there is always a kind of safety in parody. By the time we get to *Othello* everything is in question.

For it is not of course just the *misuse* of language that is at issue. The responsible writer will see that he cannot be complacent about *any* use of language. For language, to repeat, is never neutral. To make sense of the world we have to impose a pattern upon it; to speak is to make as well as to report. And very quickly we see what kind of pattern Iago is imposing: 'You ae one of those,' he tells Brabantio, 'that will not serve God if the Devil bid you . . . You'll have your daughter covered with a Barbary horse.' Even if this is not actually or even metaphorically true, it awakens echoes in the father: 'This accident is not unlike my dream. Belief of it oppresses me already.' Iago can be sure that whatever door he insists he will not open will be forced by his interlocutors, whatever image he ventures will find an echo in their dreams. Before he arrived, of course. the doors stayed shut, the dreams remained inside the dreamers' heads.

Writing about the opening scene of *The Winter's Tale*, A.D. Nuttall makes an excellent point:

> The psychoanalyst's sense of a latent ambiguity in the childhood of Leontes and Polixenes, in the sociable affect of Hermione, is, I think, really present in the play. Yet to stress this aspect is to falsify; or at least, to distort, since it transforms what is essentially background into foreground.[16]

Othello, I am suggesting, is a play which is primarily *about* such falsification and distortion.

6.   We have had Othello described to us in that first scene as 'thick-lips', and the insulting epithet, suggesting not only African origins but a kind of slowness and clumsiness of speech, at once imposes a contrast with Iago's speed of delivery and ability to change direction with the wind. And as Iago's opening words immediately give us the essence of his character, so it is with Othello: ' 'Tis better as it is,' he says when we first see him, and indeed it would be, but neither Iago nor the playwright can leave things as they are; both are committed to turning 'is' into 'becomes'.

Throughout the second scene we seem to be in quite a different world from that of the first, and it is one projected in large part by Othello's language: 'My services... shall not out-tongue his complaints.' 'I fetch my life and being From men of royal seige...' 'I would not my unhous'd free condition Put into circumscription and confine For the sea's worth.' And, finally, 'Keep up your bright swords, for the dew will rust them.' Notice the slowness of the speech, in contrast to Iago's. Silence is a crucial part of Iago's language, but it is a silence which hides what should be spoken. With Othello on the other hand, the silences come between the words, they are that out of which the words naturally spring and to which they return: they are his body, the totality of his being.

Othello, stopping the brawl, does not shout: 'Stop!' It is as if he senses that his authority externalizes itself in the deliberate quality of his words. We do not think of this as rhetoric or excess, merely as the action of his character in the public sphere. 'Were it my cue to fight, I should have known it Without a prompter,' he answers Brabantio, and we respect his authority. Iago's authority lies in what he knows: Othello's in what he is. This, of course, is an effect Shakespeare works for, and it is reinforced in the following scene, partly by the deference shown Othello by the other senators, partly by Desdemona's own response to him, partly by his great speeches in his defence. Othello, it is interesting to note, has no soliloquies – how could he have, since he exists in the public world and sees himself not as a subjectivity to be explored (like Richard II and Hamlet, who have both been prized loose from the public world and forced back on themselves), but as the doer of deeds which may be recounted?

> Most potent, grave and reverend signiors...
> Rude am I in my speech...
> And little of this great world can I speak
> More than pertains to feats of broil and battle;
> And therefore little shall I grace my cause
> In speaking for myself. Yet, by your gracious patience,
> I will a round unvarnished tale deliver
> Of my whole course of love – what drugs, what charms,
> What conjuration, and what mighty magic...
> I won his daughter.

His way of speaking in his own defence is to tell a tale. And it is through tales that he won Desdemona. He told her the story of his life, not his feelings or ideas. Othello, no less than Odysseus or any other hero from oral culture, is more than he understands, is what he can *relate*.

But this is just what Iago cannot stand. For him it seems to be an evasion, an attempt to beautify and dignify human affairs 'with bombast circumstance'. For Iago ''Tis in ourselves that we are thus or thus. Our bodies are our gardens, to the which our wills are gardeners.' For him, as for Edmund in *Lear*, we are alone in a hostile world, but if we can recognize this and are not fooled by men's rhetoric, we can make sure we remain in charge of our own destinies and eventually get to the top. Thus he urges Roderigo to cheer up and put money in his purse, for 'If sanctimony and a frail vow betwixt an erring barbarian and a supersubtle Venetian be not too hard for my wits and all the tribe of hell, thou shalt enjoy her.' Othello tells a tale: Iago sums up the characters of others, like a novelist, in two words: 'erring barbarian'; 'supersubtle Venetian'.

Indeed, like the curious reader of novels, of whom I spoke in my last lecture, Iago's motive, as it emerges from the plethora of contradictory indications with which he presents us, is simply this: the

need to bring things to an end, to have done with the uncertainty
and multiple possibilities of life and arrive at the ultimate 'truth' of
death and destruction. 'There are many events in the womb of time,
which will be delivered,' he remarks, and, at the end of the first
Act, in the soliloquy which is evidently *his* rightful medium:

> The Moor is of a free and open nature
> That thinks men honest that but seem to be so,
> And will as tenderly be led by th'nose
> As asses are.
> I have't! It is engendered! Hell and night
> Must bring this monstrous birth to the world's light.

7.   With our analysis of the first scenes behind us, it is hardly necessary to spend very much time on how Iago succeeds in poisoning
Othello's mind. It is worth noting though how the first scene of
Act II reinforces our sense of Othello's epic quality. This is the
storm scene with which Verdi starts his opera. What Verdi cannot
do of course, since he does not dream of taking the radical step of
making Iago's a non-singing part, is to differentiate between the
two men at a fundamental level. As a result his opera, for all its
flamboyance, remains mere melodrama, a story of treachery,
jealousy and death.

In this opening scene of Act II Othello's arrival in Cyprus is
heralded by Cassio with at least two speeches which make one feel
that Shakespeare must have read Homer in Greek, or at least suggest
that he must have been able to intuit the authentic epic voice through
paraphrase and translation by means of an imaginative sympathy
which it is hard for us, in our more literate and bookish age, to
understand:

> O, let the heavens
> Give him defense against the elements,
> For I have lost him on a dangerous sea!

And:

> Great Jove, Othello guard,
> And swell his sail with thine own powerful breath,
> That he may bless this bay with his tall ship.

The last line in particular, though it may not have any precise parallels
in Homer, has the authentic Homeric feel. Its significance is enhanced
by being followed by two scenes in which the contrast between Iago
and Othello is re-emphasized.

John Bayley, in a brilliant essay on the play which in many ways forestalls and complements my own remarks, has pointed out how Iago's playful verses on women already feel as though they belonged to the narrower and more cynical world of the eighteenth century.[17] But he does not stress enough, I feel, how profoundly shocked we are when we hear Iago reciting these verses and more especially when, a little later, he pretends to be drunk and 'breaks out' into song. My hesitation over how to describe his action suggests what is wrong. For the unspoken rule for such verses and songs is that they shall be *impromptu*, 'from the heart'. In his comedies Shakespeare has great fun parodying the verses of lovers, but we never doubt the sincerity, only the depth of feeling and technical skill, of those who produce such verses. And the power of music and song, throughout Shakespeare, rests on the fact that it is *natural*, that it springs directly from the occasion, even if, as is so often the case, it is in counterpoint to it. A song is listened to by a group gathered on stage, and by an audience in the theatre, and it binds the two groups together. It is, in some sense, public property, transcending the individual as does an oral tale. Song in Shakespeare has something of the same role as the chorus in Greek tragedy; it distils a mood and sends it over the rest of the play. Kierkegaard, writing about *Don Giovanni*, made the important point that Mozart has an inestimable advantage over Molière, in that he can use music to diffuse all that the Don stands for, the 'triumph of the musical erotic', over the whole action, in a way which Molière, with only the resources of the spoken language at his disposal in *Don Juan*, can never do. Shakespeare's Fools, drunken porters and songs make of his plays something closer to the drama of Aristophanes or the opera of Mozart than to the works of Molière or Ibsen. But Iago's is a private, anti-social nature, and the effect of hearing him break into a song is profoundly disturbing and divisive,[18] more painful even than the experience of hearing the Pardoner, in *The Canterbury Tales*, starting to tell his own manipulative tale – more painful because we are physically present and literally hear Iago sing.

8. Between these two episodes comes one of even greater significance, since it heralds a scene which will later prove to be the turning point of the play. Having put together his little 'Augustan' poem, Iago stands back from the action and comments upon it as he watches Desdemona and Cassio talking together:

He takes her by the palm. Ay, well said, whisper! With as little a web as this will I ensnare as great a fly as Cassio. Ay, smile upon her, do! I will gyve thee in thine own courtship...

We need to examine this little scene rather closely, for much hangs on our understanding of how it is affecting us. We are watching a play, *Othello*. But inside that play we are now watching another play, or rather, we are watching a dumb show and chorus such as we find in *Hamlet* (remember Ophelia's 'You are as good as a chorus my lord') and *Pericles*. But where we have no doubts about the authority of the chorus in these two plays, the situation here is rather different. For one thing, it is not of course strictly speaking a play or dumb show within the play: Desdemona and Cassio may be playing a game, but it is the game of good manners, not a play for an audience. At the same time of course they *are* playing for an audience, the audience which has come to watch *Othello*. But let us stay within the fiction for the time being and explore the implications of what is happening.

There is, first of all, no way for us to know what is *really* going on between the two. Nor is there any way for us to tell if Iago *really* thinks there is something between them, because this is how his mind works, or simply makes use of appearances for his own ends. But the point of the episode is more difficult to grasp than this (intellectually at least, for I believe it comes through quite clearly at an instinctive level in performance). It is that Desdemona and Cassio may not themselves know 'what is going on'.[19] One way of accommodating this is to say: they may think they are merely conversing courteously, but unconsciously they are attracted to each other; or, they may think they are merely conversing courteously, but unconsciously Cassio is attracted to Desdemona; or, just possibly, they are not in the least attracted to each other, they are just going through the social rituals expected of them. (Note that a novelist would find it difficult to avoid opting for one or the other of these explanations.)

But let us pause for a moment and ask whether we think, not of other people, but of ourselves in such clear-cut ways. The answer, I think, is no. And yet the matter is complicated by the fact that we probably feel guilty for not doing so. The trouble with our culture, which tries to live according to the ethics of sincerity and feeling is that, without realizing it, it is committed to notions of 'truth' and 'reality' underlying actions and events. There is a little Iago in all of us, perpetually asking: Is this *really* altruism? Surely you are being hypocritical! And so on. The Elizabethan age was still a period when people instinctively felt that human beings could not be understood in this way. They sensed that emotions could not be treated as self-subsistent real objects, but could only be defined in terms of public frames of reference. Hence the role of ritual and decorum, in life as in art. For a ritual acknowledges the complexity and indefinability of emotions and so establishes social channels for them. It is necessary to celebrate marriage, for example, with all due ceremony, because that turns the private and personal into the public and social and creates reasons for the couple to remain together regardless of the vagaries of the heart.

Ritual and rhetoric go together, though to define their relationship would take more skill, learning and time than I possess. On the other hand the realism of the novel is destructive of ritual. Ritual 'brings distance to life' in the words Walter Benjamin used about friendship; the novel abolishes distance. *Othello* stands poised between the two, dramatizing the clash between them. The realism of the play has this effect on us: we see something in front of us on stage, and because it is part of a play, not part of the continuum of life, we feel that it means something, that we must interpret it. But to interpret is to say: this is what is *really* happening, this is what they are *really* doing. And by putting it this way we are already playing Iago's game.

We see this clearly at the end of this very scene, when Iago and Roderigo go back in conversation over what they – and we – have just seen. Iago explains to Roderigo that Desdemona is hot for Cassio, 'her eye must be fed', she has quickly tired of the Moor, and now longs for the handsome captain. 'I cannot believe that in her,' says the bewildered Roderigo. 'She's full of most blessed condition.' 'Blessed fig's end!' retorts Iago. 'The wine she drinks is made of grapes... Blessed pudding! Did'st thou not see her paddle with the palm of his hands? Did'st thou not mark that?' 'Yes, that I did; but that was but courtesy.' 'Lechery, by this hand!' snarls Iago. 'An index and obscure prologue to the history of lust and foul thoughts.'

Is Roderigo right? Or is Iago? We too have seen the episode, and how do we adjudicate? Courtesy is too weak a concept to stand up for long against the idea of lechery. Or rather, courtesy is not a concept but part of the fabric of life, of a life where public and private are not set up against each other. But of course, as the religious history of the sixteenth century shows, once the idea has taken hold that the outer is merely outer, covering an 'inner' truth, then it is impossible to return to earlier views of man. He who would assert the validity of the outer can now only do so in a despairing Swiftian way, asserting that happiness 'is a perpetual possession of being well deceived.'[20]

In this little scene between Iago and Roderigo we can see the struggle between the two cultures, what we might call the culture of story and decorum and that of plot and truth, played out by two people who are certainly not conscious of the full implications of what they are saying and doing.

9.   This prepares us, of course, for the two great temptation scenes. As John Bayley has noticed, the first of these begins in that empty time when Desdemona is leaving the stage and Othello's thoughts are following her, though he himself remains on stage before us.

As the scene opens Cassio exits and Iago remarks, in one of his pretended asides: 'Ha! I like not that.' Othello is still distracted: 'What dost thou say?' 'Nothing, my lord...'. But, as we have repeatedly seen, to say 'nothing' is quite different from not saying anything, for nothing already conjures up a 'something' which it is negating. When Othello asks if it wasn't Cassio leaving, Iago has already won: 'Cassio, my lord? No, sure, I cannot think it, That he would steal away so guilty-like, Seeing your coming.' But we ourselves have seen Cassio and seen that there was nothing guilty about the way he left. Or was there? How *did* he look? Once an action is taken out of its place in the continuum it becomes unnatural – it becomes, that is to say, guilty.

But Iago, as we have seen, does not work only by negatives. As with Brabantio, so here, he is master of the vivid unsettling image. 'Lie –' 'With her?' asks Othello. 'With her, on her, what you will.' 'Lie with her? Lie on her?' Othello can only gasp back at him. By the middle of the scene he is practically speaking Iago's language, a language of fluid prose, dominated by notions of cause and effect, full of violent imagery. The rest, from Iago's point of view, is simple. We can almost predict it. Once again we watch a scene in dumb show, and once again we receive the ultimate shock of being forced to watch Iago simulating passion:

> Witness, you ever-burning lights above,
> You elements that clip us round about,
> Witness that Iago here doth give up
> The execution of his wit, hands, heart
> To wronged Othello's service!

10.   Let us stand back from the play for a moment and consider two things. The first is this. In classical tragedy, as we know, the dramatists choreographed their plays and wrote the music as well.

In Asian drama what an actor did with his hands, how he sat down and stood up – all this was prescribed by tradition. To some extent the same must have been true of the miracle plays, or rather, since the important thing about these was the story they were telling, and the playing area was so restricted, the action itself must have been minimal, reduced to a few stylized gestures. But on the new open space of the Elizabethan stage, who was to say how a person should enter or exit, stab a king or beat a slave? No doubt, by the time of *Othello*, certain conventions had been established, but these were essentially ad hoc practical solutions. Shakespeare, who would leave nothing unexplored, turned, in *Othello*, to exploring the validity of this as well. What does it mean to exit from the stage? What does it mean for an audience to interpret in one way rather than another so simple an action as walking away? It is a subject he would pursue into his final plays.

The second point has to do with the issues raised by Eric Havelock in his *Preface to Plato* (1963). Classical scholars have not all been convinced by Havelock's thesis that in Plato we see the triumph of the new, literate mentality, over the old oral culture of Homer. But Havelock, it seems to me, like Nietzsche before him, does at least present us with a paradigm of what might occur when there is such a clash. In *Othello* Shakespeare gives us his version, and, as Nietzsche suggested, he makes clear how vulnerable the oral culture is to the other. Shakespeare goes out of his way to suggest the play's links with an older, oral culture. The handkerchief is given to Othello's mother by an African witch: Desdemona sings a song once sung by her maid, Barbary; Venice, we are never allowed to forget, is Europe's window on the Orient. And, even in the midst of his conversion to Iago's way of seeing and talking, Othello still keeps reverting to his old ways: 'But yet the pity of it, Iago! O Iago, the pity of it, Iago.' And when he confronts Desdemona he can still, like Ulysses, only think of his life in terms of a story to be told: 'I took you for that cunning whore of Venice That married with Othello.'

11. This perhaps helps to resolve some of the problems that have notoriously beset the interpretation of the end of the play. Iago ends, as we would expect him to, asserting his privacy, that hollow centre to which others are drawn as to a magnet, and from which he will forever exclude them: 'Demand me nothing. What you know you know. From this time forth I never will speak word.' But, just as the play is seemingly all wrapped up (it could be a comedy except

for that corpse on stage), Othello stops them: 'Soft you! a word or two before you go.' And then he picks himself up, rediscovers himself as a being in action, so to speak:

> I pray you in your letters,
> When you shall these unlucky deeds relate,
> Speak of me as I am.

But what is he? He does not want them to speak of him as *being* this or that – black ram or mighty warrior. He wants them to *relate a deed* – the deed he proceeds to enact before them, killing himself as he tells how he killed another. In an extraordinary metamorphosis, suicide, which in the Christian culture to which Othello at that very moment insists that he belongs (since he implicitly contrasts himself with the 'circumcised dog' he once slew) – suicide, which is seen as the ultimate sin of pride, a final denial of the self which Christ could still redeem – suicide is here made to seem a final affirmation of the self, a final act in the public sphere (Desdemona was strangled far from the gaze of all), which will allow Othello to escape at last from Iago's net. And, as if to confirm this, the last words of the play are indeed spoken (by Lodovico, a faceless, purely representative character) from within Othello's rather than Iago's world: 'This heavy act with heavy heart *relate*.'

12. It has frequently been noticed that Iago, like the Duke in *Measure for Measure* and Prospero, is a kind of playwright or director – it is he who moves the plot forward and licks it into shape. In fact his soliloquies could frequently be taken for the dramatist's own musings as he ponders the direction in which his play is going to go:

> Cassio's a proper man. Let me see now:
> To get his place, and to plume my will
> In double knavery. How? How? Let's see...

To Roderigo he explains:

> Thou know'st we work by wit, and not by witchcraft;
> And wit depends on dilatory time.

As the plot thickens he rehearses his moves to himself:

> Two things are to be done:
> My wife must move for Cassio to her mistress;
> I'll set her on;
> Myself the while to draw the Moor apart

And bring him jump when he may Cassio find
Soliciting his wife. Ay, that's the way!
Dull not device by coldness and delay.

What this suggests is that if, in one sense, Othello triumphs in the
end, in another it is Iago who triumphs. Not just because both
Othello and Desdemona are dead, but because the making of the
play *Othello* shows the triumph of plotting over story-telling. It is
no accident that the play is so suited to grand opera (for, despite
Frye's generalizations, opera too has its history), with its villain,
early love duet, pathetic song for the heroine shortly before the end,
mislaid handkerchiefs and final, long-drawn-out deaths. Of course,
as I suggested in discussing Iago's drinking-song, the play escapes
the limitations of Verdian opera in all kinds of ways; but the fact
remains that Shakespeare, behind the scenes, is acting out a role
which is closer to that of Iago than to that of Othello.

And how could this not be so? His audience is not 'the community'. It has paid to be entertained. Shakespeare has to make sure he
keeps up their interest in a story which does not concern them
directly. As Iago says, 'there are many events in the womb of time,'
and it is the playwright's job, no less than Iago's desire, that 'they
will be delivered'. Iago merely helps this along. It is *Shakespeare*
who has Cassio leave just as Othello enters, who has Desdemona
drop her handkerchief and Emilia pick it up and give it to Iago, who
has her keep silent until it is too late. In *Othello* we watch Shakespeare
exploring, in fascinated horror, the precise implications of his chosen
vocation. From then on we will find him twisting and turning to
escape Iago's logic, the logic which says that to deliver the events
in the womb of time the dramatist must work secretly behind the
scenes, manipulating his puppets in the interests of his plot.

13.   This is particularly noticeable in *Lear* and in *Antony and
Cleopatra*. The central scenes in *Lear* are like an attempt to prolong
the moment of Othello's fit, an attempt to escape from every constraint, social and linguistic and to return to the babelic origins of
speech. But for Lear and for the playwright there is no escape and
in the end plot re-asserts itself. In the light of what I have said so
far this can only be seen as a deeply ambiguous triumph. In *Antony
and Cleopatra*, however, a decisive step has been taken. Here there
is no longer any fixed viewpoint. Each statement, each scene, is
undercut by another. At the climax, as if challenging us to compare
it with the end of *Othello*, Shakespeare makes the double death not

out of the terrible pressure of tragic inevitability, but out of hundreds of tiny contradictory elements, so that even here we have no sense of unity. That is why it is a play which has given rise to more heated argument than any other, and why, perhaps, it rarely succeeds in working in the theatre. It goes too much against those instincts which bring us to the theatre in the first place.

14.   As if aware of this, Shakespeare, in his last plays, changed tack completely. He seems in those plays determined to throw overboard all that the Elizabethan theatre had gained, all that he himself had achieved in terms of psychological motivation and the organization of plot. In *Hamlet* the dumb show had a clear dramatic function; in *Othello*, as I have tried to show, a kind of dumb show was the pivot of the action. In *Pericles* the dumb show is deliberately antitheatrical. The aged Gower, with his stumbling verses, makes no attempt to bring the audience into the action; on the contrary, he keeps us away from it. And the action itself, far from forming a plot that moves towards a climax, meanders through time, allowing us to respond to parallels and contrasts between episodes far apart in time, rather as the audience responded to *figura* in the miracle plays, never allowing us to enter the minds or feelings of the protagonists, but only to wonder at the patterns made by their actions.

Like Shakespeare's first comedy, *The Comedy of Errors*, *Pericles* is set in the traditionally magical island of Ephesus. But *Pericles* is everything *The Comedy of Errors* is not. Where that was all highly formalized New Comedy plot, identical twins and mistaken identities, this is all spectacle, story. It is as though Shakespeare, having, in *Hamlet* and *Lear*, tried to answer the questions: Who am I? What is man? – had recognized that such questions could never be answered within the work of art, and had decided not to conceal himself but to come out in front, as story-teller, between audience and play. Hamlet too, as has been remarked, acts in a sense as a mediator between the audience and a revenge tragedy. But Gower is no longer tormented by the implications of such a role: he serenely accepts it, stumbling forward on his clumsy lines:

> To sing a song that old was sung,
> From ashes ancient Gower is come...

15.   *The Winter's Tale* adds the final element. It is fitting that its analogue should be not an early comedy but *Othello* itself. The other characters in the play, instead of being broken by Leontes' jealousy,

stand resolutely up to him, insisting that he is living in a private world conjured up by his own imagination. Hermione, accused, replies firmly:

> You speak a language that I understand not:
> My life stands in the level of your dreams,
> Which I'll lay down.

But though Leontes is quick to reply: 'Your actions are my dreams', it is she who is right, and Leontes' jealous dreams cannot stand up against the pressure of events. The death of Mamilius, coming on top of Leontes' rejection of the oracle, forces the whole edifice to crumble and he recovers his sanity as quickly as he had lost it.

Leontes is the type of the tyrant, as Paulina keeps insisting, the mad king who uses his power to try and force the world to conform to his vision of it. But however powerful one is, one has ultimately to yield to the reality of the world. When the gaoler hesitates about letting Paulina leave with Hermione's new-born baby, she answers:

> You need not fear it, sir:
> This child was prisoner to the womb, and is
> By law and process of great nature, thence
> Free'd and enfranchis'd; not a party to
> The anger of the king, nor guilty of
> (If any be) the trespass of the queen.

The child is prisoner in the womb, but not in the same way as the mother is prisoner in Leontes' jail. It is the subject of the law and process of great nature, not of any earthly king. But how can nature herself be contained within the imprisoning confines of a play?

In these last plays of his, Shakespeare is careful to show us that the plots turn on chance, not manipulation or psychology. It is Autolycus, selfish, cunning, innocent Autolycus, just as much as Perdita, who is the presiding spirit here, as we move into those extraordinary last acts, with their constant reminder that what we are seeing is stranger even than an old story, no better than a tuppenny ballad. Strange but true, and true because there it is, happening in front of our eyes.

But doesn't all drama take place in front of our eyes? Well... Contrast, for example, the way Paulina sets up the last scene with the way Rosalind does so in *As You Like It*. In that play the audience knows what Rosalind but no one else knows. It is privy to all the secrets of the plot. The pleasure here, as in *Twelfth Night*, derives from seeing the characters gradually discover 'the truth', which we have known all the time. In *The Winter's Tale* Shakespeare gets rid of this aspect of the plot in a little scene where minor characters simply report and discuss the re-uniting of father and daughter. The climax is reserved for something else. Here we just sit and look. We are told our faith is required, and we give it, and watch a dead queen being conjured back to life with the help of music. This is of course what happened in Marlowe's *Doctor Faustus*. But where Helen was a spirit and Faustus and the audience doomed to be merely titillated by her, the effect of Hermione's appearance is entirely different. Like Gower, she personifies, embodies Time, and her presence before us is a gage of the bountifulness of time. In a miraculous moment Shakespeare reverses all romance conventions even as he brings them to a head: Leontes can take pleasure in his restored wife just *because* time has wrinkled her face; a Hermione unchanged in sixteen years would be a painted Hermione; that she has aged is a sign that she lives.

But there is more. This scene, in a sense, is the answer to *Othello*, and it is important to see how. In the tragedy, I suggested, Iago stands between us and a kind of dumb show, and directs us as to how we are to interpret it. We watch someone leave and are immediately made to ask ourselves: Did he look furtive? Was he guilty? To make sense of the dramatic fiction we must all become Iagos. But in these last plays Shakespeare creates a kind of drama in which the Iago within us is accepted – and dismissed. It is not a plot that breeds in the womb of time, it is human life. We have seen Hermione before. Now we see her again. We watch with awe and wonder as she performs what is after all the simplest of stage actions: she steps forward. It does not *mean* anything; the wonder lies in the fact *that it is happening*.

It is nothing: a woman walking forward. And it is everything.

16.   Nevertheless, even here, plot re-asserts itself. Hermione opens her mouth and speaks:

> You gods, look down,
> And from your sacred vials pour your graces
> Upon my daughter's head!

She asks questions; she promises explanations. And though there is still one more wonder in store for both characters and audience, the play ends with Leontes asking Paulina to

> Lead us from hence, where we may leisurely
> Each one demand and answer to his part
> Performed in this wide gap of time since first
> We were dissevered. Hastily lead away.

The fact is that Shakespeare, in spite of everything, is at ease within the rhetorical tradition. He achieves such mastery that he can bend it to suit his will, but he would not dream of destroying it or rejecting it. He seems to sense and accept the fact that he can only have everything if he has nothing.

Yet Borges' story will not leave off haunting us. Is that because we are not and cannot be the heirs of Shakespeare, but of Romanticism?

> Before a week was out he had returned to the village of his birth, where he recovered the trees and the river of his childhood, and he did not bind them to those others his muse had celebrated, those made illustrious by mythological allusions and Latin phrases.

According to Borges, Shakespeare, returning to Stratford determined to be *someone*, became a retired impresario and local businessman. But he could equally well have become a novelist. For the novel explicitly dissociates itself from mythological allusion and Latin phrases. It celebrates the trees and rivers of childhood; not that which has always been sung, but that which has never been sung before and which would have remained unsung had it not been for one person. The novel turns its back on convention and tradition and speaks about the world of each of us in our mother tongue. It is the free speech of free men.

But how free is free?

III 'Non Ego sed Democritus dixit'

1. 'O word, thou word that I lack!' With that despairing cry Schoenberg's only opera, *Moses und Aron*, breaks off at the end of the second act. The music for the third was never composed.

We are, of course, dealing with a general issue, not one particular to Schoenberg. Here, for example, is Henry James in his *Notebooks*:

> The upshot of all such reflection is that I have only to let myself *go*! So I have said to myself all my life – so I said to myself in the far-off days of my fermenting and passionate youth. Yet I have never fully done it. The sense of it – of the need of it – rolls over me at times with commanding force: it seems the formula of my salvation, of what remains to me of a future.[21]

Here is Lily Briscoe in *To the Lighthouse*:

> And she wanted to say not one thing, but everything. Little words that broke up the thought and dismembered it said nothing. 'About life, about death; about Mrs Ramsay' – no, she thought, one could say nothing to nobody. The urgency of the moment always missed its mark. Words fluttered sideways and struck the object inches too low. Then one gave up; then the idea sunk back again. . . . For how could one express in words these emotions of the body?

And here, finally, is Marcel in *A la recherche*:

> Because I wanted one day to be a writer, it was time to decide what it was I intended to write. But as soon as I asked myself that question, seeking to find a subject of infinite philosophical significance, my mind stopped functioning, my attention seemed to focus only on emptiness, I felt that I had no genius, or that perhaps a cerebral disease prevented it from coming to birth.

Why this sense of the lack of a word that would make all the difference? Why this feeling that words are incapable of expressing the emotions of the body? Why this desire to write and the simultaneous sense that the desire has only to surface to be frustrated?

These are not questions that would have troubled Shakespeare or Mozart. I suggested last week that Shakespeare's famous patience, his ability to return all our questions, is perhaps rather less bland than critical discourse often makes it appear. But any doubts he might have are absorbed in a passionately joyful refusal to come to rest in any one position. And similarly Mozart, when, for example, he gives Figaro the wonderful aria 'Non piu andrai' which ends Act I of *The Marriage of Figaro* – Mozart is happy to enter the world of martial music and plunder it of its riches, bring it to life – in ironic counterpoint of course to the action – and then move on to something else.

Such easy commerce with the tradition seems no longer possible for the writers from whom I have just quoted. Why?

2.   Let's start with one of the great fictional attempts to confront the question head-on, Thomas Mann's *Doctor Faustus*.

No reader can fail to be struck, right from the start, by the way the book moves between garrulousness and silence. The garrulousness is the narrator's, Serenus Zeitblom, latter-day Humanist and teacher; the silence is Adrian Leverkühn's, the tragic composer who is the subject of the fictional biography. On the rare occasions when Adrian does write or speak, it is nearly always in the form of parody, as though he could only give utterance in the style and voice of someone else. And, on the few occasions when he seems to speak in his own voice, we get a strong sense of the pain every word causes him, and his brief remarks are usually punctuated with a laugh, as if to dismiss as pointless and redundant whatever he has just said.

An early clue to his attitude is provided by the scene in which Adrian's father is showing some boys some of the wonders of nature. These include a beautiful shell, covered with strange markings, reminiscent of Oriental calligraphy. But though people have tried to decipher them, they have been unsuccessful. 'It has turned out to be impossible,' says old Jonathan Leverkühn, 'to get at the meaning of these marks... They refuse themselves to our understanding, and will, painfully enough, continue to do so.' And yet, he says, the very fact that the marks are there suggests 'that Nature painted these ciphers, to which we lack the key.' Something, then, is communicated here, but it is and will remain 'an inaccessible communication.' And Zeitblom comments: 'Even as a boy I clearly understood that Nature, outside of the human race, is fundamentally illiterate – that in my eyes is precisely what makes her uncanny.'

Adrian, on the other hand, finds this fascinating. Not just because he is more curious than his friend, but because he has less faith than him in the blessings of human literacy. Where Zeitblom is content to teach the classics, play the viola and respond to the beauty of works of art, Adrian is tormented by a doubt:

> The work of art? It is a fraud. It is something the burgher wishes there still were. It is contrary to truth, contrary to serious art. Genuine and serious is only the very short, the highly consistent musical moment.

Why a fraud? What has the 'burgher' to do with it? And what is Adrian implying when he remarks, immediately afterwards, that art would like 'to stop being only pretence and play'? Zeitblom, paraphrasing Adrian's first and only teacher, Wendell Kretschmar, struggles to explain:

> In a work there is much seeming and sham, one could go further and say that as 'a work' it is seeming in and for itself. Its ambition is to make one believe that it is not made, but born, like Pallas Athene in full fig and embossed armour from Jupiter's head. But that is a delusion. Never did a work come like that. It is work: art-work for appearance's sake – and now the question is whether at the present stage of our consciousness, our knowledge, our sense of the truth, this little game is still permissible, still intellectually possible..., whether all seeming, even the most beautiful, even precisely the most beautiful, has not today become a lie.

The work of art appears to be like the shell, but its marks are made by man and not by nature. And, being made by man, it must be prepared to face the question: Why? Is there any justification for it? In the first lecture I referred to Lévi-Strauss's point that there is a biological link between horse and horse, but that the only link between two axes lies in the fact that both belong to the same system of representation. The question Adrian is raising is whether we have any uses for axes in our society today, and, if not, why they still go on being made. Is there any justification for axes, no matter how beautiful, if there is no wood to cut and there are more efficient means of dealing with one's enemies?

This is the Devil's point too in the central chapter of the book. The time for masterpieces is over, he claims. Today we are too full of doubts to write in the overpowering and uninhibited fashion of a Beethoven. Adrian tries to counter this. Surely, he says, there is always 'the possibility of spontaneous harmony between a man's own needs and the moment, the possibility of "rightness", of a

natural harmony out of which one might create without a thought
or any compulsion.' But he doesn't really believe this himself, and
the Devil is really speaking for him (that, after all, is the source of
his strength), when he answers: 'My dear fellow, the situation is too
critical to be dealt with without critique.' And in case Adrian should
be tempted to think that this was purely the result of social or political
factors, which might change in time, he warns him that 'the prohibi-
tive difficulties of the work lie deep in the work itself... It no longer
tolerates pretence and play, the fiction, the self-glorification of
form.' Quite simply

> certain things are no longer possible. The pretence of feeling as
> a compositional work of art, the self-satisfied pretence of music
> itself, has become impossible, and no longer to be preserved – I
> mean the personal notion that prescribed and formalized elements
> shall be introduced as though they were the inviolable necessity
> of the single case... My friend, it cannot go on... the pretence
> of the bourgeois work of art... It is all up with the once bindingly
> valid conventions, which guaranteed freedom of play.

For what is freedom? It is only 'another word for subjectivity, and
some fine day... she despairs of the possibility of being creative out
of herself.'

The view of artistic history here presented by Mann may be over-
simplified, but it is profoundly suggestive (much more so than the
purely linear views put forward in most histories of art: Augustans
followed by Romantics followed by Victorians, etc.). Once, Mann
argues, there was an art which was linked to the cult and subservient
to it (axes were necessary because they were needed). Then, with
the collapse of the cult in the Renaissance and Reformation, there
emerged an art based on subjectivity, the art we associate with
Michaelangelo and Beethoven. Beethoven took hold of the sonata
form, which had until then been made up of roughly equal parts,
each with its precise rhetorical function, and so filled out the development section that the form itself was altered beyond recognition.
But the only rules for the making of this new kind of work were
the desires and creative imagination of the artist, and, once men had
lost Beethoven's confidence in his own will, what was there to put
in its place? The situation Leverkühn inherits is that of being Beethoven's heir without the latter's optimistic belief in himself or the
world. Beethoven shattered the playfulness of the more purely
rhetorical forms of the eighteenth century, but what he has put in
its place is no longer viable. How then is art any longer possible

for the artist who takes his calling seriously and is not content simply to pander to the tastes of the public?

3. Mann's analysis is of course meant to reflect on more than music. We can easily replace 'sonata form' by, say, Shakespearian comedy, or Beethoven by Victor Hugo. For Mann himself, though, this was his most sustained exploration of the value and meaning of the art in pursuit of which he had spent the greater part of his life – the art of the novelist.

We use the words *novel* and *roman* without giving them a thought. But those words may tell us more about the form than many a scholarly disquisition. In the Middle Ages Latin was the common language of Europe. It is difficult for us to realize the immense importance of this fact for men of the time. A recent historian gives us a glimpse of this when he writes:

> All who do not speak Latin are barbarians, don't really speak, don't have a language, merely utter cries like animals. The writers, even those who write in the vulgar tongue, imbued with a respect for 'clergie', make of Latin a synonym for language itself. In William IX of Aquitaine, as in Chretien de Troyes, the birds sing 'in their Latin' ('en leur latin').[22]

Opposed to Latin is *roman*, the romance language, the vernacular. The term soon came to apply to a literary form, but it was a long time before it lost its old meaning.

The intrusion of the vernacular tongue into the empire of *latinatas* created a crisis of which Mann's book is only one of the more recent manifestations. It is interesting in this context to recall Dante's concern to explain (to himself and to his fellow writers) why it was that he should attempt an epic to rival Virgil's not in Latin but in the vernacular, and to recall too that only fifty years after the completion of the *Commedia* Petrarch was to take the decision to write *his* epic in Latin. What Marthe Robert has called the perpetual struggle of the old and the new, which Dante, uniquely, managed to resolve, has, with Petrarch, resulted in the triumph of the old, of Authority, over the new, the vernacular, Experience.

But it was of course Experience, in the guise of the novel, which was to have the last laugh. For, as Roger Dragonetti has pointed out:

> If the word *roman* has maintained itself through so many centuries, despite its own semantic contestations, as the term which designates a genre in perpetual renewal, this is no doubt because the

revolutionary, transformational element, and especially the idea of a new language of literature, implied by the word *roman*, was more important than the content of the work.[23]

The application of these remarks to the term *novel* hardly needs underlining. In England the drama seems to have succeeded the epic as the central form in the 1590s, and to have in turn been ousted by the novel in the 1740s. Scholars have often noted the links between the rise of the novel and the social and intellectual changes of the seventeenth century. More important, perhaps, is to realize that both *roman* and *novel* imply not another genre, but an escape from all genre, from the authority of culture enshrined in the notions of *Latin* and of *art*. The novel is the free utterance of free men.

But, as I asked at the end of the last lecture, how free is free?

4.   Let us stay with this conflict between Latin and the vernacular for a moment. And let us return to Dante.

When Dante and Virgil at last leave the tenfold circlings of the penultimate pit of Hell, they find themselves in an eerie darkness, 'less than night and less than day'. Out of this darkness there emerges a dolorous sound, louder than thunder, more terrible than the sound Roland blew when Charlemagne's host was routed by the infidel. In the murky light Dante makes out an array of huge towers, but Virgil explains that these are giants, whose feet stand in the lower circle and whose upper bodies only are visible. As they approach the first of these figures the enormous mouth opens and meaningless sounds come forth: 'Raphel may amecche zabi almi.' Virgil explains to Dante:

> He is his own accuser: this is Nimrod, through whose ill thought one language only is not used in the world. Let us leave him alone and not speak in vain, for every language is to him as his is to others, which is known to none.

But Nimrod (the instigator of Babel, according to Midrashic tradition here followed by Dante) is only an extreme example of a tendency present in the *Inferno* right from the start. His sin, like that of all the damned, is essentially that of pride, placing himself before all others, and it is not surprising that this has infected his speech. For, wanting to utter that which is uniquely his, he cuts himself off from language altogether.

It seems as if our contrast of Latin and the vernacular was not as clear-cut as we had supposed. For if Latin is the language of *others*, of Authority, of the dominant culture, it does not follow that the vernacular is the opposite of these things. To use language at all is to use an instrument which is forged by others. It is not that the purely personal cannot be uttered in Latin; it cannot be uttered in language at all. Nimrod, thinking that it can – or thinking perhaps that he is speaking the language of Jonathan Leverkühn's shell, the language of nature itself – is reduced to merely uttering noises.

What then is the writer to do who, for whatever reason, has turned his back on Latin and on the whole public world of rhetoric and mythology? The question did not worry many writers before this century, but it did worry Sterne, for he placed as an epigraph to Volumes V and VI of *Tristram Shandy* a quotation, *in Latin*, from Erasmus: *'Non ego sed Democritus dixit.'* Not I but Democritus said it. And to add to the point, Sterne did not get this straight from Erasmus but via Burton's *Anatomy of Melancholy*. As it stands the epigraph is a mock excuse for any material which might offend in what follows. But it is surely more than that. Like Chaucer's similar disclaimer at the start of *The Canterbury Tales*, it is an ironic reminder to the reader who thinks he is going to read the very words of Tristram or of Sterne (for after all the book is entitled *The Life and Opinions of Tristram Shandy*), that of course he will be doing nothing of the sort. For all languages are foreign languages – foreign to us, that is to say. *I* don't say it, Democritus (or whoever) does; it is never *my* language, for 'I' have no language.

Kafka put it rather more tragically when he wrote in his diary for 19 January 1922: 'What meaning have yesterday's conclusions today? They have the same meaning as yesterday, are true, except that the blood is oozing away in the chinks between the great stones of the law.'

Words are like the stones of the law. They are what can and must be said. But the blood of the individual oozes like the minutes and seconds of his life – *his* life, the only one he has – between the stones, the words, and there is no way of turning the hardness of stone into the fluidity of blood, or of congealing blood into stone.

5.   Barthes in *S/Z*, has demonstrated with ruthless elegance the degree to which the language of the classical novel is made up of modes of discourse speaking through the writer rather than for him. I have no wish to go once again over ground he has explored so thoroughly. But perhaps the very elegance of his analysis and the hardly concealed ferocity of his onslaught on Balzac have made us focus on certain aspects of the situation at the expense of others.

At any rate, I would like to approach the problem from a slightly different angle. I want to focus not so much on the kinds of languages that get into novels as on the much bigger, more dangerous and intractable question of the writer's own sense of freedom and constraint.

I want to suggest that we should take the *dixit* in Sterne's epigraph in the widest possible sense. *Non ego sed Democritus dixit* suggests that where we thought we were free to make our destinies as individuals or as a group, we are in fact *being spoken*, or *being written*, by forces outside us. We are not speakers so much as parrots. Of course these forces do not constitute some transcendent being or historical necessity, but rather the multiplicity of conflicting and ever-changing pressures which make up what we take to be 'reality'. But the point is that the medieval optimism in history and the world as examples of God's discourse have here been ironically inverted, and the medieval notion of man as superior to the animals because capable of speech becomes God's last bad joke on us.

Let me remind you of two classic and influential nineteenth-century statements of this view. Marx's *Eighteenth Brumaire of Louis Bonaparte* opens with the famous remark: 'Hegel says somewhere that all the great events and characters of world history occur, so to speak, twice. He forgot to add: the first time as tragedy, the second as farce.' This, suggests Marx, has happened in France, with Louis Blanc, in the role of Robespierre and Louis Napoleon in that of his famous uncle. Marx goes on:

> Men make their own history, but not their own free will: not under circumstances they themselves have chosen but under the given and inherited circumstances with which they are directly confronted. The traditions of dead generations weigh like a nightmare on the minds of the living.

(Years later Eliot was to make the same point about literary tradition:

> If our predecessors cannot teach us to write better than themselves they will surely teach us to write worse; because we have never learnt to criticise Keats, Shelley and Wordsworth (poets of assured though modest merit), Keats, Shelley and Wordsworth punish us from their graves with the annual scourge of the Georgian anthology.)[24]

My second example comes from Freud. Freud's first work in psychoanalysis, the *Studies on Hysteria*, which he wrote with Breuer, contains the seeds of many of his later works. What he demonstrates here is that the patients who came to Breuer and himself suffering from hysterical paralysis were in fact acting out a personal drama *on their own bodies*. What their minds denied, their bodies affirmed. Yet part of them wished to understand what it was their bodies were concealing from them. Freud thus had to 'read' the hieroglyphics of their bodies in order to understand what they were really trying to tell him. But he could not do this on his own. He needed their collaboration. This was the origin of what one of the patients herself was to call 'the talking cure'. By talking, not necessarily telling the truth, but simply talking *to* someone, they were eventually able to give Freud enough information to allow him to reconcile their minds with their bodies and so cure them. Or so he optimistically thought at the time.

In these patients of Freud's we can see a kind of ironic echo of the Symbolist ideal of the speaking body – Yeats's admiration for Donne's line, 'one might almost say her body thought' is only the most famous example. One way of describing the relation between the two might be to say that it is rather like that between the two Napoleons. And in both the historical and the personal drama we can see a reflection of Sterne's epigraph: *Non ego sed Democritus dixit*. For it is not really *I* who speak, so much as those other, impersonal forces, forces which can perhaps best be designated by the impersonal language of Latin.

6. Freud and Marx are confident that they can tame those forces, that *their* language can encompass them, reduce them to intelligibility. The artists are less sure. 'Her painful legs' said Freud about a patient, 'began to "join in the conversation" during our analysis.' In Kafka and early Eliot too arms and legs seem to 'join in the conversation', though what exactly the conversation is about they do not know.

I don't have to remind you how meticulously Kafka describes the gestures people make. He has to be precise because these gestures always seem to be on the point of revealing something decisive about the person making them, though of course in the end they never do. And when seen from the point of view of the gesticulator they suggest a kind of anxiety, as though by the jerkiness of his movements he would find his way back to his natural environment. In a diary entry for 1922 he actually compares the gestures of the body to writing:

> Strange how make-believe, if engaged in systematically enough, can change into reality. Childish games (though I was well aware

that they were so) marked the beginning of my intellectual decline. I deliberately cultivated a facial tick, for instance, or would walk across the Graben with arms crossed behind my head. A repulsive, childish... game. (My writing began in the same way; only later on its development came to a halt, unfortunately.)

This passage suggests what many of the letters, diary entries, and of course those line drawings scattered through his diaries, all confirm: that Kafka is as though embarrassed by the number of possibilities open to him at every second of the day; not just all the possible ways of writing any one sentence, but all the possible ways of moving, nodding, waving... If there is no natural way to exist – or if I for some reason or other have never been initiated into it then is not the very basis of my existence suspect?

The early poetry of Eliot too is full of people who try to keep going by imitating the words and gestures of those around them, since they seem unable to act instinctively. Prufrock, forever climbing the stairs to where women move purposefully and talk confidently about Michaelangelo, is only the most famous of these:

And indeed there will be time
To wonder 'Do I dare?' and, 'Do I dare?'
Time to turn back and descend the stair,
With a bald spot in the middle of my hair –
(They will say: 'How his hair is growing thin!')
My morning coat, my collar mounting firmly to the chin,
My necktie rich and modest, but asserted by a simple pin –
(They will say: 'But how his arms and legs are thin!')

He is a sentient void on which articles of clothing have been hung, his very language that of the fashion magazines ('My necktie rich and modest, but *asserted* by a simple pin...'). He seems to talk about nothing but himself, yet that 'self' is made up of clothes he hardly seems to have chosen, and of words which are as external to himself as the clothes.

There are many like Prufrock in the early Eliot. Chief among them is perhaps Mr Eliot himself:

How unpleasant to meet Mr. Eliot!
With his features of clerical cut,
And his brow so grim
And his mouth so prim
And his conversation so nicely

Restricted to What Precisely
And If and Perhaps and But.
With a bobtail cur
In a coat of fur
And a porpentine cat
And a wopsical hat:
How unpleasant to meet Mr. Eliot!
    (Whether his mouth be open or shut).

7.   And yet, if the gestures of Kafka and Eliot are no more a 'true' expression of their 'true' selves than those of Louis Napoleon or Freud's patients, there is a difference. What we have here, after all, are not gestures, but poems, stories. And we read them as such, as the 'description of a struggle', to use the title of one of Kafka's earliest stories, rather than as the struggle itself.

The Chinese spy in 'The Garden of Forking Paths' thinks he is a free agent, influencing the course of history, but he is only playing his allotted role in the labyrinth which is what history really is. Borges's Shakespeare escapes from the meaningless proliferation of rhetorical exercises in the dramatic mode by retiring to Stratford and become a local business man. The hero of 'Tlön, Uqbar, Orbis Tertius' reacts to the takeover of the world by a purely idealistic universe by retreating to a lonely hotel and working on his 'uncertain Quevedian translation… of Browne's *Urn Burial*.' His Symbolist poet, Pierre Menard, takes a more aggressive attitude. Sterne had only placed his quotation from Erasmus as an epigraph. Pierre Menard devotes his life to rewriting *Don Quixote*. Not in the vulgar sense of Joyce rewriting *The Odyssey* or Anouilh rewriting Greek tragedy, but in a pure mad symbolist way:

> He did not want to compose another *Quixote* – which is easy – but *the Quixote*. It is unnecessary to add that he never envisaged a mechanical transcription of the original: he didn't propose to copy it. His admirable intention was to reproduce a few pages which would coincide word for word and line for line with those of Miguel de Cervantes.[25]

Unlike, say, the poems of Mallarmé, *Don Quixote* is full of contingent, haphazard details. To write it again would therefore entail discovering and somehow tapping not merely the inner logic of a work of art, but the very language of nature. To write *Don Quixote* – or any novel – is easy, and, in a sense, pointless. It only requires the ability to deaden one's critical instinct and a capacity for hard, unrewarding work. But to *rewrite* it would mean escaping at last from the unknown forces speaking through one, being truly master of one's destiny.

8.   Only by resolutely refusing to speak in his own voice does Pierre Menard find his voice. I have already said that Adrian Leverkühn adopts a somewhat similar solution. His silence, as I said, strikes the reader from the start. And even when he does speak or write letters, he employs a curious kind of mock sixteenth-century diction and style, as if to deny what he is saying in the very act of saying it. Zeitblom senses what is going on when, talking of a letter of Adrian's, he says that 'its style was of course intended as a parody of the grotesque Halle experiences and the language idiosyncrasies of Ehrenfried Kumpf. At the same time it both hides and reveals his own personality and stylistic leanings.' In fact, he suggests, what Leverkühn is doing is using 'quotation as disguise', 'parody as pretext.'

Parody and quotation are bound to upset the Humanist Zeitblom, for they suggest an easy alliance between self and expression, art and culture. They also clearly troubled Thomas Mann. Yet what is his own novel? Looked at in one way it seems to be an old-fashioned fictional biography, written in a straightforward linear way. But this is Zeitblom's work, not Mann's. And to Zeitblom's surprise elements keep creeping into the books which are anything but linear. Looked at a little more closely, in fact, the book seems to be constructed more on serialist than on classical lines. Not only that. It is also a huge collage of quotation, historical material, *objets trouvé*, placed next to each other, with no connecting links. If at first sight it seems to be written by Zeitblom, in the end we are left wondering if it is not perhaps Leverkühn's last, parodistic testament, merely usurping the tones and sentiments of Zeitblom as pretext and disguise.

I said last week that there would appear to be a kind of safety in parody. But perhaps we should distinguish between two kinds of parody. There is the type exemplified by Shakespeare's parody of inkhorn and bombast, which is conducted from a position of superiority, so to speak, and there is parody which is in effect collage. It can be as extreme and desperate as it is in Leverkühn's compositions or in the music-theatre works of Peter Maxwell Davies, or it can be as cool and ironic as it is in Stravinsky's neo-classical compositions. The important thing is that what we have here is an aesthetic of *making* rather than one of *expression*. The mouth is gagged but the hands are free.

9.   Let me give you some examples of such an aesthetic in action.

Consider, for instance, what Eliot is able to say by the most obvi-ous kind of making: cutting a quotation out of its place in a con-tinuum and placing it in a new context.[26] I won't go into any of the complex examples in *The Waste Land*, but will confine myself to something much simpler, to epigraphs. As you will see, that is already quite complicated enough.

The two epigraphs I have chosen are both taken from Dante, and they form ten of the first twelve lines which any reader of Eliot's *Collected Poems* will encounter. I will take the second one first. It is the epigraph to 'The Love Song of J. Alfred Prufrock', and appears, in italics, just below the title:

> S'io credesse che mia risposta fosse
> A persona che mai tornasse al mondo,
> Questa fiamma staria senza piu scosse.
> Ma perciocche giammai di questo fondo
> Non torno vivo alcun, si'i'odo il vero,
> Senza tema d'infamia ti rispondo.

Eliot's work, like that of many modern artists, has been accused of being unreal, unlocated in time or place. Nothing could be further from the truth. But its time is *now* and its place *here*. We are involved in a completely new conception of time. In most literature the words make their own sensual impact, but they also send us back and away into a unified world of time. In Eliot the gap between title and epigraph, between epigraph and first line ('Let us go then you and I') becomes something palpable, something we have to cross and something we feel ourselves crossing. The reader of early Eliot is like a steeplechaser: now a high hurdle, now a water jump, now a seductive stretch of flat. Our natural critical – self-preservative? – instinct is to remove the obstacles.[27] This is a mistake; for the obs-tacles *are* the poem.

To return to the quotation. As Hugh Kenner has said, the most important thing about these epigraphs is that they ease us into the poem so that we never know how or where or even if the poem has begun. The title speaks of a love song, but the epigraph is propelled forward by a dry crabbed logic very far removed from either love or song: 'If I thought the person I was addressing would be returning to the world above I wouldn't speak openly, as I'm now doing; but, knowing he won't, I will...'. Is the speaker then Prufrock, and is it us he is addressing, as he is to do in the opening lines of the poem? Or is it someone talking *to* Prufrock? In Dante the lines are spoken by the wily counsellor Guido to Dante himself, who will of course return to the world above, and, what's more, will write down everything Guido says for all posterity to read. So: is the speaker still Guido? And if so are we Dante? Or is Prufrock Dante? Or is Prufrock Guido? Or are both Prufrock and Guido? Or is the quote only tangentially related to the poem, giving it a particular *tone* and no more? How, in fact, *does* the epigraph relate to the poem?

To ask that is to throw into question the whole unity of the poem, of poems in general. For if we are uncertain about the relation of epigraph to poem, what of the relation of the first line of the poem proper to any of its subsequent lines?

We know the difficulty Eliot had in deciding what should go into *The Waste Land* and what should be left out. We know that Proust went on adding to the bulk of *A la recherche* until the day he died, and that at the end he had to admit to himself that what he was making was not, as he had hoped, a cathedral, but only a patchwork dress. Is not the notion of a work of art itself one of those ideas Leverkühn and the Devil felt could no longer be taken for granted? Who is to say where such a work will begin, where end, once you have discarded the rhetorical rules of form that guided a Milton, and have renounced their nineteenth-century substitutes, subjective passion and fictional plotting?

These questions hover over Eliot's poetry. The fact that generations of students have pored over the poems has somehow made it seem necessary that they mean *something*. But what if they don't mean anything? What if they exist only as an area of tension, not as repositories of meaning? Is not one's feeling on reading them more like glimpsing a snake glide through long grass? There is a stirring, then all is still. Like the magi, we have witnessed something, and that something was good, and we cannot find it again – except by rereading the poems.

The epigraph has alerted us to something in Eliot's poetry. But perhaps it is not unique to Eliot. Perhaps this is something which is true of all poetry; only in Eliot's case the poetry is stripped of the appearance of being something else.

Let me return to the other quotation. This one appears on the title page of the whole volume: *Prufrock and Other Observations*, 1917. Remember that we are dealing with the first book of poems by a little known American living in England. The title page bears a dedication: 'For Jean Verdenal, 1889-1915, mort aux Dardanelles.' then comes the quotation, in italics:

la quantitate
Puote veder del amor che a te mi scalda,
Quando dismento nostra vanitate
Trattando l'ombre come cosa salda.

Here the foreign language does not strike us as secretive so much as private. After all, a dedication is a kind of public private letter. We do not know Jean Verdenal, but clearly he was a friend of Eliot's who was killed in the Dardanelles campaign. We take this in and then almost avert our eyes from what follows, for this is even more than the usual dedication: it is a private message to someone who is dead. It has therefore all that much more authority and weight, since nothing that can now happen can make Eliot alter it.

What does it say? Roughly: 'You can see how much love I have for you when I treat the shadow as the real thing.' Verdenal is now dead, Eliot seems to be saying, but he is dedicating the book to him as to a living person, and this refusal to accept that he is dead shows how dearly he loves him. For Eliot, Verdenal will always be a living presence.

This time too we gain something, though by no means everything, from being familiar with the original and its context. Dante's poem is full of wonderful, joyful meetings: with his ancestor Cacciaguida in Heaven; with his old teacher, Brunetto Latini, in Hell; with his master Virgil at the outset. But no meeting is more full of mingled joy and sadness than the one between the two pilgrims and Statius on the upper slopes of Mt Purgatory. Statius, one of the last great poets of antiquity, a Christian like Dante but a Roman poet like Virgil, does not know who the two are who meet him, and he tells them about himself:

> I sang of Thebes, and then of great Achilles, but I fell on the way with my second burden. [He never finished his second epic.] The sparks which warmed me from the divine flame whereby more than a thousand have been kindled were the seeds of my poetic fire: I mean the *Aeneid*, which in poetry was both mother and nurse to me – without it I had achieved little of worth; and to have lived yonder when Virgil lived I would consent to one sun more than I owe to my coming forth from exile. (P.xxi.92–102)

Virgil motions to Dante to keep silent, but Statius has already caught the beginnings of a smile on his face, and asks Dante to explain the reason. When he learns who it is he has been speaking to,

> Already he was stooping to embrace my teacher's feet; but he

said to him, 'Brother, do not so, for you are a shade and a shade you see.'

And he, rising, 'Now you may comprehend the measure of the love that burns in me for you, when I forget our emptiness and treat shades as solid things.'

Statius's action and Virgil's reply is itself already a re-enactment of an episode in the *Aeneid*. This is Dante's way of paying extra, silent homage to Virgil. It is quite extraordinary to me that these lines, written in another language than his own, by another poet, spoken by a third about a fourth, should come through at the start of Eliot's volume with such heart-breaking directness: the only 'sincere' words, we could say, in the entire volume.

10.   Let us turn from poetry to prose. We open a recent novel by Muriel Spark, *Territorial Rights*, and read the following sentence (Muriel Spark seems to me to be one of the few major living writers still producing work worthy of her best, so I make no apology for placing her beside Eliot. She can survive that.):

> The bureau clerk was telephoning to the Pensione Sofia while Robert Leaver watched the water-traffic at the ferry and the off-season visitors arriving in Venice.

This appears to do its work as efficiently as any one of a hundred fairly good novels. But, though we don't fully register it at the time, I think we stumble slightly over 'telephoning to' – 'the bureau clerk was telephoning to the Pensione Sofia...' We read on, nonetheless, and a few lines later come upon the sentence:

> It was his first visit to Venice and he was young: but he had only half a mind to feel enchanted, the other half being still occupied with a personal anxiety in Paris from where he had just come.

Now there can no longer be any doubt about it. 'Occupied with a personal anxiety in Paris' is not what the narrator would say, it is what Robert would say. In a way not uncommon for novels, the narrative remains in the third person but mimes the words or thoughts of the protagonist. What is disconcerting about this book is that there is no protagonist, no central character whose way of thinking might influence the narrative. Or rather, there is such a character, but he is dead, cut in half, and buried on either side of a well-kept Venetian garden.

The narrative drives along at a firm brisk pace, but we gradually come to see that its briskness is all too suspect. It seems to have no will of its own. Without seeming to be aware of it, it accepts into itself totally incompatible modes of discourse – 'as always, full of the Curran idea'; 'That afternoon she slipped out with the courage of her wild convictions and the dissatisfaction that has no name' – leaving us with the sense of something more round the corner, something which badly needs to be said, but which never is. I cannot think of another novel which gives us so strong a sense of what Wittgenstein meant when he said: 'I cannot use language to get outside language.'

The action, as I've said, hinges on a dead body, buried in the garden of the Pensione Sofia after being cut in two, so that each of the two sisters who had loved the murdered man may have her share of his remains. The body is never uncovered, but a great deal of money, a great many words, and some affection, are made to circulate as a result of its presence. 'There's the question of the body,' one of the characters delightfully remarks. 'The rest is immaterial.'

The point is beautifully made. It is the answer to the remarks of James and Schoenberg with which I began. For them there seemed to be a fullness of language, somewhere, waiting to be grasped. Yet it would always evade them. Spark suggests that there is indeed an underlying plenitude or truth, but it is not another language, better, more truthful, richer, than the one we possess. Rather, it is the ground of all languages, that without which they would not exist, but which none of them can conjure up. As the butcher says to Robert: 'You see, *figlio mio*, they have the body in the garden, sliced in two. That's concrete. Everything else is anything you like.' Not everything is anything you like, as some recent novelists have suggested, but *everything else*, apart from the buried, dismembered body.

11.   I will draw out the implications of these remarks in a moment. But first I want to present you with two more examples of what I have called an aesthetic of making as opposed to an aesthetic of expression, one from music and one from painting.

Like Eliot and Muriel Spark, Stravinsky 'found himself' very early on in his career. After a few years of competent but unexciting late Romantic music, he suddenly changed direction and began to work, like Eliot, with small fragments, constantly repeated and starkly juxtaposed. This was to be his way of working for the rest of his long rich musical life. As Alexander Goehr has recently pointed out, each such fragment 'is defined by an absolute duration;

the manner of duration is "real" – by addition, rather than "psycho-logical".'[28] The work is built up by means of these blocks of pure time, giving Stravinsky's music that immediacy, that lack of a con-trast between foreground and background, which we have already seen at work in Eliot.

But once the approach to musical creation is conceived in this way, as the making of something, not the expression of an emotion, then the consequences are far-reaching. Schoenberg, wedded to an expressionist aesthetic, is forced to abandon his only opera for lack of that 'Word' which would be its justification. Stravinsky, we could say, does not keep reaching out *beyond*; he re-examines what is in front of him: words, sounds, and their relation. Years later he was to say about *Renard*:

> I planned the staging myself, and always with the consideration that it should not be confounded with opera. The players are to be dancing acrobats and the singers are not to be identified with them:... as in *Les Noces*, the performers, musical and mimetic, should all be together on the stage, with the singers in the centre of the musical ensemble.[29]

Les Noces is the great work of the 1912–22 period, and Stravinsky's description of what he wanted to achieve there is very illuminating:

> *Les Noces* is a suite of typical wedding episodes told through quotations of typical talk. The latter, whether the bride's, the groom's, the parents' or the guests', is always ritualistic. As a collection of clichés and quotations of typical wedding sayings, it might be compared to one of those scenes in *Ulysses* in which the reader seems to be overhearing scraps of conversation without the connecting thread of discourse. But *Les Noces* might also be compared to *Ulysses* in the larger sense that both works are trying to *present* rather than to *describe*.

'Scraps of conversation without the connecting thread of dis-course'; 'to present rather than to describe' – of course Stravinsky is talking a long time after the event, but he is accurately describing not only his own work in those years, but also that of his greatest contemporaries. The recent Picasso exhibitions, in Paris, New York and London, in which for the first time we were able to see many of the works in the artist's own collection, only served to reinforce the parallel between the painter and the composer. For what emerged so strongly from them was the paramount importance of *making* in all Picasso's art: our vision of the world is enhanced because something, no matter how small, has been made, *put together*. It is the *papiers collés* and the first made objects of the pre-war years, not the *Demoiselles d'Avignon*, we can now see, which were the heralds of the future. As with Stravinsky and Eliot, so here, one feels the excitement generated by the substitution of the notion of *pro*duction for that of *re*production. Quite rightly Daix and Rosselot, in their great catalogue of the Cubist years, point out that with the first *papiers collés*

> painting is reduced to the signifier, its material support. Neither the thing signified by perspective, nor the organising anecdote, nor a resemblance to objects or perspective intervenes in the way the spectator relates to the subject the artist submits to him. Here we have the final stages of the evolution initiated by Manet's pictorial silence: the elimination of the subject.[30]

Yet, they go on to point out, 'this is not abstract painting. It is true that it can be read as abstract painting; but it maintains very obvious connections with the concrete. Only these connections are contradictory.'

Thus if we turn to the 'Table with Wineglass and Bottle of Bass', made in Paris early in 1914 (No.656 in Daix and Rosselot), we can see that what Picasso is really doing is testing what is the minimum requirement for the viewer to be able to 'read' the work as existing in illusionist space. He draws the corner of a table in normal perspective, then, where we would expect to find the flattened parallelogram dictated by the traditional viewpoint, he places an irregularly cut square of paper which overlaps the square field left for it and forms a rough rectangular projection. This is just big enough to comprise the other corner of the table, drawn in quite a different manner from the first. On this piece of paper he places two shapes cut out of paper, a very large one for the glass and an absurdly small one for the bottle of Bass. This last is placed within a larger cutout, which reflects it like a sort of shadow. Finally, sawdust is stuck on the first two cutouts to give them a slight relief. The whole functions within a Cubist space which is both adjacent to and also within the perspective space of the table leg, which is drawn straight on to the cardboard support.

The point of all this is not, with Picasso, as it was with some of his contemporaries, mere decoration. It is part of his continued and passionate analysis of spatial syntax. Curiously, nothing succeeds in disturbing our re-creation of space – as with Sterne, we accept the most flagrant contradictions. And yet such constructions are curiously exhilarating to contemplate. They help us to rediscover the world because, depicting it other, they force us to recognize why it is as it is.

More perhaps than any of the other artists working at the time, Picasso was interested in the outside world. His question is always: How, by making something, can I discover more about the world? Making is always a step into the unknown. You start with that which is immediate, to hand, and suddenly you have left all safe ground. When Apollinaire said of him at the time that it was as if 'a new-born child were re-ordering the universe for his own personal use, and to facilitate his relationship with his fellow-men', he caught something of the excitement generated by Picasso's work, but he did not perhaps stress enough the way making, the work of the hand, contributed to discovery: for the re-ordering is perpetual, the world is remade with every canvas, every mark.

12.   It is easy to see the similarities that exist between the approaches of the artists I have been discussing: Borges, Mann, Eliot, Spark, Stravinsky, Picasso. If what I have said about them is correct then one way of describing what they are up to is to say that they have more in common with those Mann called the artists of the cult than with the artists of subjective individualism. The medieval poet was, after all, called a *maker*, and if we go back even further, to the epic poets of oral cultures, the similarities are even more striking. The epic poet put together his poem by means of blocks, the oral formulae, and he thought of himself not as having anything to express but rather as the voice and memory of the community.[31]

But we have only to put it like this to be struck at once by the enormous differences. The oral poet makes a public object; his task is to create something, which will be common property, which will fall into the established patterns and bring to life again the established traditions. But the modern artist makes – what?

This is the question to which I have been leading in the course of this lecture. There is an answer to it which is persuasive, so persuasive, in fact, that it seems to have established itself as *the* answer, but which I believe to be profoundly misleading. Let me try and sum it up for you.

Once upon a time, it goes, there were artists and there were works of art.[32] But today, because we have at last realized that a work of art is not natural, like a horse, but part of a system of representations, like an axe, we can see that this notion of an artist or author was a myth, perpetuated by a whole ideology of the subject. We know now that the artist is a maker. He puts his material together for the sheer pleasure of it, and any relation it may have with the real world is purely coincidental. A fortune-teller needs to know what the cards *mean*, says Robbe-Grillet, a bridge-player only how they are *used*. The artist is a player.

This is persuasive because it is of course partly true. And it is backed by the entire thrust of what has come to be called structuralist criticsm. But I hope my earlier discussion of Sterne, and my analysis today of other examples will have made you feel uneasy with it. The very elegance and simplicity of this model should make us suspect it. A work of art, I suggested in my first lecture, is more like a man than like an axe; it partakes of the orders of both culture and nature. What I have been suggesting today is that the modern artist, recognizing the impossibility of speaking in his own voice, is indeed a maker; but what is important about his work is not that he makes an object or plays a game, but the sense he conveys of the act of making itself.

You recall Frye's illuminating comment upon Shakespeare's impartiality:

> It is curious that we think of impartiality only as detachment, of devotion to craftsmanship only as purism, an attitude which, as in Flaubert, turns all human life into an enormously intricate still life, like the golden touch of Midas . . . Shakespeare's impartiality is a totally involved and committed impartiality: it expresses itself in bringing everything equally to life.

Now there is a view of art expressed by certain modern writers – Flaubert, Joyce, Nabokov, Robbe-Grillet, John Barth – which sees the artist as standing above the fray, indifferent, Godlike, paring his fingernails. This attitude is often taken, by both supporters and opponents of modern art, to represent its essential position. I would like to suggest that this is a misleading view, and one which is frequently given the lie by the very works of the artists who uphold it.

I suggested last week that there is a profound link between Malvolio and Iago, that Malvolio's experience precipitated Iago, so to speak. Iago is the way the self instinctively protects itself when it finds itself alone in the dark, with voices telling it it is mad. Freud would have called it the superego. And if this Iago self can be seen at work in the complex plotting of the traditional novel, it can also be seen in the retreat to a narcissistic playfulness on the part of the writers I have just mentioned. As I say, this is not necessarily the dominant aspect of their work, but it is a definite temptation, and one to which they all at one time or another succumb. It is of course a temptation to which all artists who have faced Leverkühn's crisis are particularly prone. It would be natural for Eliot or Muriel Spark to give in to it, as it seems to me in his last works Nabokov gave in to it; to say: I cannot express the unique river of my childhood, so I will play with mythology and Latin allusions in order to show that I believe in none of it.

But what we have seen in Borges and Eliot and Spark is quite another attitude: a deep desire to express, along with a recognition that it is impossible to express. 'There is a goal but no way,' says Kafka. And what he means can I think be understood by recalling Sterne's nostalgia for a time when orators had something to hide under their cloaks, and Spark's wicked novel about a corpse which is the centre of the action. There is something there, but it can never be spoken, for it is not a hidden object but the ground of all speech. We cannot find it or say it, we can only embody it in action, the action of making, of reading.

I have already mentioned the narrator of Borges's story, 'Tlön, Uqbar, Orbis Tertius', who reacts to the gradual takeover of the real world by a parallel idealist universe by retiring to a provincial hotel and getting on with his translation of Thomas Browne's *Urn Burial*. There is nothing very grandiose about that, but the point of it is that a translator is forced to submit to the reality of something outside himself. And that reality, unlike a game of cards, is not circumscribed in advance. It has definite laws, but these are laws we can never fully master. Proust too called his novel a translation and not an invention, and he too recognized that the work of translation is a giving up of the Iago-self, the hard shell of habit and self-hood, a giving up which may perhaps lead to the discovery of that full self which he had glimpsed at times and for which he always yearned.

But this giving up is never easy. The search for form in Eliot, in Virginia Woolf, is often a desperate search. How desperate we see in the figure of Lily Briscoe, and in the life and death of Virginia Woolf herself. And even tougher artists, Stravinsky, Picasso, Wallace Stevens, will at moments give in to the temptations of a lordly narcissism. It is not easy to live abandoning the safety of the Iago-ego, accepting that it is only in a making which is a perpetual breaking of the ego that true fulfilment is possible.

13. The struggle – the perpetual struggle – is very evident in the work of Beckett.

Beckett's work has always followed the pattern laid down at the end of his finest early story, 'Dante and the Lobster'. 'It's a quick death,' thinks Belaqua, watching the lobster go live into his aunt's boiling pot. For it had, we are told, 'about thirty seconds to live'. 'It is not', comes the reply, three words placed at the end of the story, impersonal, without quotation marks, the utterance of nature herself. We are not very far from Kafka's blood oozing between the great stones of the law.

Driven by the need to speak in order to utter the agony of the lobster, yet knowing that whatever he says will always only cover up that agony, render it acceptable instead of revealing it as the monstrosity it is, Beckett has moved slowly forward, shedding one skin after another in his effort to speak the truth. The Trilogy was of course the great testing ground for these matters, its very length an essential part of the process. First there was Molloy, still just about able to move; then Malone, dying in his closed room; finally the Unnamable, only able to identify himself in negative terms: not Molloy, not Malone, not Worm, only that which refuses to be named because each name, each history, will fix him, freeze him, deny him that which is most precious to him, his potential for movement, change. At the same time it is unbearable to live in a perpetual state of metamorphosis. The organism longs for stability, rest at last.

Non ego sed Democritus dixit, Sterne had copied out of Burton. In 'Not I' a mouth talks, seemingly unattached to any body. Between mouth and audience stands a shadowy figure. What is this figure? What is it doing there?

It has its instructions:

> Movement: this consists in simple sideways raising of arms from sides, and their falling back, in a gesture of helpless compassion. It lessens with each recurrence till scarcely perceptible at third. There is just enough pause to contain it as MOUTH recovers from vehement refusal to relinquish third person.

Why will the mouth not relinquish the third person? As always, there are two explanations for the same action. The mouth will not accept responsibility for what it says, denying that it is attached to any body. But it also knows that to speak in the first person is to perpetuate a falsehood, for that which is the source of utterance is always more than the ego. That is the drama. Somewhere something which is not the mouth keeps wanting it to accept to use the first person, but the only acknowledgement of that unseen force is a violent denial; and this is followed by the figure's gesture: '... and she found herself in the –... What?... who?... no!... she!... (*Pause*

and movement).' Once this is grasped we see that the compassionate
figure is deeply ambiguous: father confessor, but also judge; friend,
but also betrayer.

In *Company*, perhaps because it's a prose work and not a play, the
ambiguity is not resolved but tracked down. Again, the narrator is
unable to say 'I'. 'A voice comes to one in the dark. Imagine.' The
voice speaks, tells stories, but 'only a small part of what is said can
be verified.' All that can be ascertained is that someone is lying on
his back in the dark and a voice comes to him, telling stories:

> Use of the second person marks the voice. That of the third that
> cankerous other. Could he speak to and of whom the voice speaks
> there would be a first. But he cannot. He shall not. You cannot.
> You shall not.

Of course it would be wonderful if he could: 'What an addition to
company that would be. A voice in the first person singular. Murmuring now and then, Yes, I remember.' But though the stories
the voice tells are familiar, how is he to know if they are stories
about himself? It may simply be that the repetition has made him
imagine that they belong to himself. We say: This is how I was; or,
This is what I did – but in what sense is this 'I' oneself? All that can
be said is that to listen to the voice brings him a sense of company,
stops him being alone. All that can be said with certainty is: 'Devised
deviser devising it all for company. In the same figment dark as his
figments.' And so:

> Huddled thus you find yourself imagining you are not alone
> while knowing full well that nothing has occurred to make this
> possible. The process continues none the less lapped as it were
> in meaninglessness. You do not murmur in so many words, I
> know this doomed to fail and yet persist. No. For the first personal
> and a fortiori plural pronoun had never any place in your vocabul-
> ary.

14.   And yet, curiously, out of the writer's renewed attempts to
say 'I' and renewed refusal to come to rest in any position in which
'I' is less than his whole self, out of his perpetually repeated failure
to find that fullness of voice for which James and Virginia Woolf
longed, a certain voice does emerge. We say it is Eliot's, Muriel
Spark's, Beckett's, though it does not belong to their social and
public selves. This fullness of voice is something *we* register as we
read, but it always eludes the writer himself. He who thinks he has

it, loses it; he who goes on searching, releases it. The situation, as between writer and reader, will always be asymmetrical. For the writer it will always be the middle years[33], the time before, the time of failure, the time when it was necessary to start again. But for the reader the writer's middle years are truly that point whose centre is everywhere and whose circumference is nowhere, and in his work he sees the writer transform himself, as Mallarmé said death transforms us, into his total self: it always takes another to hear the voice, intuit the body.

15.   Since the argument of this lecture has been so dense and has ranged so widely, I would like to conclude by telling you a story.

The story concerns Dante, whose relevance to our theme has I hope been sufficiently demonstrated. I have mentioned his deep, absolutely primitive attachment to the *parlar materno*, the mother tongue. One might have thought that the fact of Dante's exile, his being forced to wander round the courts of Italy, finding shelter where it was offered, would have made it more likely that he would turn to the international language, Latin, when he came to write his epic. After all, two centuries later this was just what Erasmus did: he gave up being a native of Rotterdam and became a European citizen. Moreover, as I suggested, Dante was only too well aware of where love for the mother-tongue could lead: to the blind self-love of the giant Nimrod. Yet for Dante, as for Joyce, exile only strengthened the attachment to the speech of his childhood, and there was never really any doubt that when he came to write his life-work it would be in the vernacular. The poem itself, it would turn out, like Proust's novel, would both tell and show how he was able to do this and yet escape the Nimrod trap. And we will already find the general pattern of the entire poem in the overture, canto I of the *Inferno*, as we may find it in the overture to *A la recherche*.

Dante, you will remember, having come to in the dark wood, sees a mountain before him, with the sun shining over its summit. It is Spring, it is dawn, he is in the middle of his life. Everything says that this is a new beginning. He yearns for the light of the sun, and goes sprinting up the mountain. But at once he finds himself face to face with the three mysterious beasts, the third of which, the she-wolf

> put such heaviness upon me with the fear that came from sight of her that I lost hope of the height. And like one who is eager in winning but, when the time comes that makes him lose, weeps

and is saddened in all his thoughts, such did that peaceless beast make me, as, coming on against me, she pushed me back, little by little, to where the sun is silent.

The images are signficant here. Dante rushes up the mountain towards the source of light and salvation. But it takes only one obstacle to send him running down again just as fast. He has so little confidence in himself, so little awareness of what the journey really involves in terms of effort, of shedding the restricting layers of the self, that he is at once discouraged, 'like one who is eager in winning but, when the time comes that makes him lose, weeps and is saddened...'. He treats his action as a gamble which does not come off, a desperate throw of the dice. Ignoring the length and difficulty of the way, he tries to ignore as well the fact that it will inevitably involve him in time, in change, in a whole process which he cannot predict beforehand. He wants, somehow, to be already there. It is no surprise then that he falls back in despair, and that the wonderful synaesthetic image suggests that he falls back to a world not simply of darkness – the dark wood – but of a total, solipsistic silence: 'to where the sun is silent'.

The next lines make clear what is lacking:

While I was ruining down to the depth there appeared before me one who seemed faint through long silence. When I saw him in that vast desert I cried to him: 'Have pity on me, whoever you are, shade or living man.'

The verbs 'ruining' and 'appeared' suggest a quite passive process. Dante does not see someone; he merely becomes aware of the fact that he is not alone. His response is instinctive and immediate:

'Miserere di me,' gridai a lui.
(Have pity on me, I cried out to him.)

Miserere. A Latin word. Part of the liturgy. A small thing, but a momentous one. For in that moment Dante accepts his personal limits, accepts that he will need a guide, accepts the need *to speak*. And, accepting that, it is natural that he should speak in the language of prayer, the public language of the Church. Later he will ask Virgil to 'aiutami', to help him. Here he says: 'Pity me!'. *Miserere di me*.

The unknown 'other' is of course Virgil, though he introduces himself, rightly again, not as a great poet but as a Mantuan, born before Christ's time, and therefore debarred forever from salvation. This is as it should be. It is left to Dante to call him, in wonder,

'Oh my master and my author!' – 'lo mio maestro e il mio autore' – as it must always be the reader who responds to the writer in admiration. Dante begs Virgil, 'by that God whom you did not know', to guide him on his journey, and Virgil accepts. The first canto ends:

> Allor si mosse, e io li tenni dietro.
> (Then he moved, and I followed him.)

This word *mosse*, to move, is a key word in the *Commedia*. It is almost always associated with the word *amore*, love.[34] Dante and Virgil can move, as can the souls in Purgatory; Nimrod is stuck forever, and even the romantic lovers, Paulo and Francesca, though they are not stuck in ice, are confined to their circle, and their motions are sheer reaction as they are hurled here and there by the erratic wind.

Now Dante *can* move, and so can eventually reach his goal, because he is prepared to trust another. Which means, in the end, because he is prepared to open his mouth and speak to another. Not to affirm himself, but to say: *miserere*. In the same way Dante the author, and we the readers, can move because we are prepared to trust language, recognizing its limitations, but knowing that it is our surest path back to a lost fullness of the self. That ending to the first canto could be the epigraph to every artistic journey, the journey of the writer and that of the reader:

> Allor si mosse, e io li tenni dietro.

Only in the movement, venturing into the unknown, will Schoenberg's Moses find the word he lacks; only acknowledging the lack will make movement possible.

IV 'A Bird was in the Room'

1.   So far in these lectures I have been talking about writing which is also art, literature. Today I want to examine the implications of some scribbled notes which have been preserved because their author was a great writer, but which it would, I believe, be a mistake to treat as being for that reason somehow special, explicable in terms of genius or even talent. On the contrary, I want to suggest that they take us as far as it is possible to go in understanding the relations of writing to the body at the simplest, most banal and literal level.

2.   Let me read you a few of these scribbled notes. They are very brief:

> Aslant, that is more or less what I thought, so they can drink more; strip their leaves.
>
> A little water; these bits of pills stick in the mucus like splinters of glass.
>
> And move the lilacs into the sun.
>
> Do you have a moment? Then please lightly spray the peonies.
>
> A bird was in the room.
>
> Fear again and again.
>
> A lake doesn't flow into anything, you know.
>
> By now we have come a long way from the day in the tavern garden when we
>
> Put your hand on my forehead for a moment to give me courage.

These notes were written by Kafka. The circumstances in which he wrote them are explained by Max Brod in his note to the final pages of Kafka's *Letters to Friends, Family, and Editors*:

> During his final illness at the sanatorium in Kierling Kafka was not supposed to speak [he had developed tuberculosis of the larynx], an injunction he obeyed most of the time. He communicated with Dora Dymant, Robert Klopstock, and others, by

scribbling notes on slips of paper. Usually these notes were hints; his friends guessed the rest. A small selection has been published here from the originals in the possession of Dr. Klopstock...[35]

3.   With this information in mind, let us look at the notes again. This time I will add a few more:

Aslant, that is more or less what I thought, so they can drink more; strip their leaves.

A little water; these bits of pills stick in the mucus like splinters of glass.

And move the lilacs into the sun.

Do you have a moment? Then please lightly spray the peonies.

A bird was in the room.

Mineral water – once for fun I could

Fear again and again.

A lake doesn't flow into anything, you know.

See the lilacs, fresher than morning.

By now we have come a long way from the day in the tavern garden when we

How wonderful that is, isn't it? The lilac – dying, it drinks, goes on swilling.

That cannot be, that a dying man drinks.

I was to have gone to the Baltic with her once (along with her girl friend), but was ashamed because of my thinness and other anxieties.

Put your hand on my forehead for a moment to give me courage.

So the help goes away again without helping.

How strange and resonant they are, these fragmentary messages coming at us out of the silence of the past. Why are they so moving – almost unbearably so? (I will quite understand if at this moment anyone wants to leave: to talk about them at all may strike one as an obscenity. Yet ultimately, I hope, my few comments will only serve to liberate them from commentary.) Clearly the situation has a great deal – everything perhaps – to do with it. After all, anyone could write down: 'A bird was in the room.' Would it have the same effect on us in another context?

The temptation is to say that since this is the case we are in danger of becoming grossly sentimental, and to leave the matter at that. But I think both notes and context have much to say to us, and that we should bear in mind Kafka's remark that man's chief sin is his impatience – and so approach the matter as carefully and patiently as possible.

4. It is possible, by reading the notes through enough times, to pick out certain recurrent themes and preoccupations.

Foremost among these is the pain Kafka is suffering in his throat, which makes it impossible for him to eat, and which makes even drinking an agony. Presumably it is because of this that he is obsessed by the flowers in his room and by their ability to drink even while dying, uprooted as they have been from the soil which is their natural habitat.

All his life of course Kafka's own disgust at himself and his body had made him peculiarly aware of others, especially animals, but even inanimate objects. He must be the only writer to have explored the suffering to which bridges are exposed, stretched out between two bits of land and liable, if trampled upon, to go crashing down into the foaming water beneath. The sympathy is utterly instinctive, and often borders on masochism, as in this passage from a letter to Felice:

> To be a large piece of wood, and to be pressed against her body by the cook, who with both hands draws the knife towards her along the side of this stiff log (approximately in the region of my hip) and with all her might slices off the shavings to light the fire.

In these last notes, however, there is a new quality of attention to things, and the relation of the flowers to himself and his plight is almost never made explicit.

In those last days Kafka was also correcting the proofs of his volume of stories, *A Hunger Artist*, and some of the notes refer to that. Robert Klopstock tells how

> when he had finished working on the proofs . . . tears rolled down his cheeks for a long time. This was the first and last time I ever saw any expression of emotion of this kind in Kafka. He has always shown superhuman self-control.

And, finally, there is a third strand running through the notes, made up of memories of the past which had clearly been welling up in Kafka as he lay cocooned in silence on the hospital bed: 'I was to have gone to the Baltic with her once (along with her girl friend), but was ashamed because of my thinness and other anxieties.'

But when we have accounted for all the slips of paper in this way, discovered what they all 'refer to', we have not gone any way towards explaining their effect. What I have just told you, in other words, will not have altered your initial response at all. Where then does the effect lie?

I think we can point to the immediate cause of their strange power, though it will take us a little more time to grasp the implications of these. In part it is the very fragmentariness of the notes that makes them so striking: 'Mineral water once for fun. I could –' has a resonance that would be lacking were the sentence completed. But it is also a mysterious kind of redundancy – I can think of no other way of putting it – which contributes to the effect: 'A lake doesn't flow into anything, you know.' 'A bird was in the room.' The first is a platitude or tautology – I'm not enough of a grammarian to know just how one would describe it. The second is a plain statement of fact. Yet, written down, they seem to possess a strange resonance.

Why?

5.   What a man says in his final moments has always been seen as possessing a particular authority. There is a persistent legend, made use of by more than one writer, that in those moments our whole life flashes before us, and though I suspect that the persistence of this legend is due to that human need for a real end which I discussed in the first lecture, it is certainly beyond question that a person's final pronouncements have a special significance. For in those moments a man passes beyond the normal reticences, hypocrisies and lies, and utters what he most firmly believes. In a rather obscure though suggestive passage Walter Benjamin even suggests that the authority of the traditional tale derives from its links with death:

> It is, however, characteristic [he says] that not only a man's knowledge or wisdom, but above all his real life – and this is the stuff that stories are made of – first assumes transmissible form at the moment of his death. Just as a sequence of images is set in motion inside a man as his life comes to an end – unfolding the views of himself under which he has encountered himself without being aware of it – suddenly in his expressions and looks the unforgettable emerges and imparts to everything that concerned him that authority which even the poorest wretch in dying possesses for the living around him. This authority is at the very source of the story.[36]

Whatever the truth of this may be, it is certainly a fact that the central story in Western culture derives *its* authority from its association with death. By his death Jesus – as he is at pains to point out before-hand – sets his seal not just on his own life but on the entirety of history. He signs the book of God, so to speak, and by so doing constitutes it as a meaningful whole.[37]

Given the strength of this tradition it is not merely ironic, but profoundly shocking, that a man should be deprived of speech in those last moments. The matter becomes much more horrifying still when that man is Kafka. For if there is one thing that can be said without fear of contradiction about Kafka it is that he distrusted writing more than probably any literate person has ever done. Yet, in the end, Kafka is deprived of speech and condemned to writing.

To understand the full implications of this state of affairs for Kafka it is necessary to go back a little and trace in some detail the nature of his distrust of the written word.

6. Kafka, as we know, was never happier than when reading his stories aloud to his friends, and the one time he actually writes about himself with approval in his diary is after he has delivered a public speech on the Yiddish language at the time of the visit of the East European Jewish actors to Prague. At the same time we know what doubts he had about writing. Like all of us he turned to writing – to the blank page and the pen – when he needed to try and make sense of his life, and like all of us he was frequently visited with the thought that writing, far from making sense of anything, only led to further entanglements and greater confusion. Only with Kafka both the sense of this and the ability to express it were a hundred times more powerful than they are for any of us.

Take the first paragraph of the letter he wrote to his father at the age of thirty-six, and which grew under his hand into a seventy-five page autobiography:

Dearest Father,

You asked me recently why I maintain I am afraid of you. As usual, I was unable to think of any answer to your question, partly for the very reason that I am afraid of you, and partly because an explanation of the grounds for this fear would mean going into far more details than I could even approximately keep in mind while talking. And if I now try to give you an answer in writing, it will still be very incomplete, because even in writing this fear and its consequences hamper me in relation to you, and because the magnitude of the subject goes far beyond the scope of my memory and power of reasoning.

Nevertheless, writing, in spite of everything, is the better alternative. In the quiet of his room, far from the insistent and frightening presence of the man to whom he wants, but fears, to speak, it will be possible for him to explore their relations and explain his position. Unfortunately, just this advantage is also a grave disadvantage. For writing, being of its nature a private activity, distorts the relationship even in the process of trying to explain it. The father's absence falsifies the whole operation right from the start, for his silence in the face of his son's unending stream of accusations, is not the silence of acquiescence, but simply that of absence. It was no doubt Kafka's awareness of this which led him to give up the idea of ever sending the letter.

A similar paradox pervades his letters to the women with whom he was involved. There is no greater letter-writer than Kafka, and the letters here really were sent and received, but what were the letters *for*? He himself was well aware of the fact that the unending stream of letters to Felice and then to Milena were designed both to bind the women to him and to keep them at bay. In an extraordinary letter to Milena – but which of his letters is not extraordinary? – he writes:

> The great ease with which letters can be written must have brought into the world... a terrible dislocation of souls: it's a commerce with fantoms, not only with those of the recipient, but even with one's own; the fantom grows beneath the hand which writes, in the letter it is busy on, even more so in a series of letters where one corroborates the other and can call it to witness. Where did the idea spring from that letters would give men the means of communication? One can think of a person far away, one can hold a person who is near; the rest escapes human strength. Writing letters is presenting oneself naked before the fantoms; they avidly await the gesture. Written kisses do not reach their destination, the fantoms drink them on the way. Thanks to this nourishment they multiply at such an amazing rate.... The spirits will not die of hunger, but we will so die.

7.   Written kisses do not reach their destination, the fantoms drink them on the way. But these ever-thirsty fantoms exist not only to create havoc with the letters we address to other people; they even intercept those we address to ourselves. If Kafka's letters to those he loved were destined both to hold on to them and to keep them at bay, the same process can be seen at work, this time very much

against his wishes, in the notes he wrote to himself, his diary jottings.

In 1917 the illness which had been hovering nearer and nearer finally caught up with him. He had a haemorrhage, wrote a letter informing Felice with just a hint of triumph that this had happened to him and he could now clearly no longer seriously consider himself a candidate for marriage, and took his first long spell of sick leave from the insurance company in which he had been working for virtually the whole of his adult life. Then he went to live for a while in the country with his favourite sister, Ottla. He had been there for scarcely a week when he wrote down in his diary:

Have never understood how it is possible for almost everyone who writes to objectify his sufferings in the very midst of under-going them; thus I, for example, in the midst of my unhappiness, in all likelihood with my head still smarting from unhappiness, sit down and write to someone: I am unhappy. Yes, I can even go beyond that and with as many flourishes as I have the talent for, all of which seem to have nothing to do with my unhappiness, ring simple, or contrapuntal, or a whole orchestration of changes on my theme. And it is not a lie, and it does not still my pain; it is simply a merciful surplus of strength at a moment when suffer-ing has raked me to the bottom of my being and plainly exhausted all my strength. But then what kind of a surplus is it?

He is still pondering the mystery in 1921, for then he writes: 'Unde-niably there is a certain joy in being able calmly to write down: "Suffocation is inconceivably horrible." Of course it is inconceivable – that is why I have written nothing down.'

As always with Kafka, what is given with one hand is taken away with the other. The first passage ends with a question to which there is no answer: 'But then what kind of a surplus is it?' The second is a variant of the Cretan liar paradox which is so often the hidden form of Kafka's stories and remarks. For the phrase: 'that is why I have written nothing down' is of course itself written down. Does this mean that suffocation is then conceivable? No, for what is writ-ten down is that it is inconceivable. What is the nature of the joy one experiences in 'calmly' writing down such a sentence? What is the nature of the surplus strength which allows one to write: 'I am unhappy' in the midst of one's unhappiness? Like Derrida and his followers Kafka senses that as soon as we start to speak, to write, meaning is both made and unmade; that it escapes us even as we try to grasp it. But for him this is not a source of philosophical *interest*; it is a source of surprise and anguish.

For is writing down 'I am unhappy' in the midst of one's unhappiness a good or a bad thing? Is it a sign of imminent recovery or one more evasion, one more entanglement of the writer in his unhappiness? And from the point of view of the reader of these lines is it the genuine rendering of a painful truth or the cause of *his* entanglement in a further web of lies?

'Suffocation is inconceivably horrible.' Could a person who was really suffocating write that down? If Kafka were in fact suffocating it is doubtful whether he would have been able to write that line. But perhaps he is, after all, for only a person who *was* suffocating would realize that the experience was strictly speaking inconceivable. Besides, Kafka tells us that he has written nothing down.

A few months earlier he had jotted this in his diary:

> Anyone who cannot come to terms with his life while he is alive needs one hand to ward off a little his despair over his fate – he has little success in this – but with his other hand he can note down what he sees among the ruins, for he sees different (and more) things than do the others; after all, dead as he is in his own lifetime, he is the real survivor. This assumes that he does not need both hands, or more hands than he has, in his struggle against despair.

We have often, in the last few years, encountered the moral ambiguity of the photographer-journalist taking a newsshot of innocent civilians being gunned down by an invading army. These tell the truth to the world and may actually play a part in ending the war in question, but how much of a truth is it when the photographer is excluded from the picture? Could he not have done something for the victims rather than simply photographing them? Perhaps the issue is not confined to journalism. It is impossible, in the above passage, to tell whether the person who wards off despair with one hand and scribbles with the other is worthier than the person who needs both hands to ward off despair. Looked at from one angle it seems that to manage to keep one hand free to write means that what will be written, because it will be written in the extremity of despair, will be truer, more honest, than other writing. The person who does so, Kafka tells us, sees more and more clearly than the others; he is not only the survivor, he is the survivor who lives to tell his tale. Yet one cannot help suspecting – as Kafka too seems to suspect – that there is something theatrical, false, in this one-handed warding off. Despair that only needs one hand to ward it off may not after all be real despair, and the writing produced by the other hand may therefore be even falser than most, since it will have pretended to be truer. (I do not need to remind you how often, in recent years, we have had writing foisted on us which has tried to claim our attention and approval by its assertion of painful honesty. Our unease with such writing stems from the fact that its very existence belies these claims, without the author's apparently being in the least conscious of this.)

8.   By 1922 Kafka was no longer prepared to give writing the benefit of the doubt. In a terrible letter to Brod he writes:

> Literature helps me to live, but wouldn't it be truer to say that it furthers this sort of life? Which of course doesn't imply that my life is any better when I don't write. On the contrary, then it is much worse, quite unbearable and with no other remedy than madness. . . . Creation is a splendid reward, but for what? Last night I saw very clearly . . . that these are wages earned in the devil's service.

Why? Because writing is vanity, pride. Ultimately, Kafka sees, writing only reinforces the essential feature of pride, our stubborn belief in our own immortality. Even at the moment of death, Kafka fears, even as he says to himself: 'This is the end', that *saying* will turn him away from the truth, will turn even death itself into another story.

Writing reinforces our belief in our own immortality by helping us to avoid the acceptance of our bodies. One of the little stories that make up Kafka's first published collection, *Meditation* (the very book he was putting together when he met Felice), shows that Kafka was already aware of the central issue in 1912. The story is called 'Bachelor's Ill-Luck' and it is short enough to quote in full:

> It seems so dreadful to stay a bachelor, to become an old man struggling to keep one's dignity while begging for an invitation whenever one wants to spend an evening in company, to lie ill gazing for weeks into an empty room from the corner where one's bed is, always having to say good night at the front door, never to run up a stairway beside one's wife, to have only side-doors in one's room leading into other people's living-rooms, having to carry one's supper home in one's hand, having to admire other people's children and not even being allowed to go on saying: 'I have none myself', modelling oneself in appearance and behaviour on one or two bachelors remembered from one's youth.

That's how it will be, except that in reality, both to-day and later, one will stand there with a palpable body and a real head, a real forehead, that is, for smiting on with one's hand.

Even the real forehead, though, in this story as in all stories, is still only made of words, still only a product of the author's imagination. However much he says it is 'real', that 'real' is not real at all but only a word.

Kafka's strategy, over the next decade, consists in trying to force the reality of his body home upon his hero, as he would force it on himself and us. Take *Metamorphosis*. Everyone remembers the opening: 'As Gregor Samsa awoke one morning from uneasy dreams he found himself transformed into a gigantic insect.' And the story does not leave it at that. The paragraph continues:

> He was lying on his hard, as it were armour-plated, back and when he lifted his head a little he could see his dome-like brown belly divided into stiff arched segments on top of which the bed-quilt could hardly keep in position and was about to slide off completely. His numerous legs, which were pitifully thin compared to the rest of his bulk, waved helplessly before his eyes.

Every movement Gregor tries to make drives his condition home to him. Yet the strange thing is how readily the human mind accommodates itself to circumstances. Not even death brings Gregor to a full realization of who and what he now is. Indeed, the horror of the story lies in his – and our – inability ever to make sense of his transformed body.

Each new story of Kafka's is a fresh attempt to imagine what a real hand striking a real forehead would be like. It was perhaps in 1916, in what is no doubt his most repulsive story, that he came closest to it. You will remember that in 'In the Penal Colony' the camp commandant has devised a machine which slowly kills the guilty by cutting their indictment into their flesh. The commandant ran the colony with absolute authority, but he has been replaced by a more liberal person, and now his sole surviving disciple explains the workings of the machine to an explorer who is visiting the colony. It turns out that the condemned man does not know the sentence that has been passed on him. 'There would be no point in telling him. He'll learn it corporally, on his person,' explains the officer, who goes on to demonstrate exactly how the machine works. Basically, the idea is that little needles write the sentence all over the body of the condemned man:

Of course the script can't be a simple one; it's not supposed to kill a man straight off, but only after an interval of, on an average, twelve hours; the turning point is reckoned to come at the sixth hour.... The first six hours the condemned man stays alive almost as before, he suffers only pain...

Then, at about that time, the man suddenly starts to understand:

Enlightenment comes to the most dull-witted. It begins round the eyes. From there it radiates.... You have seen how difficult it is to decipher the script with one's eyes; but our man deciphers it with his wounds. To be sure, that is a hard task: he needs six hours to accomplish it. By that time the Harrow has pierced him quite through and casts him into the grave, where he pitches down upon the blood and water and the cotton-wool. Then the judgement has been fulfilled, and we, the soldier and I, bury him.

Anyone who, like this man, believes that judgement can be fulfilled, will welcome his end as this one does. Grasping the fact that the entire administration of the colony is turning against him as the last sole representative of the old commander and his machine, he frees the culprit and himself settles into the machine, after having placed his indictment inside it: 'Be just'. The machine, however, perhaps with a mad logic of its own, having started up again, proceeds to destroy itself and the officer along with it. The man dies as hideously as the previous victims, but this time with nothing at all having been written on his flesh: 'The Harrow was not writing, it was only jabbing, and the Bed was not turning the body over but only bringing it up quivering against the needles.' Before the explorer can do anything about it the whole hideous contraption has ground to a halt, with the dead man still stuck fast within it:

And here, almost against his will, he had to look at the face of the corpse. It was as it had been in life; no sign was visible of the promised redemption; what the others had found in the machine the officer had not found; the lips were firmly pressed together, the eyes were open, with the same expression as in life, their look was calm and convinced, through the forehead went the point of the great iron spike.

This is the final manifestation of the Renaissance ideal we began with, that of a language which would be more than words, which would speak directly, be actively inscribed upon the body. But it is important to note that the hero or protagonist of the story is not the officer, but the explorer. And he is too detached or too clear-sighted ever to imagine that such an ideal fate might be possible. The story is Kafka's most terrible dramatization of what might constitute a way out of the labyrinth of language in which he has for so long felt himself immured, unable to find any firm ground from which to launch himself into life, perpetually imbued with the sense that he has somehow not yet been born; but even as he writes it he seems to realize that it is still too Romantic in its self-destructiveness, and in his last stories the protagonist is even more peripheral to the action than the explorer. The mole in his burrow, Josephine the mouse singer, the hunger artist – they are more a source of impatience in others than anything else. No one even bothers to condemn them to death, they merely live and die on the edges of other people's consciousness, and no sooner are they dead than they are forgotten:

> So perhaps we shall not miss her so very much after all, while Josephine, redeemed from the earthly sorrows which to her thinking lay in wait for all chosen spirits, will happily lose herself in the numberless throng of the heroes of our people, and soon, since we are no historians, will rise to the heights of redemption and be forgotten like all her brothers.

9. We are now perhaps a little nearer to understanding the profound irony of Kafka's last illness. He who had always mistrusted writing, he who had always longed for a writing that would be more than mere words on paper, is now, in those last moments, reduced to communicating only by means of words on paper.

Yet we are not done with the ironies of this event. Kafka, dying of this hideous illness in which it gradually became impossible for him to eat and extremely painful for him to drink, was still able to scribble. Yet one of the central themes which run through his life and work is that of defining the precise relations between food and words.[38] To begin with, of course, you cannot both speak and eat. Food nourishes you but what do words do? The mouth mouthing words, the hand forming words – are these not being turned from their true, natural functions?

> I was, after all, depressed even by your mere physical presence [Kafka had written in the letter to his father]. I remember for instance how often we undressed together in the same bathing-hut. There was I, skinny, weakly, slight, you strong, tall, broad. Even inside the hut I felt myself a miserable specimen, and what's more not only in your eyes but in the eyes of the whole world, for you were for me the measure of all things.

But if the father's physical strength caused Kafka to be disgusted with his own puny body, that very physicality was also profoundly disgusting to him. The letter describes in grotesque detail the father's way of cutting his nails at table, his violent, unpredictable rages, his brutality with his family and employees. Seen in this light he becomes a rapacious carnivore, the creature who makes a success of his life by ruthlessly shoving aside all who try to stand in his way.

No wonder Kafka starves himself, turns vegetarian, tries to be even thinner than he is. As Canetti puts it in his moving little book on Kafka: 'One must withdraw from violence, which is unjust, by disappearing as much as possible. One makes oneself very small or one transforms oneself into an insect.'[39] Kafka most profound tendencies, he goes on, 'are to become smaller and smaller, more and more silent, lighter and lighter, till the final annihilation.'

Kafka's father was a self-made man. *His* father had been a butcher in a village in Southern Bohemia. He had got to Prague by dint of hard work and was determined to give his family the advantages he had lacked. He had no time for intellectuals or fooling around with words. But here was his son, withdrawing from him and from what he had in mind for him, and spending his time writing and reading. Yet what we have here is no simple case of a sensitive youth revolting against philistine parents. Kafka, in the letter, acknowledges that he took to writing to escape his father, yet that in the end all his writing was nothing else but a long-drawn out – indeed, a never-ending – leave-taking from him. And how could it be anything else? How could he imagine he would ever be able to get away from his father? For to get right away from him would be to enter a world of total unreality, a world of childish make-believe. The very ease with which, through writing, it is possible to create alternative worlds, is enough to condemn writing as worse than useless, a total evasion.

At the same time, by one of the twists of the knife which Kafka seems so adept at discovering, the spirit of the father enters even the world of words. We find the following in an early diary entry:

> While dictating a rather long report to the district Chief of Police, towards the end, where a climax was intended, I got stuck and could do nothing but look at K., the typist, who, in her usual way, became especially lively, moved her chair about, coughed, tapped on the table and so called the attention of the whole room to my misfortune. The sought-for idea now has the additional value that it will make her quiet, and the more valuable it becomes

> the more difficult it becomes to find it. Finally I have the word 'stigmatize' and the appropriate sentence, but still hold it all in my mouth with disgust and a sense of shame as though it were raw meat, cut out of me.

The word in his mouth is like a piece of raw meat, a portion of his own flesh. His instinctive vegetarianism, his almost anorexic behaviour later on in life, and his quite physical revulsion against words come together here in an eerie way.

Writing takes up space. To be a writer is to assert yourself at the expense of others. At the same time the words on the page are themselves assertive, elbowing others, with an equal right to be there, off the page. Kafka wants to curl up into a ball like a hedgehog, but in writing all he does is spread himself out until, like his father for the child Franz, he covers the entire world. The peculiar pathos of his last story, 'The Hunger Artist', lies in this. The crowd-dispelling fasting showman finally dies and is quickly cleared away to make place for the healthy and active panther, in whose jaws the spirit of freedom and health seem to lurk. But in the very writing of this story Kafka turns from fasting showman into carnivorous panther. And though this could be seen as the ultimate triumph of art, that would be to see it from the father's point of view. From Kafka's it is the ultimate failure of life, his life. And remember that it was the proofs of this that Kafka was correcting on his death-bed. Has there ever been such a tangling of truth and falsehood, such an interpenetration of motive?

10.   Kafka's father, I have said, was a self-made man, and he was determined that his children would not have to look back to the poverty and degradation he had known in his native village, but should absorb the dominant German culture and move ever forwards and up in the world. But for Kafka the whole thing seemed upside down. For him everything that is made only by the self is an imposition on the world, without meaning, and a sign of dehumanization in that it implies the crushing of another human being. The self-made man uses tradition for his own ends. Hence Kafka's horror at his father's purely social Judaism and his almost physical reaction to his father's use of a traditional expression when he found his son consorting with an unsavoury East European Jewish actor (who no doubt reminded him of a past he would rather forget): 'He who sleeps with dogs picks up fleas.' In the same way Iago had used proverbs for his own ends, while he busily worked upon the world to make it yield up the plot he needed from it.

But tradition is precisely that which is *not* questioned, that which is taken on trust. As Erich Heller has recently, and beautifully, put it:

> Every tradition, as long as it is intact, is a miniature paradise.... Not because tradition knows no suffering, far from it; but because it does not know the kind of curiosity that the serpent aroused in Eve.... For tradition is, among a thousand other things, the silent and unconsciously wise agreement to curb one's curiosity...[40]

But this is not quite right. As we saw when looking at *Othello*, curiosity cannot be curbed; tradition exists when curiosity is absent. Heller senses this, for he goes on to quote the end of Kafka's little story, 'The Test':

> He asked me several things, but I couldn't answer, indeed I didn't even understand his questions. So I said: Perhaps you are sorry now that you invited me, so I'd better go, and I was about to get up. But he stretched out his hand over the table and pressed me down. Stay, he said, that was only a test. He who does not answer the question has passed the test.

And Heller remarks: 'Perhaps it is the test of a tradition not even to ask [questions].'

It would be wrong to imagine that Heller is talking about anything abstract or esoteric. He is talking about what we experience every day of our lives. For it is not the case that there first is 'the tradition' and that then it vanishes. There are countless traditions, as many perhaps as there are Wittgensteinian language-games. Thus to the person who has been brought up celebrating Christmas as a family affair the sudden decision to turn New Year's Day into a holiday will seem odd; but to the person who has been brought up to think of the family midwinter celebration as taking place on New Year's Day, there is something incomprehensible and slightly comic about the way people rush around getting worked up about Christmas. Kafka's father had seen the degradation to which immersion in a web of traditions can bring one; he was determined to break out of this web, to forge a clean uncluttered future for himself and his children. In this he was of course typical of many Jews of his time, as Kafka himself fully realized. He also, like his generation of central European Jews, perhaps had a good deal in common with those Englishmen of the seventeenth and eighteenth century of whom Iago was a kind of precursor and in whose midst the novel first emerged.

Kafka realized too that if all hope of salvation lay with such East

European Jews as the actor Lowy and, indeed, the whole milieu from which his father was so keen to separate himself, he, Franz Kafka, could not partake of that salvation. In a letter to Milena he puts the matter quite clearly:

> We both know well many typical examples of Occidental Jews; of them all I am, as far as I know, the most typical; that is to say, exaggerating a little, that I don't have one second's peace, that nothing is given for me, that it is necessary for me to acquire everything, not only the present and the future, but also the past, that thing of which all men freely receive a portion; it too I must acquire, that is perhaps the hardest task...

This is the burden of all Kafka's work, and of all his actions. He would re-enter the tradition, or traditions, in which he might feel himself come alive, but such entry cannot start from him: he must be called in. And he knows that no one will call him. This is the drama of his love affairs and successive engagements. He wants to be married – but he cannot marry, because that demands a decision *from him*, and so abolishes precisely what he hopes to gain by marrying. The most one can do in this life, he tells his father, is to marry and raise a family and protect them against the world. But marriage, which would allow him to stand on the same footing as his father, and thus in one stroke set right the relations between them, would also turn him into the equivalent of his father, and that is one thing he instinctively will never do.

11.   Ultimately, he tells his father, marriage might prove to be his salvation, but what if it didn't? What if all it did was to make it impossible for him to write?

For writing, in spite of everything, is sensed instinctively as a good. And yet is that not to make writing the greatest betrayer of all? Writing mimes oneness with the tradition while all the time it is the product only of one man and his wilfulness. How can Kafka not view this with distrust, even with disgust?

12.   It is time to return to the slips of paper Kafka scribbled on as he lay in the Kierling sanatorium, unable to speak. I want to suggest that why they are so moving is that, in the face of all I have said so far, of everything we have learnt about the place of writing in Kafka's life, and which should make of them only a bitter and ironic inversion of all our notions about the solemnity and authoritativeness of death – they are actually nothing of the sort. I began by pointing out how

Kafka's being condemned to write down words on paper instead of speaking his last thoughts shows that we are never free of the labyrinthine ambiguities of writing, that there is no end to them. But it is also possible to say that what happens here is that, amazingly enough, writing itself is transformed into something supremely authoritative, and thus, when it is too late, allows Kafka to achieve what he had sought for all his life.

13. 'Mineral water once for fun. I could   '

The meaning, or the impact, comes from the fact that the message is broken off. What we understand is not the result of our *filling out* the sentence, completing it. It is the result of our feeling that the sentence could *never* be adequately filled out.

'A lake doesn't flow into anything, you know.'

Nothing here is being said that we didn't know. Why then do we feel that so much more is being said here than we ever knew before?

What these brief messages make manifest is this: human beings are always closed off to each other. What they convey in speech and writing is always both more and less than the words suggest. The well-made work is unsatisfactory precisely because it implies that meaning is complete, that nothing more needs to be said. But, as Kafka said to Janouch one day, there is always something left unaccounted for. The catch is that it must be left unaccounted for only after we have tried to account for everything. Otherwise it is merely unaccounted for by an oversight, because we have simply been impatient.

In these fragments that is no longer the case. 'A bird was in the room.' No one is allowed to say this, it is cheating, it is the cheapest trick of language. No one who feels a responsibility to language and to truth will simply write that down. If it is written and wasn't the case, then it is a lie. If it was the case, so what? No one, except Kafka, in this situation. He has earned the right, so to speak, to say what cannot otherwise be said. And when he writes that down what it conveys is not an element of fact, but a sensation of *wonder*. *That* Kafka should have chosen to record this, then, makes it something for us to wonder at. What it conveys is not meaning, not a message, but a person: Kafka. His longings, his ineluctable privacy, his inability to say what it is he wants to say.

Kafka's enforced silence is what speaks loudest to us. I suspect that it is also what we hear when we read any book that moves us. We listen to it as we don't to our friends. Proust was right to criticize

Sainte-Beuve and Ruskin for refusing to distinguish art from conversation. In conversation we respond to the immediate. In art the immediate always has another dimension: we sense that it has been written. And written not by a computer or a penal settlement machines or in a universal language, but by a mortal man in a natural language.

Kafka had jotted down in his journal: 'My life a hesitation before birth.' And he had called Milena 'Mother Milena', half begging her to bring him to birth. Of course she could not do this. In a strange way, though, as we read him, we bring him to life within us. But we can only do this because as he writes he is about to die. And as we read we too are about to die, and so can experience what it is he experiences.

One of Kafka's most mysterious little stories concerns Odradek, that strange creature formed like one of those flat star-shaped spools, with odd bits of wood sticking out of it at angles. 'He lurks by turns in the garrett, the stairway, the lobbies, the entrance hall.' When one asks him where he lives, he replies: 'No fixed address', and laughs. 'I ask myself, to no purpose, what is likely to happen to him? Can he possibly die? Anything that dies has had some kind of aim in life, some kind of activity, which has worn out; but that does not apply to Odradek.' Neither Czech nor German, neither man nor object, always on the move, unable to die, Odradek is the crystallization of Kafka the imaginer of stories, one more example of the multitude of symbolic bodies he projects. But Kafka differs from Odradek by the simple fact, which we can experience but which, in a sense, Kafka can't, that he will die, that he is indeed now dead. It is because of this that Kafka's words come to us charged in a way those of Odradek could never be.

14.   But there is something else which is conveyed by those last notes. I find it difficult to be clear about it, but I think it is this: Kafka, who had always been so suspicious of writing, is, we have seen, forced in the end to rely upon it. And he is prepared to do so because he knows that someone will read what he has written: Dora Dymant, Robert Klopstock. What these fragments finally convey is the centrality of trust; they are an icon of trust.

To write down 'A bird was in the room' is to wish to share something with another person. It is not perhaps an important fact that is shared, but this is precisely why it demonstrates what it does. Kafka, who all his life had distrusted his own fluency, his own manipulative skill with words, who had felt as we have seen, that he was forever debarred from all traditions, forced to start everything from himself, through an effort of his own will – Kafka has here arrived at the point where there is either silence or the manifestation of trust. Because Klopstock is *there*, Kafka writes. It is as simple as that.

15.   But here we come to the strangest thing of all. We see acted out before us, in slow motion and exaggerated form, so to speak, something which had always been the case, but which, without this, it might have been difficult to focus on. Kafka writes at this point, we have said, because of his trust in the friends who surround him. But why then, given all his doubts did he keep writing all his life?

Trust here takes on another dimension. It is trust simply in the ability of the hand to keep moving forward over the page. It is, finally, trust, against all the evidence, in the beneficial aspect of time, in movement as opposed to stasis.

I talked last week about the relation of trust to motion in Dante. Dante provided a beautiful illustration of this in the first canto of the *Commedia*. Kafka's life and death reveal it to us not as an idea or an insight, but as a simple fact.

You may remember that Kafka's ape, in his lecture to the Academy, told the august members of that assembly that he had never looked for freedom, only for a way out. He wanted simply to survive, and in circumstances a little less grim than he seemed to be condemned to. His way of doing so was to imitate the language of men. And so with Kafka. He too learned to imitate the language of men. But he often despaired of it. For language, it seemed, was utterly dependent on metaphor, on the girl who tends the fire, on the cat warming himself in front of the fire. Why reduplicate an already well-stocked world? Yet he went on needing a way out. And he found it by turning metaphor into metamorphosis.

Metaphor implies a fixed position from which we judge, choose and select.[41] Metaphor leads to the compulsive imagining of the self as symbolic body: beetle, bridge, Odradek or mutilated corpse. And the end of such compulsive imagining is autism, catalepsy, suicide. But if images belong to the dead world of metaphor, the writing itself is metamorphosis, continuous transformation.

At basis all writing is the metamorphosis of the mechanical movement of the hand into the infinite variety which constitutes letters, words, sentences. And just because Kafka's refusal to accept *any* tradition on trust was so absolute, his final acceptance of *this* is all the more moving. He may not have trusted the world, or language, or literature, but his hand moved unthinkingly over the paper, forming words. His moving hand was his Autolycus, no longer clearly labelled Fool or disguised heroine, but a being possessed of the instinct for survival and a trust in the bountifulness of time which nature cannot let go unrewarded.

16. We have reached rock bottom. Any movement we now make will have to be sideways. And there are of course a number of such movements which are open to us. We could explore the contrast between the constant metamorphosis of the moving hand in writing and the mechanical repetition of masturbation, and go on to develop a set of contrasts between an Oedipal organization, genital sexuality and repressiveness on the one hand, and freedom from such organization, polymorphous perversity and perpetual foreplay on the other. I think there is something in this kind of contrast, but that what it tends to do is to polarise matters into good and bad where instead I have tried to show the constant interplay of forces and the perpetual contamination of the one by the other, and to suggest that all gains are bought at a cost.[42]

It would be possible, and perhaps more fruitful, to turn to the kind of work being done by Luria and Sacks.[43] Freud had suggested that the language of hysteria corresponded only to an imaginative image of the body and not to any physiological reality. An arm, murderous only in fantasy, is punished by paralysis, though physically there is nothing wrong with it. Sacks has developed this insight in his studies of migraine and Parkinsonism. Here, he has shown, 'the symptoms are fixed and bounded by physiological connections', but 'they can constitute a bodily alphabet, or proto-language, which may subsequently be used as a symbolic language.' Here, then, and nowhere else, do we find the lived reality of that language of the Academy of Lagado which I discussed in my first lecture, a language that transcends words and speaks with reality itself. But the sufferer, of course, is more like the damned souls in Dante's *Inferno* than like Dante and Virgil. Though the distinction is a narrow one, and at times impossible to apply in practice, it is nonetheless a crucial one, for it is the distinction between the freedom to fulfil one's potential and the condemnation to an everlasting and compulsive repetition.

Yet the work of both Luria and Sacks suggests that the boundaries have constantly to be redrawn. In *The Man With the Shattered Skull* Luria examines the case of a young soldier who had part of his brain shot away in the war and spent the next twenty-five years laboriously trying to put together the pieces of his shattered world, to little avail.

His extraordinary account of his attempts, beautifully edited and commented upon by Luria, show as does nothing else I know what a miracle human thought, memory and language are, though we take them so much for granted. Especially interesting is Luria's account of how Zasetsky was finally enabled to write when Luria persuaded him to stop worrying about the formation of individual letters, which was causing him terrible difficulty and anxiety, and instead to trust his pen, so to speak. 'Kinetic melody' is how Luria describes our normal habit of writing, and that beautiful phrase sums up a great deal of what I have been trying to say.

The work of Luria and Sacks also draws our attention to an important aspect of modern art. For, as I have suggested, the victims of disease and accident about whom they write, people who cannot remember anything, cannot forget anything, speak too fast or much too slowly – these alert us to what we take for granted most of the time: the incredible complexity of even the simplest mechanisms of speech, movement and writing. What we get from these accounts, though, is very much what we get from the best modern writing, and what we experience when we read Kafka's scribbled notes: 'A lake doesn't flow into anything you know.' 'A bird was in the room.' A sense of awe and wonder.

Few writers have been able to speak directly about these things. Wallace Stevens, in his last poems, those poems, as Randall Jarrell said, 'from the other side of existence, the poems of someone who sees things in steady accustomedness, as we do not; and who sees their accustomedness, and them, as about to perish' – Wallace Stevens is one of the few. Looking back, at over seventy, and asking himself what it had all been about, he gave a diversity of answers. One was the poem, 'The Planet on the Table':

> Ariel was glad he had written his poems.
> They were of a remembered time
> Or of something seen that he liked.
>
> Other makings of the sun
> Were waste and welter
> And the ripe shrub writhed.
>
> His self and the sun were one
> And his poems, although the makings of the self,
> Were no less makings of the sun.
>
> It was not important that they survive.
> What mattered was that they should bear
> Some lineament or character,

> Some affluence, if only half-perceived,
> In the poverty of their words,
> Of the planet of which they were a part.

In the old days, at the time of 'The Man With the Blue Guitar',
Stevens had worried about whether it is up to the poet to make the
world, to discover its true shape, or whether such making is a distortion. In a sense he has passed beyond such questions now. The
planet is on the table, for it is only conjured up in his poem. It is
there, like a child's globe perhaps, to be turned this way and that.
But the 'it' which we turn about, the poem there before us, is also
an acknowledgement that it is only a part of the world, one more
element within it. And yet not a 'mere' part, but a part in the sense
of 'playing a part'. 'That's it'. Stevens had understood as he was
finishing 'Auroras of Autumn', 'The lover writes, the believer hears,
The poet mumbles, the painter sees,   Each one, his fated eccentricity,
As a part, but tenacious particle,   Of the Skeleton of the ether, the
total...'.

The poet mumbles, but this is not a wholly private activity. In
'To an Old Philosopher in Rome' Stevens apostrophizes Santayana,
urging him

> Be orator but with an accurate tongue
> And without eloquence, O half-asleep,
> Of the pity that is the memorial of this room
>
> So that we feel, in this illumined large,
> The veritable small, so that each of us
> Beholds himself in you, and hears his voice
> In yours, master and comiserable man.

As we read these lines we are the old philosopher in Rome, and we
are Stevens as he imaginatively enters the old man's world. But we
are also, strangely, more ourselves than we were before. Each of us
hears his voice in Stevens's, and this means that we hear ourselves
saying what we did not know we could say, in a tone we didn't
know was ours, but which, hearing, we recognize as the actualizing
of what had always been latent. The same thing happens, I would
suggest, when we read, at the end of the volume of Kafka's letters:
'A bird was in the room.' Saying it, we are Kafka in that room, in
that loneliness. And so that loneliness is something shared.

17.   In conclusion, I would like to make two points. The first has
to do with the notion of trust which has figured so prominently in

these lectures. It seems to me to be a concept which it is easier for a Jew than for a Christian, especially a Protestant, to understand. Ignaz Maybaum, in a fine lecture on the binding of Isaac, made the point that for the Jew the story is, at a profound level, never in doubt.[44] He trusts God as Isaac trusts his father; as Isaac says 'Here am I', when his father calls him, so Abraham says 'Here am I' when God calls him. But for Kierkegaard, as for Paul before him, all is a matter of crisis, faith, a faith beyond the bounds of reason.

This is very suggestive. I bring it in not to claim Kafka for Judaism, which would be nonsense. I hope I have shown that trust is ultimately something instinctively human, lying somewhere in the region between brain and wrist, and that it has nothing to do with ethnic or religious affiliations. But if I have been right in the general historical trend of my argument, if there was indeed a shift of consciousness in the sixteenth and seventeenth centuries, and if Iago and Malvolio are typical of the new spirit which will take nothing on trust, then it may be helpful to bring to the fore this opposition between trust and faith. Perhaps by stressing the Jewishness of the concept of trust[45] I am only trying to highlight its opposite, which for convenience we can call the Protestant spirit, and which seems to infect all thinking men in the course of the years 1500 to 1700.

I am, in a sense, only repeating what Nietzsche argued, and what recent thinkers like Dan Sperber have suggested[46], that the will to truth, to interpretation, is not a given, but is an aspect of our culture, a culture forged in the sixteenth and seventeenth centuries. 'The attribution of sense is an essential aspect of symbolic development in our culture' is how Sperber puts it. The difficulty with such notions is that the very vocabulary with which we deal with these matters is itself derived from this culture. Our problem is to get behind that and to discover why it came about and what aspects of life it hides or distorts.

And it is here that I come to my second point. Imaginative literature can help us with our task as nothing else can. My exploration of *Tristram Shandy* and *Othello* will, I hope, have made that plain. It will also have been evident to you that in the course of these lectures I have not hesitated to make use of Freud, or to borrow from anthropologists and philosophers when it suited me. Purists may feel that I have been employing the vocabulary or concepts of other disciplines in too loose and unsystematic a fashion. I make no apology. Literary criticism has for too long, it seems to me, been overimpressed by what it sees as other, 'harder', more 'relevant' disciplines. It has felt that it cannot understand the works of the imagination unless it first masters the thought and vocabulary of linguistics or psychoanalysis. But is this not just one more example of the lack of trust, of the Iago–ego at work? George Craig, in the essay on Proust to which I referred in my first lecture, made a very important point when he began a sentence with the words: 'We can, with Freud and Lacan – and a little imagination...'. Nothing I have been talking about has to do with any kind of specialized discipline: a little imagination, a little attention, that is all that is required. Naturally, if there are imaginative and brilliant men working in other fields, it would be folly to ignore them. But if I am correct in what I have been saying, it may be that the taking of so much on trust, the perpetual lack of certainty which is the hallmark of the imagination, may be *truer to the facts* than the certainties of scientists and philosophers.

18.   In keeping with this credo, let me end not with a statement or a summary, but with a brief commentary on one of the endings of a writer who knew all about endings.

The most moving moment in Shakespeare is not the death of Hamlet or Othello. It is not even the death of Lear. It is the moment when Lear talks to himself over the dead body of Cordelia. It is so moving because it is seen only in profile, as it were. It is not something we hear but, like Kafka's last notes, something we overhear. Nothing that Lear says at this point advances the plot, nothing is, in a sense, necessary. What Lear says is simple too, far from the great poetry of so much of the play; and, besides, he is fooling himself. But it is just because the language is inadequate to the situation, just because we sense in Lear's blindness a dramatization of our own perpetual and incorrigible blindness, that we are so deeply moved. Though Shakespeare is wonderfully tactful with his ending, Edgar's last words in particular can only strike us as too full and confident for what has gone before. They face us directly, so to speak, guiding our responses, filling in the gaps for us, denying the emptiness we have just glimpsed, which may after all be the space we really need if we are to become fully alive.

Shakespeare never quite found a way of making full use of what the happy accident of the plotting of *Lear* had given him. But something of that feeling is conjured up again, though seemingly in a very different guise, at the very end of his last play. Prospero comes forward and addresses the audience:

Now my charms are all o'erthrown,
And what strength I have's mine own,
Which is most faint: 'tis true,
I must be here confined by you,
Or sent to Naples. Let me not,
Since I have my dukedom got,
And pardoned the deceiver, dwell
In this bare island by your spell:
But release me from my bands
With the help of your good hands:
Gentle breath of yours my sails
Must fill, or else my project fails,
Which was to please. Now I want
Spirits to enforce, Art to enchant;
And my ending is despair,
Unless I be relieved by prayer,
Which pierces so, that it assaults
Mercy itself, and frees all faults.
    As you from crimes would pardoned be,
    Let your indulgence set me free.

We know this so well that it is perhaps difficult to see it for what it is. We all know how Victorian critics read it as Shakespeare's farewell, not Prospero's, and such critics have come in for a lot of stick in the past fifty years. I have no wish to take their side. Yet certain conclusions seem inescapable.

Prospero is speaking. Many references in the passage link it firmly to the play we have just seen. On the other hand it is a new Prospero, not the one we have had before us so far. What strength he has is now his own. He has buried his magic book and is now an ordinary mortal. At this point he makes an odd appeal to the audience: 'Let me not, Since I have my dukedom got, And pardon'd the deceiver, dwell In this bare island by your spell. . .' It is now we, the audience, who wield the magic power, and Prospero who is at our mercy as Caliban was at his. Imperceptibly, too, we have been moving out of the fiction. Now it is the actor who says: So far I have been speaking someone else's lines, now I speak to you in my own words, and I need your help – though of course he accepts that the help we give him is conditional on his having entertained us earlier.

And now, imperceptibly again, we move into yet another context. 'Release me from my bands With the help of your good hands' is straightforward enough. 'Gentle breath of yours my sails Must fill, or else my project fails' is just about conceivable as a call to the audience to cheer as well as clap. But 'my ending is despair, Unless I be relieved by prayer' is something new. We could say that Shakespeare is here emerging from the figure of the actor who has himself emerged from the figure of Prospero. But the lines haunt us just because *he cannot quite emerge*. Just as the actor, having dropped his Prospero voice or removed his Prospero cloak, can never quite dispel the awareness that even these lines have been written for him, are not 'really' his; so whoever or whatever is behind Prospero, even though he substitutes simple octosyllabics for the more usual pentameter, can never quite speak *in propria persona*. The gap remains. It is the necessary fiction, for 'even the absence of imagination had itself to be imagined', as Stevens said. And just as Stevens ends one of his great last poems with the injunction: 'call it, again and again, The river that flows nowhere, like a sea'; so here Shakespeare ends with an injunction: 'As you from crimes would pardoned be, Let your indulgence set me free.'

And so we clap and the actors take their bows. But their freedom is ambiguous, both desired and dreaded, a release from the constraints of the role, but a release into what? Tomorrow they will return to the liberating prisons of those roles.

Shakespeare lives in Prospero, yet he also dies a little behind the mask. The actor too both lives and dies. He discovers possibilities within himself as he speaks the lines of another, and it is we, the audience, who help him do this: because *we* are there, *he* is. And we too, watching, then applauding, undergo a similar process, moving perpetually between constraint and freedom, and between a constraint that releases and a freedom that imprisons.

19.   Shakespeare is, in the end, ready to accept the constraints. The epilogue is, after all, an accepted part of any play. Shakespeare may almost break its mould, but he will never break it completely; he is too conscious of the benefits of remaining within it. Modern writers, equally conscious perhaps, have nevertheless felt it necessary to break and to go on breaking all the moulds. And yet, as Kafka said, there is always something left unaccounted for. I too have attempted to get as close as possible to a certain truth which it seemed important to try and articulate, but I have had, ultimately, to content myself with what may well be seen as a series of tallish stories. In the end I have to trust you to make up for yourselves what can never be said.

Notes

1 The Bible in Focus

Charles Martindale read a draft of this essay and made many helpful comments. I am greatly indebted to him.

1 Roland H. Bainton, 'The Bible in the Reformation', in *The Cambridge History of the Bible*, vol.III: *The West from the Reformation to the Present Day* (ed. S.L. Greenslade; Cambridge: Cambridge University Press, 1963), pp.1-37. The quotations from Luther and other Reformation writers in the first half of this essay come from Bainton's article.

2 The example is Bainton's, *loc. cit.*

3 For Franck see Bainton, *loc. cit.*

4 Quoted in 'The Criticism and Theological Use of the Bible, 1700-1900' by W. Neil, *The Cambridge History of the Bible*, vol.III, pp.238-93.

5 For Simon see 'The Religion of the Protestants' by Norman Sykes, *The Cambridge History of the Bible*, vol.III, pp.175-98.

6 W. Neil, *loc. cit.*

7 W. Neil, *loc. cit.*

8 Norman Sykes, *loc. cit.*

9 Erich Auerbach (*Mimesis*, trans. Williard Trask; New York, 1957), p.7.

10 *Mimesis*, p.12.

11 I use the Loeb translations throughout.

12 Norman Austin, *Archery at the Dark of the Moon* (Berkeley, 1975), p.223.

13 S. Kierkegaard, *Either/Or* (trans. D.F. and L.A. Swenson; New York, 1959), I, pp.153-54.

14 Hermann Frankel, quoted in James M. Redfield, *Nature and Culture in the Iliad* (Chicago, 1975), pp.20-21.

15 Martha Nussbaum, *The Fragility of Goodness* (Cambridge University Press, 1986).

16 My attention was drawn to the Talmud passage by a fine article by Henri Atlan: 'La mémoire du rite: métaphore et fécondation', in *Mémoire et histoire: Données et débats presentés par Jean Halperin et Georges Lévitte* (Paris, 1986), pp.29-49.

2 Eating Your Words: Dante as Modernist

1 See John Freccero, 'The Pilgrim in the Gyre' in *Dante: The Poetics of Conversion* (Harvard, 1986).

2 Singleton, 'In Exitu Israel de Aegypto' in John Freccero (ed.), *Dante: A Collection of Critical Essays* (Englewood Cliffs, 1965).

3 I use Singleton's lucid prose translation throughout: *The Divine Comedy, Translated, with a Commentary by Charles S. Singleton* (Princeton, 1971-3).

4 Heaney's volume *The Haw Lantern* (London, 1987) contains a beautiful translation of *Beowulf*, lines 26-52, which shows a much more personal and relaxed attitude to the translation of ancient poems than does his Ugolini translation, and is consequently much more successful, it seems to me.

5 Freccero, 'Bestial Sign and Bread of Angels' in *Dante: The Poetics of Conversion*.

6 Freud, *Studies on Hysteria*, The Pelican Freud Library Vol. III (Harmondsworth, 1974), p.217.

3 Reflections on Echo

1 This and subsequent quotations are from Ovid, *Metamorphoses*, iii, 338-511, trans. Rolphe Humphries (Bloomington and London, 1955).

2 Wordsworth has changed the punctuation here and there in the *Prelude* version. I quote from the earlier version, as printed in *William Wordsworth: The Poems*, 2 vols, ed. John O. Hayden (Penguin English Poets, 1977), I, pp.362-3.

3 See John Mepham, 'Mourning and Modernism', in Patricia Clements and Isobel Grundy (eds), *Virginia Woolf: New Critical Essays* (London, 1983) and John Kerrigan, 'Knowing the Dead', *Essays in Criticism*, 37 (1987), pp.11-42.

4 See Ch.6, 'Hawthorne: Allegory and Compulsion', of my *The World and the Book* (2nd edn, London, 1979).

5 All references to *A la recherche du temps perdu*, 3 vols, ed. Pierre Clarac and André Ferré (Pléiade, Paris, 1954).

4 Maurice Blanchot

Unless otherwise indicated, all the quotations in English may be found in Gabriel Josipovici (ed.), *Maurice Blanchot: The Sirens' Song*, trans. Sacha Rabinovitch (Brighton: Harvester, 1982).

1 'Ou maintenant? Qui maintenant?', *Le Livre à venir* (Paris, 1959), pp. 256-64.

2 'L'échec de Baudelaire', *La Part du feu* (Paris, 1949), p.133. Not in *The Sirens' Song*.

3 I have developed this point at greater length in 'Text and Voice', see pp.114-37 above.

4 'Le mythe de Mallarmé', *La Part du feu*, p.35. Not in *The Sirens' Song*.

5 'Gide et la littérature d'expérience', *La Part du feu*, p.213. Not in *The Sirens' Song*.

6   'Kafka et l'exigence de l'oeuvre', *L'Espace littéraire* (Paris, 1955), p.57.
7   'Rilke et l'exigence de la mort', *L'Espace littéraire*, p.165.
8   'La Douleur du diologue', *Le Livre à venir*, pp.185-94.
9   'Le Livre à venir', *Le Livre à venir*, p.237.
10 'Ars nova', *L'Entretien infini* (Paris, 1969), pp.506-14.
11 'L'Expérience de Proust', *Le Livre à venir*, pp.18-34.
12 Martin Heidegger, *Poetry, Language, Thought*, trans. Albert Hofstadter (New York, 1971), pp. 46, 92, 228, 148, 215, 182.
13 'L'infini littéraire: L'Aleph', *Le Livre à venir*, p.116.
14 Françoise Collin, *Maurice Blanchot et la question de l'écriture* (Paris, 1971), p.75.
15 *L'Écriture du désastre* (Paris, 1980), p.98. Not in *The Sirens' Song*.

5 Samuel Beckett: The Need to Fail

1   For this and other biographical information I have drawn on Deirdre Bair's biography, *Samuel Beckett* (London, 1978).

6 The Balzac of M. Barthes and the Balzac of M. de Guermantes

1   Roland Barthes, *Mythologies* (Paris, 1970), p.29.
2   Ibid., p.182.
3   Roland Barthes, *Le degré zéro de l'écriture* (Paris, 1974), p.32.
4   Roland Barthes, *S/Z* (Paris, 1976), pp.174-5.
5   Ibid., pp.222-3.
6   Ibid.
7   Ibid., pp.22-3.
8   Marcel Proust, *Contre Sainte-Beuve*, ed. Bernard de Fallois (Paris, 1954), pp.237-8.
9   Ibid.
10 Ibid., pp.196-7.
11 Ibid., pp.302-3.
12 Roland Barthes, *Fragments d'un discours amoureux* (Paris, 1977), p.41.
13 Roland Barthes, *La chambre claire* (Paris, 1980), p.168.
14 Roland Barthes, *Essais critiques* (Paris, 1981), p.131.

7 Text and Voice

1   Quoted in *Nouveau Roman: hier, aujourd'hui*, 2 vols. (Paris, 1972), vol.I, p.140.
2   Edward Said, *Beginnings* (New York, 1975), p.299.
3   Jacques Derrida, *Positions* (Paris, 1972), p.46.

4   I am greatly indebted to John Mepham for his help in the writing of this essay. The following paragraph in particular makes use of his brilliant essay, 'The Structuralist Sciences and Philosophy', in D. Robey (ed.), *Structuralism* (London, 1972).
5   Quoted in Mepham, 'The Structuralist Sciences', p.111.
6   Quoted in ibid., p.112.
7   Roland Barthes, *Essais critiques* (Paris, 1964), p.185.
8   Roland Barthes, *Critique et verité* (Paris, 1966), pp.56-7.
9   Northrop Frye, *Anatomy of Criticism* (Princeton, 1957), p.133.
10 Quoted in *Nouveau Roman: hier, aujourd'hui*, vol.I, p.140.
11 *Nouveau Roman: hier, aujourd'hui*, vol.I, pp.252-3.
12 Roland Barthes, *S/Z* (Paris, 1970), pp.21-2.
13 Ibid., p.211.
14 *Nouveau Roman: hier, aujourd'hui*, 2 vols. (Paris, 1972).
15 Ibid., vol.I, p.10.
16 Ibid., vol.I, p.99.
17 Ibid., vol.I, pp.122-3.
18 Ibid., vol.I, pp.123-4.
19 Ibid., vol.I, pp.127-8.
20 Ibid., vol.II, p.32.
21 Ibid., vol.II, pp.51-2.
22 Ibid., vol.I, p.221.
23 Ibid., vol.II, p.313.
24 Ibid., vol.II, p.314.
25 Ibid., vol.II, pp.318-19.
26 Ibid., vol.II, pp.323-4.
27 Alain Robbe-Grillet, *Dans le labyrinthe* (Paris, 1964), pp.9-10.
28 Ibid., p.10.
29 Ibid., pp.13-14.
30 Ibid., pp.15-17.
31 Ibid., p.17.
32 Ibid., pp.238-9.
33 Robert Pinget, *Passacaille* (Paris, 1969), pp.7-8.
34 Ibid., pp.130-3.
35 *Positions*, pp. 37-8.
36 *S/Z*, pp.48-9.
37 Norbert Lynton made this point in a recent (unpublished) lecture.
38 *Inferno*, I. 79-87.

8 Perec's *La Vie mode d'emploi*

1   Georges Perec, *La Vie mode d'emploi* (Paris, 1978). Page references are to this edition.
2   For the layout of the building, see the plan on p.145 above.
3   Roland Barthes' *S/Z* is the pioneer here, of course. But see also the

extension of his work to paintings by Norman Bryson in *Vision and Painting* (London, 1983), and in the first chapter of *Word and Image* (Cambridge, 1981).

4 'Quatres figures pour *La Vie mode d'emploi*, *L'Arc* 76 (1979), pp.50-53; reprinted with an additional section in *OULIPO: Atlas de littérature potentielle* (Paris, 1981), pp.387-95. The classic study of magic squares is W.S. Andrews, *Magic Squares and Cubes* (New York, 1917; enlarged edn, 1960). Martin Gardner gave publicity to the surprising discovery of the ten-by-ten Graeco-Latin square in his column in *Scientific American* (November, 1959), pp.181-7.

5 Note that the bottom left-hand square is unused, giving us ninety-nine and not a hundred chapters. Part of the reason for this is to be found on p.394, at the junction of Chapters 65 and 66.

6 David Roberts, *Contact* 23 (1981), p.28.

7 Keith Albarn et al., *The Language of Pattern* (London, 1974), p.48.

8 Wallace Stevens, 'To an Old Philosopher in Rome', *Collected Poems* (London, 1955), p.510.

9 Erwin Panofsky, *The Life and Art of Albrecht Dürer* (Princeton, 1971, paperback edn), p.168.

Writing and the Body

1 'The Garden of Forking Paths', in *Labyrinths*, eds D.A. Yates and J.E. Irby (Harmondsworth, 1970).

2 *Gulliver's Travels*, Book III, Ch.V. The passage is so interesting it is worth quoting in full:

> The other, was a scheme for entirely abolishing all words whatsoever: And this was urged as a great advantage in point of health as well as brevity. For, it is plain, that every word we speak is in some degree of diminution of our lungs by corrosion; and consequently contributes to the shortening of our lives. An expedient was therefore offered, that since words are only names for *things*, it would be more convenient for all men to carry about them, such *things* as were necessary to express the particular business they are to discourse on. And this invention would certainly have taken place, to the great ease as well as health of the subject, if the women in conjunction with the vulgar and illiterate had not threatened to raise a rebellion, unless they might be allowed the liberty to speak their tongues.... However, many of the most learned and wise adhere to the new scheme of expressing themselves by *things*; which hath only this inconvenience attending it; that if a man's business be very great, and of various kinds, he must be obliged in proportion to carry a greater bundle of *things* upon his back, unless he can afford one or two strong servants to attend him. I have often beheld two of those sages almost sinking under the weight of their packs, like pedlars among us; who, when

they met in the streets would lay down their loads, open their sacks, and hold a conversation for an hour together; then put up their implements, help each other to resume their burthens, and take their leave.

3   Reprinted in *Dialogues and a Diary* (London, 1968). See also Calvino's *Note* to his *The Castle of Crossed Destinies*, trans. William Weaver (London, 1977).

4   Quoted in John Mepham, 'The Structuralist Sciences and Philosophy', in D. Robey (ed.), *Structuralism* (London, 1972).

5   In *The World and the Book* (London, 1971), especially Ch. 4, 'Rabelais: Language and Laughter'. Terence Cave, *The Cornucopian Text* (Oxford, 1979).

6   See the fascinating essay by Roger Moss, 'Sterne's Punctuation', *Eighteenth Century Studies* 15:2 (Winter 1981-2), pp. 179-200. It overlaps with my own discussion of Sterne in more than one place.

7   George Craig, 'The "Petite Phase" and the sentence', *Journal of the History of European Ideas* I:3 (1981), pp. 259-76.

8   In the first draft of 'What is Epic Theatre?', in *Understanding Brecht*, trans. Anna Bostock (London, 1975).

9   'Theses on the Philosophy of History'. In *Illuminations*, trans. Harry Zohn (London, 1970).

10 A splendid description of a *ceilidh* or Highland story-telling session, is quoted from Alexander Carmichael's *Carmina Gadelica* in the introduction to Katharine Briggs's *British Folk Tales and Legends: A Sampler* (London, 1977):

> The house of the story-teller is already full, and it is difficult to get inside and away from the cold wind and sleet without. But with that politeness native to the people, the stranger is pressed to come forward and occupy the seat vacated for him beside the houseman. The house is roomy and clean, if homely, with its bright peat fire in the middle of the floor. There are many present – men and women, boys and girls. All the women are seated, and most of the men. Girls are crouched between the knees of fathers or brothers or friends, while boys are perched wherever – boy-like – they can climb. . . . The houseman is twisting twigs of heather into ropes to hold down thatch, a neighbour crofter is twining quicken roots into cords to tie cows, while another is plaiting bent grass into baskets to hold meal. The housewife is spinning, a daughter is carding, another daughter is teasing, while a third daughter, supposed to be working, is away in the background conversing in low whispers with the son of a neighbouring crofter. Neighbour wives or neighbour daughters are knitting, sewing or embroidering. The conversation is general.

Other vivid examples of the atmosphere of oral story-telling are to be found in David Thomson's marvellous *The People of the Sea* (London, 1965). I suspect that most of the critical and philosophical problems that arise in the study of works of literature stem from the fact that when we read a book we can do nothing else, while when we listen to a story being told our hands can be active. The apparently only partial attention accorded the story-teller in the above quotation may perhaps be a better way of taking in stories than the full attention educational institutions tend to try to foster.

11 See the interesting essay by J. Paul Hunter, 'The Loneliness of the Long-Distance Reader', *Genre*, vol. X, No. 4, from which the following examples are taken.

12 In *Labyrinths*. I have preferred the translation by Mildred Boyer in *Dreamtigers*, London, 1973.

13 In *Encounter*, November 1964.

14 'Recognition and the Reader' in *Comparative Criticism, A Yearbook*, ed. E. Shaffer (Cambridge, 1980).

15 *The Diary of Virginia Woolf. Volume III: 1925-1930* (London, 1980) pp. 300-301. It is interesting that an earlier entry in the same volume (p. 182) registers a resistance to Shakespeare's verbalism, and with specific reference to *Othello*:

> I was reading Othello last night, and was impressed by the volley and volume and tumble of his words: too many I should say, were I reviewing for the Times. He put them in when tension was slack. In the great scenes, everything fits like a glove. The mind tumbles and splashes among words when it is not being urged on: I mean, the mind of a very great master of words who is writing with one hand. He abounds. The lesser writers stint.

16 A. D. Nuttall, *William Shakespeare: The Winter's Tale* (London, 1966).

17 John Bayley, *The Characters of Love* (London, 1960), Ch. 3.

18 *Twelfth Night* once again provides us with a version of this, in the comic mode: Malvolio appearing before Olivia in festive dress, smiling 'his face into more lines than is in the new map with the augmentation of the Indies' (III, ii, 91-3). Like Iago, Malvolio is only *imitating* jollity, but he is ridiculous rather than threatening because he is not the deceiver but the deceived.

19 Compare Nuttall's comments on Act I of *The Winter's Tale*, op. cit.

20 See *A Tale of a Tub*, the 'Digression on Madness'.

21 *The Notebooks of Henry James*, eds F. C. Matthiessen and K. B. Murdock (New York, 1961), p. 106. Similar outbursts punctuate the pages of the *Notebooks*.

22 Jaques Le Goff, *La civilisation de L'Occident mediéval* (Paris, 1972) p. 342.

23 Dragonetti, 'Dante face a Nemrod', *Critique*, August-September 1979, p. 691. The whole issue is devoted to 'Le mythe de la langue universelle' and contains many interesting articles apart from Dragonetti's.

24 Quoted in Hugh Kenner, *The Invisible Poet* (London, 1960)

25 'Pierre Menard, Author of the Quixote', in *Labyrinths*.

26 Antoine Compagnon's *La seconde main* (Paris, 1979) unfortunately

came to my notice after these lectures were written. It is a detailed study of 'le travail de la citation' and touches on many of the themes dealt with in this lecture.

27 For a discussion of this in relation to *Ulysses*, see Roger Moss, 'Difficult language' in G. Josipovici (ed.) *The Modern English Novel* (London, 1976).

28 Alexander Goehr, 'Some thoughts about Stravinsky', in the programme for the Stravinsky Festival, Part II, Royal Festival Hall, January-February 1981.

29 *Expositions and Developments* (London, 1962) pp.122, 115.

30 Daix and Rosselot, *Picasso: The Cubist Years, 1907-1916* (London, 1980).

31 See especially, in the wake of Parry and Lord, G. Nagler, *Spontaneity and Tradition* (Berkeley, 1974), and B. Peabody, *The Winged Word* (Albany, 1975).

32 For a fuller discussion of what follows see 'Text and Voice', above, pp.114-137.

33 The reference is of course to James's great short story, especially to its marvellous closing pages.

34 The third word in the cluster is *tornare*. Those in Purgatory have shown, in life, a suppleness, an ability to change, to move, to turn, which is not to be found among the rigid souls in Hell.

35 The note is on p.493 of the English edition. The 'Conversation Slips' occupy pages 416-23.

36 Walter Benjamin, 'The Storyteller', in *Illuminations*.

37 See Ch. IX, 'Dialogue and Distance' in my *The Book of God* (London, 1988).

38 There are some suggestive remarks on this topic in G. Deleuze and F. Guattari, *Kafka, pour une littérature mineure* (Paris, 1975).

39 Canetti, *Kafka's Other Trial*, trans. C. Middleton (London, 1974). This now forms the Preface to the Penguin edition of the *Letters to Felice*.

40 Erich Heller, 'Investigations of a Dog and Other Matters', in J.P. Stern (ed.), *The World of Franz Kafka* (London, 1980).

41 For a different view of metaphor – closer, in fact, to my concept of metamorphosis, see Bernard Harrison's 'Metaphor and Interpretation'. My own argument depends on a much more naive and physical notion of metaphor and metamorphosis than philosophers would probably be willing to accept.

42 I am thinking in particular of the work of Norman Brown and Deleuze and Guattari. Jakobson, who is one of the few linguists never to have shied away from considering language in relation to the body, has also been very clear about the cost to the child of acquiring speech. In *Child Language, Aphasia and Phonological Universals*, for example, he argues that the babble of the child contains all sounds but that most of these are lost with the first acquisition of speech. He goes on:

In place of the phonetic abundance of babbling, the phonemic poverty of the first linguistic stages appears, a kind of deflation which transforms the so-called 'wild-sounds' of the babbling period into entities of linguistic value.

He proceeds to show that a full grasp of language, both active and passive, depends on articulation and so on the ability to differentiate. The crucial moment is when the child moves from the undifferentiated cry (*aaaa*) which is pure emotional expression, to the call (*mama*), which is his entry into the world of language, culture and symbolism. What this suggests is that a loss of self, a sacrifice of the immediate and the physical is required in the interests of long-term gains. But ambiguities abound. One remembers how Freud came to see repetition itself as a manifestation of the death wish; yet the denial of the physical involved in articulation can itself lead to the permanent installation of the super-ego and thus of the death-wish in another form.

43 Luria died in 1977. In his fascinating article, 'Witty Ticcy Ray', in the *London Review of Books*, Vol.3, No.4, March 1981, Sacks talks a little about the relation of the two men. The quotations from Sacks come from the revised edition of *Migraine* (London, 1981).

44 Ignaz Maybaum, *The Sacrifice of Isaac* (London, 1959).

45 See Ch. IX, 'Dialogue and Distance' in my *The Book Of God*, and 'The Irreducible Word' in the special issue of *European Judaism* on the Bible, ed. Jonathan Magonet, Autumn 1981.

46 Dan Sperber, *Rethinking Symbolism* (Cambridge, 1975).

Index of Names

Island 162; *La Vie mode
d'emploi* 138-63; *W ou le
souvenir d'enfance* 157, 162
Petrarch, F. 226
Picasso, Pablo 135, 239-41, 243
Pinget, Robert 10, 119, 123-4,
128-30, 132; *Passacaille* 123,
128-30
Plato 21, 26, 68, 215
Poe, Edgar Allan 10, 54-8, 59;
'The Fall of the House of
Usher' 54-7; 'William Wilson'
57-8
Proust, Marcel 9, 10, 32,
58-61, 62, 63, 74-6, 86, 96,
102-8, 109-24 *passim*, 130,
151, 162, 189, 243, 246, 265-6,
272; *Contre Sainte-Beuve* 102,
103, 104-8, 111; *Pastiches et
mélanges* 138; *A la Recherche du
temps perdu* 58-61, 75-6, 107-8,
111, 119, 128, 138, 169, 170,
188, 195, 222, 235, 246; *Jean
Santeuil* 75-6, 111

Queneau, Raymond 97, 108,
112-3; *Zazie dans le métro* 147

Rabelais, François 181
Ricardou, Jean 10, 119-21,
124, 131; *La Prise de
Constantinople* 120, 123
Richardson, Samuel *Clarissa*
181, 182
Rimbaud, Arthur 63
Rilke, Rainer Maria 70, 71, 76,
78
Robbe-Grillet, Alain 10, 63,
97, 108, 118, 119, 120-2, 124,
135, 136, 242; *Dans le laby-
rinthe* 121, 124-8, 130; *Les
Gommes* 121; *La Jalousie* 121,

122, 127; *La Maison de rendez-
vous* 123; *Le Voyeur* 120, 121,
127
Robert, Marthe 226
Roberts, David 144
Ronsard, Pierre de 179
Roussel, Raymond 120, 121
Ruskin, John 200, 266
Russell, Bertrand (and
Whitehead) *Principia
Mathematica* 176

Sacks, Oliver 268-9
Sainte-Beuve, Charles Augustin
104, 266
Sarraute, Nathalie 119, 120,
122-3
Sartre, Jean-Paul 65, 108
Schoenberg, Arnold 97, 238,
239; *Moses und Aron* 222, 239,
248
Scherer, Jacques 74
Schwarz, Delmore 200
Simon, Claude 119; *Les Corps
conducteurs* 123
Simon, Richard 18
Shakespeare, William 10, 96,
169, 179, 181, 199-221, 223,
226, 233, 272, 274; *Anthony
and Cleopatra* 217-18; *As You
Like It* 219; *Hamlet* 18, 203,
206, 212, 272; *Henry IV* 207;
Henry VIII 201; *King Lear* 217,
272; *Love's Labour's Lost* 207;
Measure for Measure 216; *The
Merchant of Venice* 206; *Othello*
202, 204, 205-17, 262-3, 271,
272, 281 n.15; *Pericles* 202,
212, 218; *The Tempest* 202,
206, 272-4; *Twelfth Night* 202,
204-5, 219, 281 n.18; *The
Winter's Tale* 218-21, 268

The Seattle School
2510 Elliott Ave.
Seattle, WA 98121
theseattleschool.edu